Strand

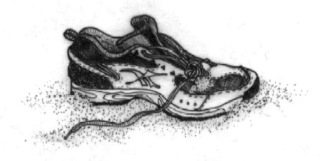

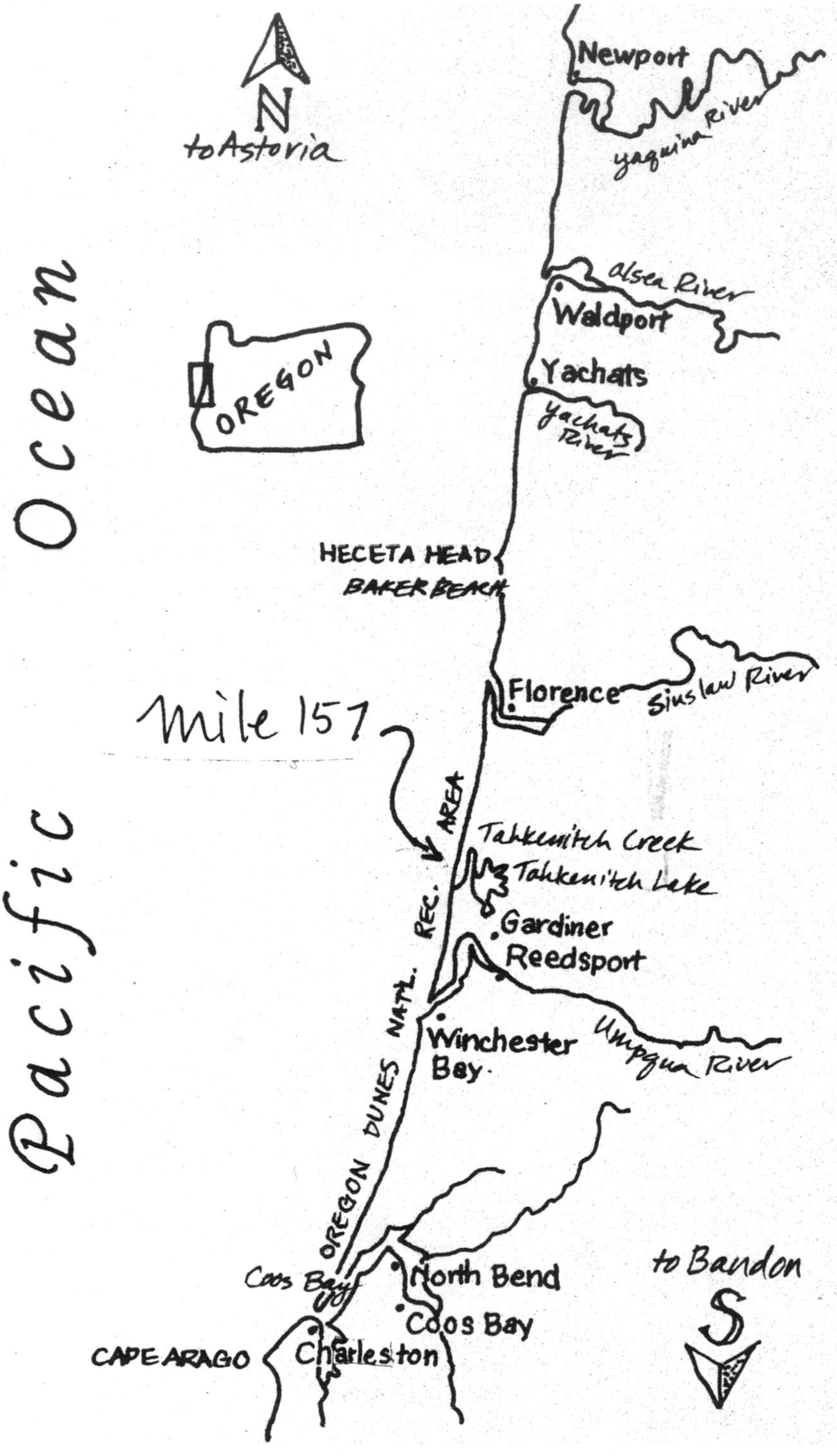

N
to Astoria
Pacific Ocean
OREGON
Newport
Yaquina River
Alsea River
Waldport
Yachats
Yachats River
HECETA HEAD
BAKER BEACH
Florence
Siuslaw River
Mile 157
OREGON DUNES NATL. REC. AREA
Tahkenitch Creek
Tahkenitch Lake
Gardiner
Reedsport
Winchester Bay
Umpqua River
Coos Bay
North Bend
Coos Bay
CAPE ARAGO
Charleston
to Bandon
S

Strand

An Odyssey of Pacific Ocean Debris

Bonnie Henderson

Oregon State University Press
Corvallis

The paper in this book meets the guidelines for permanence and
durability of the Committee on Production Guidelines for Book
Longevity of the Council on Library Resources and the minimum
requirements of the American National Standard for Permanence of
Paper for Printed Library Materials Z39.48-1984.

Library of Congress Cataloging-in-Publication Data
Henderson, Bonnie.
  Strand : an odyssey of Pacific Ocean debris / Bonnie Henderson.
      p. cm.
  Includes bibliographical references and index.
  ISBN 978-0-87071-299-9 (alk. paper)
  1. Outdoor recreation--Oregon--Pacific Coast--Guidebooks. 2.
Recreation areas--Oregon--Pacific Coast--Guidebooks. 3. Pacific Coast
(Or.)--Guidebooks. I. Title.
  GV191.42.O7H48 2008
  796.509795--dc22

                        2008020948

First published in 2008 by Oregon State University Press
Printed in the United States of America

 Oregon State University Press
121 The Valley Library
Corvallis OR 97331-4501
541-737-3166 • fax 541-737-3170
http://oregonstate.edu/dept/press

n. Strand: The land bordering a body of water; a beach …
One of the elements woven together to make an intricate
whole, such as the plot of a novel. *v.intr.* 1. To be driven
or run ashore or aground.
—*The American Heritage Dictionary of the English
    Language,* Fourth Edition (Houghton Mifflin Company,
    2004)

I learned early on that if you tell people what you see …
they'll think you're exaggerating or lying when you're
actually just explaining strange and wonderful things as
clearly as you can.
— From *The Highest Tide,* by Jim Lynch

My suspicion is that the universe is not only queerer than
we suppose, but queerer than we can suppose.
—From *Possible Worlds,* by J. B. S. Haldane

RUSSIA

UNITED
STATES

CANADA

Bering Sea

ALASKA Current

Gulf of
Alaska

PRIBILOF·
ISLANDS

INTERNATIONAL   DATE   LINE

ALEUTIAN ISLANDS

SUBARCTIC CURRENT

PACIFIC CURRENT

VANCOUVER ISLAND   Vancouver
TATOOSH ISLAND
SAN JUAN ISLANDS
Ocean Shores   Seattle
Astoria

Mile 157

UNITED
STATES

San Francisco

CALIFORNIA Current

Los Angeles

MEXICO

Ocean

·MIDWAY
ISLANDS

HAWAIIAN
ISLANDS

CURRENT

Contents

Introduction:
A Thoroughly Modern Midden

SEPTEMBER 4, 2000: Labor Day may be the worst day of the year to go beachcombing on the Oregon coast. Storms from the west and southwest are what drive wrack—nature's debris and humanity's flotsam and jetsam—onto the beach, and Labor Day typically follows a summer's worth of steady but light northwest winds, yielding little of interest.

But that's the beauty of beachcombing: you never get what you expect. On this mostly sunny day following an unseasonable late-summer storm, the beach was littered: plastic and glass bottles, long strands of kelp wrested from offshore "forests," a broken insulated cooler, foam floats escaped from fishermen's nets, shells of big Dungeness crabs and little mole crabs. Three dead birds, one of them a horned grebe, if I wasn't mistaken, its wings tucked flush at its sides and one clear red eye open to the sky. Two shoes—not a pair, but two different makes and sizes, colonized with gooseneck barnacles suggesting an ocean journey. And that mystery boat again, the one we'd first discovered buried in sand a year and a half earlier. All traces of it had disappeared after that first spring sighting. But here it was again, the weathered fragments of its bow and stern jutting from the beach, its rusted engine block mired amidships, its charred sides tracing parentheses in the sand. They may as well have been question marks. How, we wondered, and when and *why* did this boat end up on this beach? What about the shoes, and the horned grebe, for that matter—what were their stories?

My own story—what brought me again and again in all seasons to what I'd come to know as Mile 157—had begun five years earlier, one winter afternoon some 4,800 feet above sea level in Oregon's Cascade Range, when a friend of a friend cornered me in the lobby of a ski lodge. "You like the coast," she accused. I couldn't deny it. I'd walked every mile of Oregon beach, hiked every trail. I'd lived on the north coast at one time and dreamed of moving back. My house is cluttered with jars and baskets full of agates, beach glass, shells. I don't know what happened to my favorite toys and books of childhood, but I still have the vials of sand I collected on family vacations. What draws some people to the desert, others to the mountains, others to the shore? I can't explain it, but I know there is nothing I would rather do than spend a day, alone or with company, walking the beach.

"You should join CoastWatch," she continued. It was a fledgling volunteer organization, she explained, an offshoot of the advocacy group Oregon Shores Conservation Coalition. Each volunteer "adopted" one mile of coastline; all you had to do, she said, was visit your mile at least four times a year, briefly reporting seasonal changes and keeping an eye out for any potential problems: proposed developments on fragile estuaries and dunes, changes to management plans in state parks and national forests, anything threatening the public's access to Oregon's publicly owned beaches.

So I did, drafting a friend to adopt an adjacent mile. Jack took Mile 156, the beach immediately north of the mouth of Tahkenitch Creek, and I took the next mile north of his—identical but for the creek mouth. We developed a routine: hike out to the beach, walk both of our miles, stop for lunch along Tahkenitch estuary, walk back to the car. Jack brought the sandwiches; I brought the cookies.

Never a very attentive bird-watcher, I came to know the ducks that rode winter waves, the pelicans that skimmed the waves in July, and the shorebirds that foraged at the water's edge fall through spring. More than once we came across the decomposing carcass of a dead sea lion, and one bright December day we watched migrating salmon dodge the seals to struggle into the creek at its shallow mouth. Sometimes we could see fishing boats, and we'd speculate on their catch: in winter, maybe crab: in summer, salmon. Storms chewed up the seabed and spit rocks onto the beach: pieces of dark gray shale riddled with the borings of piddock clams, knobby agates in sunset hues, and occasionally a split-open geode sparkling with quartz crystals. Once three ultralight planes buzzed us as we paused for lunch on the bank of the sinuous, tannin-stained creek; virtually every lunch stop was marked by the low rumble of a helicopter approaching from the south—the Coast Guard on a routine midday run out of the air station at North Bend, near the mouth of Coos Bay.

There is absolutely nothing extraordinary about Mile 157, little to distinguish this mile from the other forty or fifty miles of beach bordering Oregon Dunes National Recreation Area, an undeveloped swath of shoreline between the mouths of Coos Bay and the Siuslaw River. A broad band of fine sand—dark gray and almost as hard as concrete just above the wash of waves—slopes up gently, becoming taupe-colored and soft where the wind shifts the fine, dry grains north and south with the seasons. Beyond the beach itself is a low sand bluff fringed with clumps of yellow-green beach grass. That foredune bluff falls away to a marshy depression, and behind it is a dense coastal forest of salal and evergreen huckleberry, knicknick and rhododendron, shore pine and Sitka spruce. There are no high rocks or offshore islands compelling seabirds to rest and nest, no tidepools offering twice-daily glimpses into the habitat of sculpin and hermit crab and chiton. Elsewhere in the dunes, two rivers and a handful of creeks cut through the sand bluffs and empty into the sea, inviting salmon to spawn. No creek splits the beach on Mile 157.

In winter, storm waves pull sand off the beach; in summer, waves move that sand back onto the beach. It's a little colder and rainier here in the winter, a little warmer and drier in the summer, but the pines and spruces stay green year-round, and the ocean stays cold—about 48 degrees in winter, "warming" to 57 in summer. Rarely will you run into another human on the beach here; it's a one-mile walk from the highway to the beach via the quickest route, a combination of narrow footpath and wooden boardwalk and, on the open sand, wooden posts marking the route. Other than the small overlook platform perched in the forest high above the beach, there is no sign of civilization.

None, that is, except that borne by wind and waves and stranded in the drift line. Among the broken shells and crab molt, twigs and logs, feathers and bones, clumps of green and brown kelp, and shreds of other seaweeds stranded by the high tide is a sampling of refuse. Little or none has been left by those few hikers who make it out here. The leavings of the world sweep in on the tide. Fishing nets and tangles of rope and plastic floats. Shotgun shells and plastic caps from summer fireworks. Plastic buckets and bottles of motor oil. Water bottles and detergent bottles. Glass bottles made for whiskey and sake, beer and soda. Tires. Lumber. Plywood. Busted styrofoam ice chests. Plastic toys. Metal tanks. Tarps and plastic bags. Light bulbs, inexplicably intact.

Ours is not the first generation to dump garbage here. Prehistory is written in refuse. The only evidence left of the earliest known inhabitants of this part of the coast is found in ancient midden heaps along the shore of nearby Tahkenitch Lake—domestic trash piles at least eight thousand years old. Bones of tomcod and hake and sculpin, clam and mussel shells, and charcoal from cooking fires. Until 2003, when archaeologists found older prehistoric middens sixty miles to the south near the town of Bandon, these bits of ancient refuse at Tahkenitch Landing were the oldest evidence of human life found on the Oregon coast.

The wrack line on the beach is a kind of modern midden, albeit a fleeting one. In addition to the native plants and birds and mammals and fish whose remains periodically are stranded in the tide line are plenty of remnants of human activity. Unlike ancient middens, though, this one isn't a reliable reflection of daily living in the immediate vicinity. The glass and, mostly, plastic debris that floats in may have traveled for hundreds or even thousands of miles and may have been at sea for years before wind and current conspired to dump it at this place, on this day.

"Forensic CoastWatchers," we started to call ourselves, as we speculated out loud about the origins of what we found: plants and animals, living and dead, part and whole, and the manufactured things discarded or lost by someone, somewhere. Now and then we'd find a genuine treasure, worthy of display on the windowsill at home: an unusually large, clear agate, or—just once—a glass fishing float.

Ultimately, it was stories I prized most. Everything on the beach has one—every discarded bottle, every dead seabird chick. Even when you can't get the whole story, the quest becomes a story in itself. And in the end, those are the best stories anyway.

Chapter One: *Gomi*

ANYONE WHO'S PROWLED SOUVENIR SHOPS or stopped for clam chowder at a café on the Oregon or Washington coast has seen glass fishing floats: sturdy, hollow spheres mostly the size of softballs but some as big as beach balls, mostly in shades of green and blue-green, sorted by price and heaped in bins or suspended on a wall or from a ceiling, some still encased in a filigree of rope as they were when fishermen attached them to their nets to buoy those nets at sea. Escapees mostly from Japanese fishing operations, the floats used to roll in on the tides by the dozens back in the fifties and sixties, or so I'd heard. I didn't think anyone found them any more since plastic had replaced glass. Certainly, I had never found one on any of my beach walks, anywhere.

But here it was, in the soft sand above the tide line, on a sunny May afternoon following more than a week of rainy weather. It was pale blue, the blue of a Bombay Sapphire gin bottle but shot with fine bubbles and etched with pale pink diamonds in a not-quite-symmetrical pattern, unlike any glass float I had ever seen. A few grains of fine sand clung to the pink parts in places, and faint concentric rings circled the glass, most visible at what you might call—if it were a fruit—the blossom end, with an irregular blob of glass at the stem end. It was smaller than a baseball, a little more than two inches in diameter, almost small enough for me to wrap my fingers around. It seemed much too pretty to have hung on the edge of a fishing net, too pretty for a day's hard work at sea, too pretty to be cast into the ocean for any purpose. I felt certain this was no fisherman's float. I had found an original work of art.

It was, after all, spring of 2000, four months after the turn of the millennium, a turning point in history that, in retrospect, seemed to have tapped into people's core emotions, from paranoia and fear—of widespread economic collapse and social breakdown—to generosity and hope. Artist and part-time Waldport resident Bryan Duncan fell into that latter category, or so it seemed from a newspaper article I'd read. One afternoon in 1997, he was sitting on his porch and musing about the coming turn of the millennium, thinking that it would be fun to mark it with some kind of big art project, when his wife walked out and, apropos of nothing, said something to the effect of, "Gosh, nobody finds glass floats on the beach anymore." With that comment, Duncan said, it just clicked: two thousand glass floats for the year 2000, no two alike, on the beach for people to stumble across unexpectedly, a gift of art when and where you least expect it, serendipity and generosity trumping fear and greed. He was an amateur glassblower himself, and he assembled a team and got to work producing a hundred glass balls to help him share his vision and drum up financial support.

The local convention and visitors bureau loved the idea and was more than willing to buy the globes and the advertising to tell tourists all about it, luring them to the beach in the off-season for a kind of Easter egg hunt on the sand. By the time 2000 rolled around, the Festival of Glass concept was rolling as a brilliant marketing gimmick for tourism on the central coast, and Duncan had lost all control of his millennial art project.

I had not seen any of these millennium floats, those made by Duncan or by any of the other artists who had joined the project, but I was fairly certain I'd found one that May day. It was the only logical explanation. Even if genuine glass fishing floats still washed up on Northwest beaches now and then, I didn't think they looked like what we'd found, a pretty sapphire-and-pink bauble. I called the Lincoln City Visitor and Convention Bureau and described the small float I'd found.

"Doesn't sound like one of ours," I was told. The contemporary artist-blown floats were bigger—at least twice the size of mine—and had a flat button on the bottom, allowing them to stand on a shelf without rolling away. And the flat buttons were clearly stamped with the year "2000" and the artist's name.

There were no numbers on this float, no name, no markings of any kind, and no flat button to keep it from rolling. Just a plug of pink-frosted blue glass, chipped on one side like a bitten nail and centered on a little elliptical bubble of glass that, if you held it right, looked like a tiny eye.

STU FARNSWORTH'S HOUSE NORTH OF SALEM is in a modern suburban development sprung seemingly overnight from the farmland that edged nearly to his street. New and well kempt outside, pin-neat inside; not what I expected at the home of an inveterate beachcomber and glass-float collector. Then he walked me into his garage. It's well-organized and neat there, too, just very crowded, with blue plastic lidded boxes piled everywhere, boxes filled with glass fishing floats, stacked to the ceiling, along every wall, two and three rows deep. These are just his spares, he explained—his trading stock. He led me into the house and up the carpeted stairs to his office, where his best floats—those small enough to fit on shelves—were displayed in a glass case, each nested in a wooden curtain ring. The range of colors was astonishing. There were blue and green balls in hues I'd never seen in a float: amethyst and olive amber, aquamarine and cobalt. And there were brown floats, red floats, purple and orange and clear floats. One little yellow sphere shot with bubbles looked so much like a piece of hard candy, it made my mouth water. A red one was textured like snakeskin. One pale blue float was sealed with a button of royal blue. Most were round, but some were elongated—rolling pins, or rollers, he called them—and a few larger ones, outside the case, were dumbbell-shaped or were double spheres, twinned: two round glass floats fused together. A few floats had water inside. One had a thin spindle of glass stretched across the hollow interior, formed, he explained, when a drop of molten glass dripped as the float was being sealed. He had a separate case of European floats— his new passion—but my eye was drawn to the better-lit case of vibrantly colored Japanese floats nearer the window.

"I mean, you've never seen a color 'til you've seen this!" he exclaimed, pointing to a plum-colored globe. He pointed to another that he said is his favorite, then to another as his most valuable, then to the rarest one; like children, each one seemed to be his favorite.

It is from this office that he corresponds, mainly by e-mail, with other collectors in this country and in Europe and Japan. He monitors the Internet, mostly eBay, looking for rare floats and keeping an eye on price trends. The Internet had led me to him and to his book, coauthored with Alan Rammer, *Glass Fishing Floats of the World: The Collectors Price Guide and Identification Handbook.*

Tall and broad-shouldered, with a salt-and-pepper crew cut, Farnsworth looks like a Marine but with a pixieish smile that animates his face, cutting deep grooves in his cheeks, especially when he's on his favorite topic. I pulled out the float I'd found—four years had passed since the day we found it on the beach, and in that time the pink frosting had mostly faded to a milky white against the clear blue glass—and told him about stumbling upon it among the bits of driftwood high up on the beach. He tilted his head a bit and busted open that smile.

"Weren't you excited?" he asked, beaming. He reached for the float and held it up to the light from the window, turning it slowly in his hand.

"That's an oldie," he said, then pointed to the white patches where, he suggested, sand had scoured the once-smooth glass to a rough, matte texture. " See the net marks? It probably got caught up in the Aleutian Islands for a while and got 'sandblasted.' "

The pink color, now nearly gone but for spots of it on the bump of glass—the seal button, he called it—was actually a type of algae, he said. A crustose alga, I learned later, probably in the family *Peysonnellia,* related to the sometimes fan-like, sometimes branching pink seaweeds that grow deep in the rocky intertidal zone, revealed to beachcombers only on the lowest tides. It was definitely a Japanese float, he said; he could tell from the smooth, symmetrical shape indicating it was blown, not molded, and from the fairly neat seal button. I asked which fishery he thought it had been used for. Salmon gillnetting maybe, he said. "It was probably used up in the Aleutians, probably caught up somewhere on the shore and blasted with sand with the net still on it." How old was it? From the size—he called it golf-ball size, though according to the specs in his book, it fell into the baseball size category—it probably dated from the 1950s or early '60s, when many floats this size were made, he said.

But who really knew? "If you were to pick up one of these floats on a Northwest beach, it might have been lost anytime from 1910 to last year," I read in *Beachcombing for Japanese Glass Floats,* a dog-eared paperback I'd found in a secondhand bookstore. "If it did not contain a trademark, it still might be difficult to trace it to any ten-year calendar period." At any rate, Farnsworth didn't seem too keen on history; his interest in floats was centered on aesthetics and the serendipitous spirit of collecting. He was doing his best to answer my questions and help me solve a mystery, but I sensed that his answers—just educated guesses, really—were not so much about setting the record straight as they were about not wanting me to go away empty handed.

"In Japan they call 'em *gomi*—junk," he said. "They think we're funny for collecting them."

As a child, Farnsworth used to hunt arrowheads in the eastern Oregon desert with his dad; his wife grew up beachcombing with her family on the Oregon coast. He still remembers the first time a float caught his attention, nearly thirty years ago: a basketball-sized orange glass orb, shining like the sun itself, hanging from the ceiling at his in-laws' beach house at Netarts, on the north coast. His wife's grandmother had found it one morning more than forty years earlier, in the 1930s near Sand Lake, where her family farmed. It had stormed the night before, and the beach was littered with driftwood and seaweed, including a pile of kelp with a glint of gold within that happened to catch her eye. Farnsworth dates his own passion for collecting floats to a morning in the late 1970s when he and his wife were walking the beach south of Cape Lookout. They happened upon an old man with a gunnysack. In it were three glass floats the man had just found on the sand: the morning's harvest, free for the picking. As Farnsworth puts it, "I was bitten by the bug."

It wasn't long before beachcombing was beginning to organize his life and even influence his career path. He took a job as a manager at a large discount chain store, a job that allowed him to set his own schedule. Whenever conditions were right, he'd head to the beach, an hour's drive to the west.

"I know this sounds crazy," he said, "but you can smell it in the air." A west wind is what you wait for, he said, grinning broadly. "Oh yeah, believe me. When the *Velella velella* starts coming, that's great," he said, referring to the inch-long, violet-blue members of the jellyfish family better known by their common name, by-the-wind sailors, that strand by the millions on the beach each spring. "Whenever you find driftwood with gooseneck barnacles on it, that means it's been at sea a long time, it means you know it's coming in. When there's a good, solid, 15-mile-an-hour west wind, you'd better be on the beach, because the stuff's going to start coming in." First come the big floats, he said, then smaller and smaller floats, and finally the rolling pins.

The very best time to be out, he said, is early in the morning or even in the middle of the night—1 or 2 a.m.—at high tide, at the height of the storm, when it's raining so hard you can barely see, when the rain leaks through your rain gear and starts running down the back of your neck, when your feet are soaked and you have to lean forward to make progress against the gale. That's when you really find the floats, he said. "That's hard-core beachcombing."

As a new collector, he amassed a pretty fair number of floats by walking the beach on those stormy nights, most of them ordinary blue and green softball-sized floats, "a bunch of nothing floats," he says dismissively. In the back of his mind, however, was a big amber-colored float he'd spotted in a gift shop in the town of Rockaway. "I really wanted it bad," he says. The shop owner had priced it at something like $300, "which was a lot of money, I mean a *huge* amount of money back then. So I amassed a collection of about $300-worth of common floats, and I went in and asked her, 'Would you take these common floats, which you can probably sell easier than this big one, and give me that one?' And she said, 'Sure.'

"So that got me going, that was my technique. That's how I built up my collection. I would trade quantity for quality."

Soon Farnsworth and his collection were a regular fixture at beachcomber festivals in small towns along the Northwest coast: Seaside and Netarts in Oregon, and Grayland and Ocean Shores, Washington. That's how he got acquainted with Amos Wood, the dean of Pacific Northwest beachcombing. Wood, a Boeing aircraft engineer, was the author of *Beachcombing for Japanese Glass Floats*, the paperback I'd found secondhand. It was the first guide of its kind and an instant classic. It summarized his findings from years of "vacation beachcombing" and included interviews with fellow beachcombers and correspondence with glass-float makers in Japan. Until his book came out in 1967, glass floats were a complete mystery to virtually everyone who found them on the beach on the eastern side of the Pacific, and the theories about their origins ranged from the pragmatic to the near-mythical: *They were made by fishermen aboard fishing boats. They erupted from the summit of Mt. Fuji. They were made by street vendors in Tokyo. They were used to transport opium.* He began quizzing friends of friends returning from trips to Japan. He sent scores of letters to Japan but got no response. Finally, a breakthrough: at a dinner party, he explained his quest to a fellow guest, and she put him in touch with a friend of hers in Japan, an elderly woman "of some circumstance and influence" who lived near a fishing village. Soon his mailbox in Seattle was filled with photographs and letters from Japanese glass-float manufacturers detailing their operations.

Japanese fishermen were not the first to use glass rather than wood or cork floats, he learned. Glass floats were introduced in Japan in about 1910 but had been used in Norway as early as the 1840s. Through his correspondence with Japanese glass manufacturers, Wood learned how fishing floats were made, in large and small factories, by artisans free-blowing glass globes into hemispherical shaping molds to size them for different needs, or in the case of rollers, blowing them into fully enclosed molds, then sealing the floats with plugs of molten glass and hardening them in brick annealing ovens. He learned why there were so many different sizes: big, extra-buoyant floats were for long-line tuna fishing, medium-sized floats suspended from tangle nets were used in bottom fishing, and some of the smallest floats held up salmon gillnets. Before World War II, there was such demand for glass floats in Japan that ten factories specialized in their manufacture, a number that had dwindled to six by the early sixties. By 1967 plastic had supplanted glass on many Japanese fishing boats, but glassworks in that country were still producing some two million fishing floats a year. He also confirmed what some beachcombers had suspected: Japanese fishermen lost or discarded roughly half of their stock of floats every year. Given those figures and others he had gathered, Wood estimated that as of the mid-1960s there were still some ten million Japanese fishing floats circulating on the currents of the North Pacific.

"So if you have yet to find an Oriental glass ball, just keep looking," he concluded. "Plenty of them are merely waiting to be thrust ashore, and plenty more are being turned out daily from the ovens of the Japanese glassblowers."

"He was a huge celebrity, he was the main guy," Farnsworth recalled of Wood. So was Farnsworth, who was courted by organizers of beachcombing fairs. "They wanted me to set up my collection to display, because I was real serious into it, and he wanted to set up next to me, which was quite an honor.

"He taught me a lot," Farnsworth continued. "He was so nice. Never had a bad word to say about anybody. He would share any knowledge he had with anybody." Wood died in 1989. By then *Beachcombing for Japanese Glass Floats* was in its third edition; it would remain in print until 1991.

"See, back in those times, float collecting was, you go out on the beach, you walk the beach," he explained. "You're out and it's pouring down rain or it's sleeting or hailing and the winds are blowing hard, and you're just loving it, you're having so much fun—it's exciting, you know?

"Amos used to sit next to me and I would pick his brain; we would talk and talk and talk and talk and talk. Once I had a purple float, and I asked him, 'How much do you think this is worth?' And he says, 'Probably about $300.' 'Amos,' I'd go, 'That's ridiculous, this is worth a lot more than $300!' 'Stu,' he'd say, 'that's a 32-cent piece of glass right there. What makes you say that that float's worth more than $300? I'm saying it's a 32-cent piece of glass, and I'm telling you it's worth $300, which is a lot of money compared to 32 cents. What makes it worth more to you?' 'Because it's rare.' 'OK,' he says, 'that's why it's worth $300.'

"He'd be very sad to see what it's become, because it's all about eBay now," Farnsworth said. These days collectors from Miami to Kansas City buy their floats from dealers who buy from fishermen who pick floats out of the water on their way back to the fish processor from the open sea, or from American servicemen stationed in Japan who spend their days off prowling the beaches of Hokkaido and northern Honshu and pawing through piles of discarded glass floats in Japanese fishermen's gear shacks. "There's this one guy—he's a big, big float collector—he told me once, 'Why should I go out on the beach? I can buy them in stores, junk shops, and on eBay. Why would I want to go out on the beach?'" Farnsworth recounted.

"The thing is, you go out on the beach to smell the fresh air, to listen to the ocean roaring, to have the sleet pelt you in the face, to have it rain so hard that it's going down your shirt even though you've got rain gear on—that's half the fun of it! Or coming up to a creek that you have to go across that's maybe 4 feet deep and it's rushing out into the ocean."

What you're *not* doing is driving on the beach, as float collectors do nowadays, anywhere it's allowed, mainly on the broad beaches north and south of the mouth of the Columbia—Gearhart, Oregon, and the Long Beach Peninsula—and on the beaches of the central Washington coast. And competing for floats on eBay is not the same as beachcombing.

"ebay has changed everything," he mourned. "With eBay there are more and more collectors. When prices were reasonable, it was fun. But it's gotten so out of hand." Collectors today, he said, "don't even have to get wet anymore."

Farnsworth's book was his attempt to bring some sanity to float prices, which he established after asking twenty-four collectors of various income levels what they would pay for specific types of floats. But price ranges and guidebooks are for ordinary collectors, not for those memorable characters who have made the hobby "crazy," collectors like Jim Watson.

"Jim was a dear friend," Farnsworth insists. "Very rich. Very nice, and very rich." When he came on the float-collecting scene in the 1980s, Watson was something brand new. He didn't prowl the beaches at 2 a.m., Farnsworth said; he hired people to do it for him. And if there was a float for sale that he wanted, money was no object. Like the day Watson showed up at Farnsworth's house holding a shoebox; Farnsworth figured it held some small floats to trade, and he invited him up to his office.

"Tell you what, Stu," Farnsworth recalls Watson saying, "I got an idea." Watson opened Farnsworth's glass display case and pulled out a teal-colored rolling pin, one Farnsworth knew Watson had coveted for some time. Then Watson sat down on the plush carpet of Farnsworth's home office and opened the shoebox. It contained not floats but stacks of $100 bills, paper-clipped together in piles of ten. Watson, staring at the teal roller, reached in the box and pulled out first one packet of bills, and then a second: $2,000, sitting on the carpet, waiting for Farnsworth to pick it up.

But that seven-inch teal roller had great sentimental value to Farnsworth. He'd spotted it by chance in his rearview mirror on a drive through the Willamette Valley town of Lebanon, where it was one of a pile of floats stashed in an old garage; it had taken him years to get his hands on it. "I really can't do it," Farnsworth told Watson, "but it's an awfully nice offer, I really thank you."

"Well, OK," Watson said, and he pulled out two more packets, setting them on the carpet: $4,000.

"Jim, you know, that's an incredible offer; I'd be stupid not to take it," Farnsworth recalled telling Watson, "but it has sentimental value. I could never replace it, so I don't want to do it."

"You're turning down $4,000 for that float?" Watson asked.

"'Yeah, I'm turning down $4,000 for that float.'"

So Watson reached in the display case and grabbed a grooved roller that Farnsworth had received in trade from a close friend who had made him swear he would never, ever trade it or sell it to anyone else. Watson laid the grooved roller on the floor next to the teal roller and pulled out three more packets of $100 bills. Now there was $7,000 on Farnsworth's carpet.

"I'm thinking to myself, Stu, you would be a real idiot not to take $7,000 for these two floats that Amos Wood said are worth 32 cents apiece. But then I'm thinking, if this guy is willing to pay this much money for them, then they must be pretty rare, and it's kind of fun to have something that somebody else wants—the trump card." When Farnsworth said no to the $7,000, he recalled, Watson "wasn't real happy.

"Because when he made up his mind he wanted something, 99 percent of the time he got it."

Watson didn't give up on the teal roller. Another time, he offered to give Farnsworth a pair of first-class round-trip airline tickets to Hawaii for Farnsworth and his wife and ten days at Watson's beachfront island house in exchange for that single float. He was flabbergasted when Farnsworth turned him down. But Farnsworth wasn't even tempted. Sure, a trip like that would be fun, he said, but then it would be over, and he'd be back at home with, as he put it, "nothing to show for it."

"I miss Jim," Farnsworth said. Watson had died of cancer several years earlier. "He made the hobby crazy, and he's one of the reasons I went to collecting European floats instead of Japanese floats. But I miss him."

I asked Farnsworth if he'd ever been to Japan; I figured he had, given his familiarity with Japanese geography and the collecting scene there. The question seemed to catch him by surprise.

"No, I never did do that," he said. His face took on an expression of wonder and puzzlement, as if he had never really thought about it and now wasn't entirely sure why. "The cost is prohibitive," he mused. "I don't speak the language. What would I do?"

I was as surprised by his answer as he was by the question. We were in a room full of glass floats so rare, so prized by collectors, that one or two of them might have paid for a round-trip ticket to Sapporo. But then, I suppose, the trip would be over, and he'd be back in his home office surrounded by his collection, staring at the glass case holding all his favorites, save for one empty space—like the room of a child who'd run away and never returned.

And I, as greedy for good stories as Jim Watson was for rare floats, stood there holding a single little sand-scoured blue glass float—with no identification markings, no net attached, no water inside, it wasn't worth more than $5 to $10, according to Farnsworth's price guide—and found myself wondering how I could parlay this single little float into a research trip to Japan.

"Do people still find floats on the beach?" I asked. How much of a fluke was our find?

"When I started collecting I used to be able to find them all the time, but not so much now," he said vaguely, shaking his head. "There aren't as many, and the competition is absolutely fierce," especially in places like Ocean Shores and Long Beach, Washington, where cars are allowed to drive on the beach and beachcombers prowl the beach all night from behind the wheel. "When the floats are coming in on the Long Beach Peninsula," he said, "it's like Interstate 5 on Thanksgiving weekend."

So are glass floats still being made in Japan? I probed further. Amos Wood said they were in the 1960s, but that was forty years ago. Are they still being used by fishermen in Japan? Farnsworth shook his head, uncertain. He loved glass floats—loved to find them, to look at them, to trade them, to discover unusual shapes and colors. He apparently hadn't spent so much time thinking about where they came from.

Then suddenly he brightened. "You should talk with Walt Pich."

IT HAD BEEN A LONG DRIVE, up the Oregon coast and across the bridge at Astoria and north on winding two-lane highways through miles of heavily logged forest, to reach the slender south-pointing finger of land that was Ocean Shores, Washington. The annual Beachcomber Fun Fair wouldn't get under way until the morning, but the community's brand-new convention center was already busy with arriving vendors and exhibitors setting up their displays. I turned off Ocean Shores Boulevard and onto West Chance a la Mer Street, then pulled over to stretch my legs: the air was full of the mewing of gulls and the burnt-sugar smell of seaside candy shops. The beachfront motels and concentration of shops that constituted the city center were clustered here at the peninsula's north end; to the south stretched a labyrinth of canals and streets named for every possible coastal cliché: Driftwood, Sea Urchin, Sand Dollar, Starfish, Butter Clam, Barnacle, Gull, Tall Ships, Spinnaker, Mizzen, Frigate, Trade Wind, Diamond Head. One house caught my eye with its front landscape devoted entirely to an arrangement of round beach stones and Styrofoam fishing floats. This was indeed a beachcombing town.

In its nineteenth year, the Fun Fair wasn't much older than the town itself. There had been tourist motels in nearby Moclips and Pacific Beach at the turn of the century, but fifty years later the flat, six-mile-long peninsula was still nothing but ranchland—the first white homesteader had shown up in 1860—and accreted tideland. Then in 1960 a group of investors bought the entire six thousand-acre peninsula from the grandson of an early rancher for $1 million. They started planning a community and selling lots, and in 1970, the city of Ocean Shores was incorporated. Thirty-six years after the town's incorporation, its mostly modest houses were among the most affordable beach places on the Oregon and Washington coasts. With house after house lining Ocean Shores' winding streets, it seems those who bought this peninsula for a cool million got a bit of *chance à la mer* themselves.

It was nearly sunset, so I turned my car west, toward the beach, intending to park and stroll, but before I knew it I'd rolled right past the small parking area and was driving on the beach—I'd forgotten it was legal here. It's not only legal—it's embedded in the culture: "Like I-5 on Thanksgiving," as Stu Farnsworth had said of the nearby Long Beach

Peninsula, but he could just as well have been talking about the beach at Ocean Shores during glass float-yielding storms. The beach was long and wide and nearly hard as pavement; the dozen or more cars parked here this evening in early March were all pointing west, and there were more headlights in the distance to the north and south. The setting sun had slipped into an opening below a line of scudding clouds and a thick bank of cottony clouds hanging on the horizon and was painting a mural in turquoise and orange and gold.

I was among the small crowd waiting in the convention center lobby the next morning for the exhibit hall doors to open: locals, mostly, and a few out-of-towners, judging from the conversations. One neat, middle-aged man was holding a purple glass float, softball sized, with "snakeskin"— an intentional texture some float-blowers added in an effort to attract squid, he explained when I asked. The float also had some curious white calcite inlays, like bits of shell, and patches of rainbow iridescence, like gasoline floating on water. It's part of a collection from the Marshall Islands that he bought over the Internet, he said; he had driven down from his home on Vancouver Island, British Columbia, hoping to make a trade here. He does some beachcombing near his home, but the beaches are rocky, and nearly all he finds of glass floats are "nubs"—the seal button, after the float itself has shattered. "It's global now," he says of the collectors' market for glass fishing floats. He went to Japan a few years ago and spent three weeks prowling the east coast of Hokkaido. "We found so many it was crazy."

"Are you a collector?" he asked me.

Hardly. "I've just found one," I said. Then I remembered the green softball-sized float I'd received in trade for a hiking book a year earlier. Shirley Loeffel had found it one day in 1995 at the mouth of Grant Creek, near her home in Newport. "And," I added, "I ... *acquired* another."

He looked me in the eye and smiled knowingly, nodding slowly. "There will be more *acquirements.*"

The doors opened, and I started circling the large exhibit hall. Along the walls were tables filled with exhibits; county fair-style, they'd been submitted in advance, judged, and awarded ribbons. The categories were listed on a sheet I'd picked up at the entrance:

Class I: Floats—maximum of 10 floats in collections, strictly enforced

A-1. Individual glass float, with or without net

A-2. Glass float collection, maximum 10 floats

A-3. Float collection, other than glass, maximum 10 floats

A-4. Glass floats not found on Pacific Northwest beaches, maximum 10 floats

The list of class categories went on: "collections of beachcombed items," "mosaics and collages," "finished driftwood," "natural driftwood," "zoo review" (driftwood that looked like an animal and was arranged to heighten that effect), "household furnishings made from beachcombed items," "most unusual beachcombed items," and the catch-all, "potpourri."

Any doubts I had about whether glass floats still appeared on Northwest beaches in 2006 were quickly quashed. "Super ball—found Sunday, Feb. 5, 2006" read a label accompanying a green float at least eighteen inches in diameter with a faint tracing of red in its green glass, sporting a third-place ribbon; that had been found just four weeks earlier. "Wild waves brought this cranberry swirls float up to the beach in Westport, Washington" read the tag on another large float; Westport is just on the other side of the entrance to Grays Harbor from Ocean Shores. The label continued: "I have also found four rolling pins since that big storm. 2006 is turning into a great year for beachcombing!" Glass floats weren't the only beachcombed treasures on display. Honorable mentions had gone to a collection of thirty-three construction helmets found on the beach and to a century-old brown glass Purex bottle found along Grays Harbor two months earlier.

The middle of the exhibit hall was occupied with booths, including those of several glass-float dealers. A cranberry-colored "basketball" was priced at $1,250, and a small purple roller was marked $395. A swirly-textured cobalt sphere six inches in diameter had a $950 price tag. There were plenty of lesser floats as well, but values had clearly risen since Farnsworth and Rammer had published their price guide in 2001. Floats the same size and color as mine, with or without the kinds of net marks mine had, with no identifying figures stamped on the seal button, were now fetching $25 to $35. Groups such as Grays Harbor Audubon and the Ocean Shores Interpretive Center and Westport Maritime Museum had set up tables and display boards and were handing out information about their activities. A handful of prominent beachcombers had set up elaborate displays showing off gems from their collections.

I found Walt Pich right inside the entrance, holding court from a folding chair in the midst of a display of huge green floats—beachball-sized spheres, a good two feet in diameter, still encased in knotwork of thick rope, stacked above his head. His eyes were what most struck me about his appearance; they scanned, peered, twinkled when he smiled, but they never stopped looking. A parade of friends and acquaintances dropped by to greet him and exchange news; some got an invitation to a party at his beachfront house that evening. Collectors stopped in to show him floats they'd found or bought, asking what he knew about them; most left with an autographed copy of *Glass Ball: A Comprehensive Guide for Oriental Glass Fishing Floats Found on Pacific Beaches*, the second of his two self-published books on beachcombing.

Pich had been part of the Beachcomber Fun Fair nearly from the beginning. Doc Bedillion, a local beachcombing legend and Pich's neighbor in Ocean Shores, started the Fun Fair in collaboration with Alan Rammer, Stu Farnsworth's co-author; Bedillion soon roped in Pich to help as well. Bedillion had died a decade earlier, but his widow, Irma, was still involved with the fair; she, Pich, and Rammer served as judges of this year's fair entries.

Pich's books *are* comprehensive: they are the result of more than thirty years of intensive, almost frenzied, beachcombing in Oregon and Washington, Alaska, and finally Asia, "by yacht, Zodiac, sea kayak, airplane, helicopter, backpack, wetsuit, surfboard and climbing rope," as he writes in his 1997 book, *Beachcombers Guide to the Northwest*.

"The damn glass balls are worse than drugs," he said with a self-satisfied grin. "Normal people go to Disneyland. I go to some wild beach. I'm not normal. It used to be I was looking for floats every second I had."

An environmental consultant, Pich split his time between his home in Federal Way, south of Seattle, and the beach house he built in Ocean Shores in the early 1980s. He'd grown up in New Jersey, gone to college in California, got a job with logging giant Weyerhaeuser in southern California after college, and been transferred to Tacoma in 1973. That same year he took his first backpacking trip on Washington's remote Olympic coast. It was on that trip that he happened upon his first glass fishing float.

"I found it on a pile of kelp," he recalls. "It was a standard blue-green, three-inch baseball. The next trip I went out there I found another glass ball, and it was the second or third trip I found a rolling pin. That kind of sealed everything. By the third or fourth time, I was hopelessly addicted."

He first combed the nearby beaches of the Washington coast, then started exploring north: Vancouver Island, the Queen Charlotte Islands, and up into southeastern Alaska. He walked. He kayaked. He partnered with a friend in the charter boat business in Alaska and motored out to even more remote beaches and islands.

Other collectors followed, urged on in part, perhaps, by the articles Pich had begun to write for outdoor magazines. But by the mid-1990s, he says, "It got to the point where we were finding absolutely nothing." Other collectors had beaten him to the sweet spots and taken everything of any value off the beach. "The cookie-jar beaches were deserted."

Then he was contacted by an American in Japan who taught school for the Department of Defense and had read Pich's articles. He invited Pich to join him for some collecting. Pich flew to Japan and spent a few days beachcombing on northern Honshu but was not very impressed by the results. Then the two of them headed north, to the northern tip of Hokkaido, and began working their way down the beaches on the large island's northeast coast.

What Pich found was mind-boggling even to an experienced beachcomber like himself. Photographs in his 2004 book tell it best: the author sitting on a grassy dune surrounded by several thousand five-inch floats, abandoned—he was told—more than forty years earlier; an acquaintance of Pich's perched on the edge of a wooden crib that corralled six thousand or more rolling-pin floats in a Hokkaido fishing village. The first three or four times he went to Japan he searched for floats just by beachcombing. Then, having studied a little Japanese, he started talking with fishermen and poking through their sheds, finding even more float treasures. As his proficiency with the Japanese language improved, he was able to ask more questions of the fishermen he met and, increasingly, to understand their answers.

"I'll sort through fifteen, twenty thousand balls a trip to look for colors or shapes or oddities," he explained, adding that he brings home only what he's allowed to check as luggage, making him very selective. "There's lots there. It's just like here—only there's a lot more floats to pick through, and you have to walk a whole lot less to find a whole lot more."

As he collected floats, washed up on beaches or abandoned in piles in the dunes or stashed in fishermen's sheds, he began collecting background information far beyond what Amos Wood, who hadn't visited Japan himself, had compiled: how different kinds of floats were made and what various shapes and sizes were used for. Pich returned to Japan again and again, sometimes making several trips a year, each time picking up a little more of the language and a little more information about glass fishing floats.

Pich even tracked down Yoshi Asahara, a third-generation glassblower in Otaru, a port city near Sapporo; Asahara's grandfather, Kiyukichi Asahara, had started what he said was the first glass-float factory in Japan and the largest ever on Hokkaido. From Asahara he learned more about the origins and evolution of glass-float manufacturing in Japan; with few exceptions, Japanese floats were individually blown in factories scattered up and down the Japanese seacoast. Pich learned more about the uses of different sizes and styles of Japanese floats. He learned about the identifying marks some manufacturers put on their floats (though Asahara-made floats bore no such marks). And though Asahara had no accurate production records from those early years, Pich learned that the number of floats made by his and other Japanese factories—some of which, Pich had confirmed with his own observations and conversations with fishermen, were still in use off Japan—was huge.

"When asked how many balls were produced over the last three generations," Pich writes in *Glass Ball,* Asahara "thought for a moment, looked up, moved his arm in a slow skyward arc, responding, 'Like the stars.'"

"Researching the history of glass ball production in Japan is an extremely daunting project," he adds in *Glass Ball*. "Not only was there a devastating war where much of the country was destroyed, but the glass factories kept limited records.

"The only sources of accurate information," he continues, "are interviews with veteran fishermen and glass-factory employees as well as statistical information generated from old abandoned piles of floats in fishing villages." Over the years, Pich says, he interviewed hundreds of fishermen. "Every so often," he writes, "maybe one interview in ten will yield a bit of information that answers one of the many questions. It is this process of searching through old gear and interviewing fishermen, and interpolations and extrapolations based on these methods, that gives us the little history we have."

Without ever visiting Japan, Amos Wood had nudged open a window on the mysteries of Japanese glass floats for American collectors in the 1960s. Some thirty years later, Pich came along and flung that window wide open. By the time the nineteenth Beachcomber Fun Fair rolled around, Pich was making plans for his twenty-fifth trip to Asia later that spring.

A visitor ambled up to Pich with a question: Were rollers really used to transport narcotics, as she'd heard? Not true, Pich responded with a patient smile. Giant rolling pins in particular are still rumored to have been made for that purpose, he said, but in fact they were made for use in the Japanese sardine fishery in the 1950s. She picked up a copy of his book, flipping through it silently for several minutes. He autographed it while she wrote him a check.

Another woman approached holding a clear-glass rolling pin. He took it in at a glance. "Shark roller," he said. "They use these for shark gillnetting." Her face lit up with a smile. He turned it to examine the marks in the seal button. "That's *katakana*," he said, without further explanation. Maybe she knew that *katakana* is one of three writing systems used by the Japanese, or maybe she didn't care. "You have a treasure there," he added with a grin. She promptly bought both of his books. "I've been on the Internet looking at this stuff," she said, beaming. "I'm so excited to be here! We're from Oregon." She and her husband—trailing her through the convention center—had found ten floats since moving to South Beach, just south of Newport, four years before. Now her husband piped up. "In November I found a soccer ball-sized float one morning," he said, "and that afternoon I went back out—I wasn't even looking for anything—and I found one a third again bigger." The wife then revealed the rest of the contents of the basket hooked over her arm: an assortment of green and clear floats of various shapes, mostly small. "These," Pich said, pointing to a modest green roller, "are from Hokkaido. It's been a big year for rolling pins. They use these for octopus." He launched into an explanation of how the floats are used to line the octopus nets, how the fishermen catch the octopus with unbaited hooks. But she didn't seem to be listening; she just stared at her modest collection with added fondness.

From the wealth of recent finds displayed in the exhibit hall, it was clear that glass floats were indeed still appearing on Northwest beaches, if not in the numbers they once did. Photographs in Pich's books provided ample evidence of the large stockpile of glass floats still found in Japanese fishing villages, and his conversations with fishermen there indicated that, even in 2006, glass floats were still in use, at least by some. I wondered if glass floats were still being manufactured, adding to the world's supply and, ultimately, ending up floating free in the Pacific Ocean.

"The Chinese make 'em, and the Japanese make a few," he said and pointed to a collection of floats on an adjacent display table: smooth green glass orbs, basketball sized, with longitudinal lines indicating that they had been blown into a closed mold, not free-blown into a shaping bowl as most Japanese floats were. "Those are Chinese, recent, for long-lining tuna and salmon." Probably 95 percent of the floats used by Japanese fishermen these days are plastic, he estimated, but many fishermen still have stockpiles of glass floats stored in their sheds, to sell to collectors or to have on hand should they need them. Chinese glassworks are now starting to make reproduction fishing floats in a variety of colors and shapes, even rollers, Pich said.

In fact, one of the most puzzling glass-float mysteries involves some of the newest floats. In the mid-1990s, as Pich details in *Glass Ball,* he began finding a new kind of float on the beaches of western Japan: the size and squat shape of a pumpkin, anywhere from seven to eighteen inches in diameter, in a brilliant array of colors, with a curiously sunken seal button and odd dabs of glass stuck to the outside here and there. Within a year or so, they started appearing on Japan's Pacific side, and by the turn of the millennium they were washing onto the beaches of Oregon and Washington. Then, three years later, they all but disappeared. They were too crude to have come from a Japanese glass factory; they had never been seen by collectors on Chinese or South Korean beaches, as far as Pich knew. Were they of North Korean origin, perhaps, or the work of an individual glassblower in some obscure hamlet in China or Russia?

"Pumpkin floats." It's astounding that in the Age of Information when deep mysteries such as the structure of DNA are being unlocked, so little is known about something so mundane as a kind of glass float produced somewhere, for some reason, in obvious profusion. Something crosses the ocean, and in that process, separated from its original purpose, becomes unfathomable to others. Picture something you use every day, perhaps something made locally or not, a simple tool or utensil. A garlic press. A porcelain egg cup. A bulb planter. A windshield ice scraper. A grapefruit spoon with its serrated edge. Something that speaks instantly to you of its utility but is unintelligible to someone from another culture, where there is no ice in winter, or no windshields to see through, no grapefruit. Were it to appear on the beach an ocean away, divorced from its function, it could be utterly unknowable. It would take travel, and language, and sometimes something more—a cultural bridge of some kind—to make sense of it. When that thing that appears on the beach is also a thing of beauty, glistening with seawater and glinting in the sun, there is absolutely nothing about it that is not magical. This is the sort of mystery, the sense of surprise, that Bryan Duncan sought to rekindle with his millennial glass-float project, a mystery he was carefully crafting in the late 1990s—utterly unaware that another glass-float mystery, a real one, was bobbing just offshore, shaped like a pumpkin, maybe even rolling onto the beach a few steps away from him at that very moment.

OTARU IS A PORT CITY of about one hundred forty thousand people located thirty-six minutes by rapid train west of Sapporo on Hokkaido, the large island north of Honshu, site of Tokyo. It's in the crook of the elbow of the northwestern Hokkaido coastline. The waterfront is busy with small cargo ships and large ferry boats and pleasure craft and a few fishing boats—long, slim octopus boats with large electric lightbulbs strung in a line and suspended over the working deck. From the water, the town rises steeply on a series of hills. Locals prize their town's architectural heritage, particularly the nineteenth-century tile-roofed stone warehouses found along the waterfront, and a few *nishin goten*— "herring mansions"—large homes built by herring fishery magnates in the late nineteenth and early twentieth centuries to house not only their own families but their businesses and employees. But present-day Otaru is characterized by boxy modern buildings, metal-roofed to handle the heavy load of snow that falls every winter.

With the demise of herring fishing as the town's economic engine, Otaru is trying to position itself as a tourist attraction, capitalizing in large part on its heritage as a center of glassblowing. The streets near the waterfront are lined with glass-related tourist shops: galleries of exquisite art glass, souvenir shops with glass knickknacks, "hot shops" with working furnaces where you can see glass being blown or even— with lots of help from the young staff— blow your own little bottle or vase.

The factory that put Otaru on the map as a glassblowing center— Asahara Glass Factory—is nowhere near the galleries and studios on the waterfront. To reach it, I followed the verdant banks of the Katsunai River up toward the folded green hills above town, past block after block of small one- or two-story houses with opaque glass windows or, seen through clear windows, shoji screens and new compact cars in small driveways. Trees and rose bushes in the small front gardens of the houses were trim and well-tended, as were marigolds and violets in pots on the front steps. A tiny Shinto temple, squeezed between a couple of houses, was approached through a series of red *tori* gates; it was roofed for protection from the elements, and just outside the front entrance was a table holding a small white vase with a clutch of fresh boxwood branches. Weeds sprouted through cracks in the pavement, but there was no litter, anywhere.

My interpreter and I arrived at a neat ocher-colored, two-story home; across a gravel driveway stood a gray concrete-block building—a garage with a little office in the front corner. A half-dozen floats in knotted ropes hung outside the front office window; there was no need for further signage. Presently Yoshi Asahara emerged slowly from his house and waved us into the office, where we sat down to wait for him. ("He must take his medicine," my interpreter explained.) The office had the clean smell of a place that's well-aged but not often used. A tall kerosene heater stood on the floor, not necessary this hot day in early July. A large wooden desk was littered with dusty glass fishing floats, vases and cups, and stacks of papers; no one had been working here much lately. On a wooden tripod stood a pale blue-glass candle lantern, round like a fishing float but with a large opening at the top. It looked like the lanterns photographed for the posters tacked high on the opposite wall: little points of light bobbing in the black stream of Otaru's waterfront canal on a winter night. "Otaru Snow Gleaming Festival," each poster read in English and Japanese; they were arranged chronologically from the first—in December 1999—to the most recent, 2005. High on the near wall, above the desk, were a series of framed black-and-white photographs: of Mr. Asahara as a young man, lips pursed at one end of a long steel pipe with an orb of molten glass billowing at the other end, and more formal portraits of his father and grandfather.

I had been warned that it would be hard to find an interpreter in Otaru—that, unlike in Tokyo, English is not widely spoken on Hokkaido. But the host at the hostel where I was staying was conversant in English and had put me in touch with Tomoko Wahei, a tall, engaging, middle-aged woman who eked out a living running a little tea room, arranging study-abroad programs in New Zealand for local high school students, teaching English to a handful of adult learners, and picking up the occasional interpreting job. She had been abroad, briefly, a few times herself, in the unlikely pattern of the traveler who follows not fashion but personal connections and opportunity: Helena, Montana; San Francisco; and Dunedin, Otaru's sister city in New Zealand, where she served as interpreter for the mayor of Otaru on an official visit. Her business, Tea Room Merino, was decorated in a Kiwi theme and served black tea in dainty china cups and saucers. Her English wasn't perfect, but it was good, and she was earnest and intent, a good listener; you could almost see the new words being added to her store of English vocabulary in every conversation we had.

"I thought that he was an artisan, but he looks like a teacher!" Tomoko whispered as Asahara-san emerged from his house and walked slowly toward the garage in soft house slippers. He wore dark gray slacks, a neat dark orange shirt, and zippered khaki jacket, and his gray hair was neatly combed. We bowed, and he nodded and settled into the chair at the desk, gazing past us, toward the window, as he listened to Tomoko translate my questions and he formulated his responses.

It was in the Meiji period—the nearly fifty-year era ending in 1912—when fishermen in Japan began looking for a better way to float their nets, he said. For generations they had used wooden and cork floats—I had seen examples of them in the historical museum on Otaru's waterfront—but over time wood and cork lose buoyancy as they absorb water.

By Asahara's account, glass floats were already being used by fishermen on the West Coast of the United States at the turn of the twentieth century, and groups of Japanese fishermen from Hokkaido had visited the United States soon after 1900 to find out how they were made. No doubt ocean currents had carried these or even early Scandinavian glass floats to Japanese shores, just as they later carried Japanese floats to America. The fishermen returned from America without much information, perhaps because—according to research Amos Wood had done—those first glass floats used by American fishermen were actually made in Germany. But the Japanese fishermen brought examples of those floats to Asahara's grandfather, Kiyukichi Asahara, who in 1900 had started the Asahara Glass Factory, then in the center of town. It produced small jars, lanterns for gas lamps, and other household items in high demand before the days of electric lights and plastic. Could Asahara also try to make hollow glass balls, *ukidama,* to line the edge of fishing nets, they asked, balls that would never absorb water and, if enclosed in a sturdy lacework of rope, would hold up for many, many fishing trips?

"He tried many ways to find out how to make the glass like that," Tomoko translated. "So, trials and errors for him." Those trials led him to develop steel shaping bowls, hemispheres that glassblowers used to efficiently shape floats into smooth spheres of specific sizes. The technique would allow him to produce large numbers of floats inexpensively. About 1910, the elder Asahara gave an early run of baseball-sized glass floats to a group of crab fishermen heading out to the North Pacific, east of the Kamchatka Peninsula, where huge fleets of Japanese boats fished in those days. "Those groups carried the glass balls as a trial, and it was successful—*really* popular and successful," Tomoko translated.

Japanese fishermen began abandoning wood and cork floats, and it wasn't long before virtually all floats used to line Japanese fishing nets were made of glass. Soon *Asahara Garasu Seizou-sho* had more business than it could possibly handle, so Kiyukichi Asahara offered his techniques to other glass manufacturers, and other Asahara family members scattered to open more factories: in Hakodate on southern Hokkaido, and in Aomori prefecture at the northern tip of Honshu. Manufacture and use of glass fishing floats spread south, to Sendai, on the Pacific side of Honshu, and Akita, on the eastern coast.

"As you can see," Tomoko translated for Asahara, who swept his hand north, toward the waterfront, "Japan is surrounded by sea." Nearly 18,500 miles of coastline, in fact, almost as much as the entire continental United States. At the height of glass fishing-float use prior to World War II, Asahara said, some eight million glass floats were being produced annually by factories in the cities of Otaru and Hakodate and in Aomori prefecture alone. "So the factories are all over Japan," Tomoko continued. "All the factories got really busy producing glass balls."

So busy that the neighbors complained. In those days, the furnaces that melted the glass and the ovens that hardened the finished floats were fueled with coal. As Otaru's population grew, so did complaints about the smoke from the glass factory. So, in 1934—the year Yoshi Asahara was born—his grandfather and his father, who was by then helping run the business, moved the factory to what was then the outskirts of town, a good four miles up the Katsunai River from the waterfront. The factory switched to using fuel oil in the 1950s.

Asahara paused to light a cigarette. He had been very ill with heart trouble, Tomoko had told me as we waited for him in his office; he'd spent four months in the hospital earlier in the year. I was guessing congestive heart failure: the slow gait, the fatigue, the deep, hacking cough, and the four Kents he smoked in the course of our interview.

When did the factory stop making glass floats? I asked. Tomoko translated. Asahara, his expression almost stoic up to this point, cracked a smile as he answered.

"He is still making glass floats for fishermen!" Tomoko said, gleeful— by now as caught up in solving the mysteries of glass floats as was I.

Production of glass floats did indeed decline after the war, notably in the 1960s, as plastic began to replace glass in everything from housewares to fishing gear. Plastic floats are lighter, thus easier to handle and much cheaper to make. One by one, the other factories on Hokkaido and in Aomori prefecture quit making fishermen's floats. But not every fisherman had given up glass floats. Plastic is cheaper, but glass floats are actually more durable. Exposure to saltwater, sunshine, and rough use is much harder on plastic than on glass, which, unless it's broken, can last indefinitely. And it tends to endure if it is properly enclosed in rope. So glass is still used by many fishermen along Japan's west coast, the Sea of Japan side—near Otaru, for example—and in such places as Sendai on northern Honshu, according to Asahara. Glass floats are also used extensively in inland aquaculture.

"Answering strong demand from fishermen," Tomoko said, consulting the notes she'd scribbled as Asahara spoke, "he has to keep making glass balls for fishermen." Since 1965, floats have been the only products made by Asahara Glass Factory. Though production had slowly declined, his shop still produced about twenty thousand floats every year, for Japanese fishermen on Hokkaido and all along the Sea of Japan.

Was it true, I asked, that fishermen used to throw their nets, glass floats and all, overboard once the ship's hold was full of fish? It's a story that American float collectors often mention, one that seemed unthinkable to me.

"It was the practice in the days when north sea fisheries were flourishing," Tomoko translates. "That was quite common in offshore fishing, particularly tuna fishing, not coastal fishing. Every time they went fishing they threw the nets and glass balls overboard to make room for the fish." Tuna floats, he explained, are the big 30-centimeter floats—*basketballs,* in American collectors' parlance. Asahara Glass Factory made—still, as of 2005, he said—forty different sizes of floats, from tiny 3-centimeter floats used to float octopus nets to jumbo 45-centimeter floats that mark the location of crab pots sitting on the floor of the Sea of Japan as much as one kilometer below the surface. Medium-sized floats are sometimes threaded partway up a net that is hanging deep in the ocean; they support the work of larger floats that bob on the surface, at the upper edge of the net.

Would Asahara-san mind if I looked around his factory? He rose slowly from his chair, and Tomoko and I followed him outside to a large concrete slab, half of it bare, the other half covered with a metal framework and draped with a tattered patchwork of blue and clear plastic tarps, rattling and flapping in the wind. The factory actually burned down in 1988, he explained; since then, he'd met the limited demand for glass floats in this half-rebuilt structure. To our left was a pile of empty and discarded milk bottles as tall as my shoulders—his current raw material, he said. These days he starts with clear glass and adds color. When demand was at its peak, the factory was always in need of glass and used anything it could get—recycled milk bottles, sake bottles, even beer bottles, he said. But the beer bottles didn't work out too well. "He heard from the fishermen that the fish avoid areas if they can see the floats," Tomoko translated, "so the color should be the same color as the sea." To the fish, he was told, the beer bottle-brown floats looked black, and the fish steered clear.

We tucked through a slit in the tarp-covered wall and into the diffused light of the tarp-roofed glassworks. In the middle were brick furnaces for melting and heating glass; at one end stood a pair of brick annealing ovens, where just-blown floats would be baked and very slowly cooled, a process to harden and strengthen the glass. On shelves along the far wall and piled here and there were steel shaping bowls in all sizes, now rusty with old rainwater, catching glints of sun through the tarps.

"Now glass balls are quite popular, and tourists buy them," Tomoko said, translating for Asahara. Aware of American collectors' interest in *ukidama,* Asahara said, some fishermen who had switched to plastic still hoarded their old glass floats in their warehouses, waiting to sell them.

Does Asahara-san plan to continue to make floats? I asked. What does the future hold for Asahara Glass Factory? The third-generation master glass float maker's eyes crinkled in a quiet smile. There would be no fourth-generation float maker; Asahara had two sons, but both were involved in other businesses and had no interest in manufacturing glass floats for fishermen. As for Asahara himself, he still believed in glass.

"As long as you don't break it, it lasts for many, many years," as Tomoko phrased his response. "Even though you throw them away." I had met a friend of Tomoko's who lived in the nearby fishing village of Oshoro and who said she frequently finds grapefruit-sized glass balls in the earth behind her house as she digs her garden; she figured fishermen probably buried them there with the rest of their trash, back when they made a switch to plastic.

"It's not the cause of pollution!" Tomoko said, echoing Asahara's defiant tone. "It returns to the sand." Glass will rise again, he predicted, after the world realizes the harm plastic is doing to the environment. "Then," Tomoko translated as Asahara listened, smiling, "glass will be needed. That's why he continues to make glass floats, no matter how small the production."

I pulled the float I had found in Oregon from my bag and held it up, telling him—with Tomoko's help—the story of finding it that May day on the beach. Is there anything Asahara could tell me about it? I asked. Gingerly he took the small orb from me and fingered it, turning it slowly over and over in one hand. "Rocks and sand," Tomoko translated, as he pointed to the opaque white patches on the otherwise transparent blue glass. "The rubbing produced that, nature produced that," she said. "It may be very old!" she added. "He thinks it took many, many years to get to Oregon."

Why are there bubbles in the glass, in this float and in the float Tomoko's friend found in her garden and in others, but not in the new lantern floats Asahara-san produced for Otaru's winter festival? It's about the temperature of the molten glass, he explained. Coal fuel didn't get the glass hot enough to disperse all the bubbles; since the switch to fuel oil in the 1950s the glass is no longer bubbly.

Walt Pich had written that, unlike the floats from some Japanese factories, Asahara floats have no signature on the seal button. Is that true? "His was the first one, so he has no markings," Tomoko translated, while Asahara continued to scrutinize the little blue float.

"He could not find any mark on it," Tomoko said, "so he doesn't know much about the ball, about who made it." She stopped to listen as he spoke up again, then burst into a wide smile, translating quickly. "He says it might be, possibly be, his! He's not sure!"

Asahara's definite *maybe* was a more definitive explanation of the float's provenance than I ever thought I'd get.

"He says when he gets better, he will return to making floats," Tomoko told me as we ducked through an opening in the tarp wall and stepped back outside. "If he doesn't get better, he won't!" she continued, her voice oddly cheerful—pleased, surely, not about Asahara-san's grave prognosis but about the success of the day's interpreting and her role in helping me solve the mysteries that had brought me from Oregon to Otaru. She paused, frowning slightly, apparently searching for just the right English idiom to succinctly sum up Asahara's situation—his poor health, and the glass factory's iffy future. Then finding it, she brightened.

"Sink or swim!"

THE NEXT DAY I TOOK a twenty-minute bus ride to the aquarium, east of Otaru proper; it was actually in the little fishing village of Shukutsu, at the last in a series of crescent beaches and accessible harbors that ended at a tall headland and cliffs that marched south. I didn't have high hopes for this small aquarium. I was more interested in visiting the restored herring mansion on the hill, now a museum; it reminded me of the mythical bathhouse in *anime* filmmaker Hayao Miyazaki's *Spirited Away*. And truth be told, I was hoping to find glass floats. I'd walked the entire Otaru waterfront and had come up empty-handed. Ditto for the town of Oshoro, where Tomoko's friend had found the floats in her garden; they may be buried in the earth, but on a visit there I didn't find any during a stroll at the port and along the back streets. A tourism poster plastered all around Otaru—including the corridor wall leading to the bathroom at the hostel where I was staying—showed the city's waterfront at night, in a misty blue light. "Otaru," it read in the slightly off-center English I'd grown accustomed to finding in Hokkaido tourist literature: "If you go, you will find what you are looking for—the journey you have been searching for." I hoped it was true. I had the feeling the floats were there, right around the corner, and I was just not looking in the right places; perhaps I was not yet searching for the right journey.

A narrow beach curved about a mile between two headlands defining Shukutsu. Long, slender, open fishing boats were lined up on the beach, with huge piles of plastic floats and sheds behind each one. More boats floated in a marina at the west end of the beach, where even bigger boats were hauled out. Fishermen making repairs hunched over nets spread on the docks in the sunshine. There were plastic floats everywhere, corralled in bamboo cages taller than my head and dumped in spreading piles on the docks: basketball-size floats in black and red and yellow, shiny-new and glinting like obsidian, like red car fenders, or dull and faded to pale hues and mottled with algae and the remains of barnacles. Nets of different kinds were folded neatly and piled in tall stacks by type.

A long breakwater enclosed the harbor, with a wide concrete dock lining the inside. A couple of fishing boats were tied up there, with what looked like piles of gear stacked nearby. A few tourists strolled the dock or scrambled on the breakwater. The day was sunny and hot but for a faint, cool breeze blowing off the water. I headed down the dock toward the tall orange-tiled tower topped by a navigation light at the harbor's mouth.

That's where I found them: not in loose piles, as I'd been led to expect from the pictures in Walt Pich's book, but nestled in bunches of angel hair-fine, green and white nets stuffed into blue plastic crates like laundry hampers stacked against the breakwater's concrete wall. Baseball-sized glass floats, just a little larger than the float I'd found, glinting like gems in their net nests, more floats than I'd ever seen in one place, than I ever really thought I'd see. Unlike my old float, the glass in these apparently newish floats was smooth and bubble-free. Some were colorless but most were in shades of blue and green, every shade of sea: the sapphire of the water's edge at a rocky sunlit shore, the dark olivey green of the deep water over a kelp bed on a cloudy day. Each was crisscrossed with a crude lace of twisted gray cord, and that cord was tied to a stouter blue and pink cord lining the edge of the net. Snagged in the nets were remnants of nearshore life—tiny clam shells and parts of small crabs, bleached white; matted blades of green and brown seaweed. Mixed among the floats, also attached firmly to the nets, were a few short, cylindrical red and blue Styrofoam floats and lots of brown-glazed cylindrical ceramic weights. The net-filled, float-filled crates, dozens of them, were stacked in groups, apparently belonging to different boats. Were they still in use? There was garbage piled with the crates too, or seemed to be: empty bottles, tires, old cans of paint, empty foil snack bags, a smashed beer can, a pair of stout brown rubber gloves, both halves of a broken shovel. Trash. Surely the faded nets and their floats were discards.

I wanted one.

Just one. Not to expand my collection—I didn't have one, really, and these small, ordinary, newish floats were of no particular value to a collector—but to memorialize the moment. If they were discards, and they clearly were, no one would miss just one, right? There was no one around to ask permission. A lone sport fisherman stood nearby, casting into the green water of the harbor. A couple of guys climbed out of a sports car to take pictures of one another on top of the breakwater. I reached out and tentatively fingered a float in a fluff of net; it was firmly attached. They all were. To take one I'd need a tool, would need to sever it from the net in an act of will. That seemed just a little too larcenous.

Instead, I wandered back to the beach opposite the breakwater where I knew how to satisfy this sudden yearning for *acquirements.* I might not acquire a float, but a handful of beach-polished sea glass would be a satisfying consolation prize. As I expected, the pebbly shore there was littered with "gems" in brown and green and blue—and wave-tumbled shards of broken pottery in celadon and floral patterns of blue and white.

I stuffed my pockets.

I returned to Shukutsu the next day, dragging with me an Australian college student I'd met in Otaru who had six months of Japanese language class under her belt. The crates of fine nets and floats were still there, but they'd been moved, and there were not as many. So they weren't discards, after all; they were working stock. We wandered over to the front street between the fishing sheds and boats lining the beach and the first row of houses in the neighborhood that stretched away from the beach and up the hillside. Now I saw glass floats everywhere: scattered beside houses, tucked in bunches alongside sheds. It was as if the first glimpse unlocked a door into a world where glass floats existed as commonly as rocks and shells, as plastic floats. A fisherman and his wife were unloading gear from the back of a pickup truck into their garage: crates of nets not quite as fine as those on the breakwater, but also strung with blue and green glass floats. "What did they use these nets to fish for?" Emily asked in her most precise Japanese. The wife smiled and pointed at a shallow metal pan on the garage floor, where the day's catch—flat flounders and other small bottom fish—lay in a sandy pool. How about the nets in crates along the breakwater, the really fine nets? What were they for?

"*Shako,*" the fisherman answered. Emily didn't understand.

"*Shako,*" the wife repeated. Emily shook her head slowly, a puzzled, apologetic expression on her face, mentally flipping through her Japanese vocabulary. *Shako?*

"*Shako!*" the wife insisted, then trotted into the house, emerging with a Ziploc bag of what appeared to be a half-dozen good-sized frozen prawns.

"Squilla—mantis shrimp!" Tomoko later translated when we showed her our "catch." We had never heard of that either. It's a local specialty, she said. *Shako* spoils quickly, so it's never eaten raw, only cooked. That night Tomoko took Emily and me out to a *yataimura,* a little cluster of tiny food booths off a corner of downtown Otaru's covered shopping arcade. It was a warm night. Red lanterns hung over the courtyard, illuminating a cluster of picnic tables where groups of men in dark business suits smoked and drank beer. The three of us squeezed into a little booth and sipped cold sake and ate *shako* sushi, the purple-mantled shrimp meat draped on neat bricks of sticky white rice, and I was glad the glass floats I had found that day hadn't been used to net sea slugs, or pufferfish.

IN 1991 WORLD-RENOWNED GLASS ARTIST Dale Chihuly—whose brilliantly colored, fantastically shaped blown-glass sculptures can be seen in permanent installations from Las Vegas to London—set out to create a series of works inspired by childhood memories of the glass fishing floats he used to see on the beach after storms in Tacoma, Washington, where he had grown up. I'd run across mention of the *Niijima Night Floats* in the course of my glass float research and had seen photographs of the series on display in Honolulu and in Palm Desert, California. They were pretty, a bit like big croquet balls on a lawn, or night lights in a garden. Prior to launching the project at a glassblowing center on the Japanese island of Niijima, I'd read, Chihuly had sought out the "last living master of blown-glass fishing floats." I figured that had to be Asahara-san.

Yes, Tomoko had confirmed as Mr. Asahara nodded gravely when I asked. "When Mr. Chihuly visited the factory," she translated, "he did not clearly mention his project, but he had his photographer take many photos of Mr. Asahara at work, and Mr. Chihuly was looking eagerly at the process of making glass floats." I was surprised to learn, then, that that was the last Asahara heard about the project. "Mr. Asahara thought that he was trying to get the technique of making glass floats," Tomoko explained. "Mr. Asahara hasn't seen any photos of Mr. Chihuly's works he might have made after his visit to the factory."

On a whim, back in the States, I called Tacoma's Museum of Glass—opened in 2002 as an ode to the Pacific Northwest's, and particularly native son Chihuly's, leading role in the contemporary studio glass movement—to find out if the installation might be on display there. Not anymore, I was told, but it *was* in Tacoma, on display next door at the Tacoma Art Museum. I made plans to see it on an upcoming trip to Seattle.

The *Niijima Night Floats* were scattered on a curved stone surface filling the museum's central courtyard, an irregular quadrangle enclosed with windows and exposed to the sky. I had expected to be underwhelmed; these were *faux* floats, after all, floats that never did a day's work, never spent any time at sea, and I had by this time seen hundreds of the real thing. But in that first moment, I was simply stunned to the point of tears: dazzled and overwhelmed by an intense feeling of well-being that was completely familiar.

It was the same feeling I get while walking the beach—not searching or beachcombing with a purpose, necessarily, but simply walking, and wondering what will appear, what unexpected, unexplained, undeserved treasure will reveal itself. Here were three dozen or so floats, large and small. Unlike on the beach, there were no logs, no rocks, no tangled piles of kelp or dead birds to hide them. The tall windows surrounding the courtyard created a mirror effect, and the floats seemed to ricochet off in every direction. They were all out in the open, and still I had the sense that I wasn't seeing them all.

Of course they looked more like the "floats" artisans now make and Oregon coastal chambers of commerce hide on the beach to draw tourists than like ordinary fishermen's floats. However, in this setting, they *felt* more like something you might stumble upon randomly: gifts from the sea, at once human and luminous. Turquoise with tracings of pale lavender in lines and spots like the branches and blossoms of a cherry tree. Ochre obscuring a fiery globe of orange and umber, like a cooling ball of molten metal. A golden float marbled with brown like an ancient urn. Cobalt clouded with slate striations like the moons of Jupiter, and a smaller cobalt sphere scudded with white like whitecaps at sea. Spirals of orange and blue, orange and yellow, indigo and lime. Some had a little depression at the top, the blossom end, where the day's rain was pooling. The scene was as compelling as the beach itself after a winter storm: stuff *everywhere.* They were planets of glass, flower buds of glass, perfect and imperfect spheres like fishermen's floats, with a brilliance you rarely see in functional glass floats but with all their variety and distinction.

The floats were arrayed in seemingly random order on a concave curve of granite tiles, like a bumpy skateboard park—gray as the beach is gray, the sand composed of grains of so many colors that it surrenders to a collective gray. They were on what is known as the "stone wave," a sculpture by Seattle-based artist Richard Rhodes, made of stones gathered from an ancient road in southern China's Fujian Province, where new road construction had made the stone road obsolete.

"The open-air stone garden brings the metaphor of water to the museum's core," an explanatory sign read. "The sculpture's form is a silent wave, and the undulating curves and textured stone appear to dissolve into the sky in the reflective glass and steel above." From where I stood, however, it felt more like a beach. Most of the floats seem to have congregated in the low point of the beach; others were scattered higher on the slope, as though pushed there by the tide.

A museum staff member sidled up to me; it would have been hard to ignore how enchanted I was by the installation. "When the sun shines it's pretty," she said. But I was glad it was a rainy day, a day more like those when a real float might appear. The rain was leaving matchstick streaks on the windows and hitting the pool formed in the depression at the top of a squat, dappled jade-and-crimson sphere. Wind ruffled the surface of the tiny pool, and through the water I could see a spot of iridescent blue, like a window of sky.

I continued around the courtyard on a gradually ascending walkway, then turned to survey the exhibit from this new, higher perspective. Like the sea itself, the demeanor of the stone wave had changed. Now the floats did indeed appear to be bobbing on the sea on a big, gray wave. They animated the stone wave, the play of light making water of the hard rock. I reached for the rail in front of the window, dizzied by the sight and even a bit queasy. A few more steps and I'd reached the corridor's high point, above the tip of the wave, and I was looking at the floats from above. Now I'd become a seabird, soaring over the ocean. The mirrored glass multiplied the wave into more waves and sent them off in every direction, and I felt, for a moment, that it would not be so hard to keep rising, higher and higher, watching as the floats crowding this wave shrank smaller and smaller and finally just disappeared into the wide, gray sea.

YOSHI ASAHARA DIED JAN. 12, 2007

Chapter Two: COMU

DEATH ON THE BEACH IS NOT UNUSUAL. Death and garbage are the beachcomber's bread and butter. Every few visits to Mile 157 we seemed to stumble across a dead bird or two. Years earlier, on a mid-December beach walk, we'd found six. I had had a field guide to the birds with me on that December walk and took a stab at identifying them. A scoter of some kind, maybe? The book said there were lots of them on the Oregon coast in the wintertime, especially surf scoters. A northern fulmar, or was it a shearwater? It was hard to tell. Most had been dead for a while, their feathers matted and bodies ravaged by scavengers; one wasn't actually dead but dying. None looked anything like the pictures in the bird book: plump and alert, standing or perching in profile or soaring, the palette of colors on their feathers stark and bright. They were, in the field guide, their best selves, idealized for easy identification. On the beach that cold day at the juncture of fall and winter, water and wind and the hunger of other animals had obscured their distinguishing characteristics, turning each of them into a heap of dark and light feathers, with necks and legs and wings at awkward angles.

But on this mid-September day in 2005, the breadth of dead birds was beyond anything we'd seen previously—or noticed, anyway. Not a scene of slaughter, no blood; in fact, it took a few minutes to realize that the little piles of wrack scattered across the beach *were* birds. Then our eyes adjusted, and we started seeing them everywhere. Dead, waterlogged birds, too many to miss even on a casual stroll. Dead birds all over the beach, high in the soft dunes and low on the flat, hard, wet sand. If we weren't careful, we'd step on them.

This time it was pretty easy to tell that most, if not all, the dead birds were common murres. My field guide described them as members of the auk, or alcid, family. They were small and stocky, the size of a small duck, with a dark head, a short, dark neck and back, a white breast, and dark wings brushed with white on the underside, "counter shading," as the book described it, possibly camouflaging them from their prey— fish—and from their predators such as sea lions and orca whales. Murres are seabirds; they live on the sea, get all their food from the sea, and come ashore only to breed. But unlike albatrosses, shearwaters, and other oceanic seabirds that spend most of their lives on the open sea far from shore and migrate tens of thousands of miles, the murres—like pelicans and cormorants, gulls and terns—are *neritic* seabirds, sticking close to shore, seldom venturing out past the narrow continental shelf. And, presumably, more likely than, say, an albatross to die near the shore and wind up in a heap on the beach.

The murres on the beach that day ranged from freshly dead to nearly decomposed. Those not yet found by scavengers were still plump, the short, white feathers covering the bird's breast curling softly like the hair on a baby's sweaty head, with dark wings bent sharply, as if still in a dive. If predators had beat us to the bird, the breast and wing bones looked like a picked-over chicken carcass, and all that was left of the neck and spine was a string of delicate bones, one tiny vertebra after another lined up like a necklace. The purple-black feet were generally intact, the webs between the three long, slender toes folded like a closed fan. The bill, among those birds with heads still attached, was black and sharp and a little shorter than my thumb. Some corpses were obscured by sand and seaweed; even so, it was easy to see they were birds. Sometimes all we found was a wing.

Visitation, they call it in obituaries when family and friends are invited to view the body of the loved one before burial. That's the word that came to mind. It was as if the birds were laid out for viewing before retrieval by the tide, or before becoming some other bird's dinner. At one point in our walk down the beach we looked up to see a bald eagle perhaps a hundred yards ahead, ripping into the carcass of a dead murre and attended by a trio of crows standing at a respectful distance. When we got to within fifty yards or so, the eagle spooked and, clutching the murre in its talons, lifted off and flapped into the dunes. Dangling from the eagle's claws, the dead bird's body unfolded, its wings stretched out, angular and limp, dark against the pale gray sky. Then the eagle lost its grip, or maybe it dropped the bird intentionally, planning to return later to feed. The murre plummeted to earth in its final dive, disappearing into the pale green swells of beach grass.

I wasn't altogether surprised to find all the dead birds; I'd read a front-page story in *The Oregonian* newspaper a month before about a big die-off of common murres, but at the time I didn't even know what a common murre looked like in life, off the pages of the field guide, let alone what a big murre die-off looked like. Now I knew: charcoal-and-white, football-shaped, duck-size birds and parts of birds, birds entangled in weeds and birds by themselves. And in the driftline, along with bits of wood and shell and remnants of green seaweed, lots and lots of small, matted, charcoal and white feathers.

COMMON MURRES ARE JUST THAT—common on every coast of the northern hemisphere where there are also plenty of little fishes and crustaceans. They nest on rocks and cliffs along the western coast of North America, from the Bering Sea coast of Alaska down to the Pacific coast off central California. In winter they spread out over the ocean, never too far from shore, generally staying above the continental shelf, sometimes venturing as far south as the northern coast of Baja California. There are more murres in Alaska than in Oregon, but there's more coastline in Alaska. With more than seven hundred thousand common murres breeding on offshore rocks in the summertime, Oregon is where the common murre is truly common. It is by far the most numerous nesting seabird on the Oregon coast.

Which surprised me when I first read it. Gulls seemed the most common seabird; they were certainly the commonest bird on the beaches I walked, not including the silvery flocks of little shorebirds that forage at the water's edge fall through spring. But the beach is obvious gull habitat. There are easy pickings on the beach: worms, stray potato chips, crabs washed to shore, dead fish, even dead murres. But murres like their fish live, so they dive underwater—and they do so better than almost any other bird, nearly as well as penguins. There is nothing of interest to murres on the beach; they come ashore only to breed, and they do that on high, rocky ledges along mainland cliffs or, more often, rocky islands just offshore—rocks off-limits to humans thanks to their status as wildlife refuges. No wonder I had no acquaintance with murres, the commonest of Oregon coast birds. To me, *coast* mainly means beach, long and lonely. To a murre, *coast* means a high rock, crowded with kin.

Very crowded. No other bird nests more densely than the common murrre, with the possible exception of penguins. In fact, in this and other respects, murres bear a striking resemblance to penguins. Standing, a common murre has the same alert posture as an Adélie penguin, and similar markings—the tuxedo-like white breast and black back—though at sixteen or seventeen inches from bill tip to tail, the common murre is smaller than all but the smallest penguin species. Some penguins build nests of pebbles; murres "nest" on bare rock. And both birds are expert swimmers, virtually flying underwater, propelled through the water almost entirely by their flapping wings. While other underwater diving birds—loons, for example— swim mostly by kicking their webbed feet, the murre's webbed feet are merely rudders, helping them steer; their horsepower comes from their short, stubby wings. Penguins have evolved into such efficient swimmers that they've lost the ability to fly. Murres fly—barely. If they were any bigger, any better evolved for maneuvering under water, the balance would likely tip, as it has for penguins, toward flightlessness. But for murres and penguins, it's a case of parallel evolution; they are distant relatives at best.

Common murres live and sleep at sea, often in rafts of hundreds of birds, tucking their heads into the feathers at their shoulders. In winter murres migrate, but not too far—not compared to the epic seasonal voyages of shearwaters and albatrosses and the like. Rather, they disperse, fanning out over the nearshore ocean, usually no farther west than the outer limits of the continental shelf, looking for food. The murres that breed in Oregon may head north, up to the plume of food-rich waters where the Columbia empties into the Pacific, or farther still, to the Strait of Juan de Fuca south of Washington's San Juan Islands. There is no southern Washington murre population, because other than Cape Disappointment, at the mouth of the Columbia, there are no large offshore rocks—murre habitat—on the southern Washington coast.

Oregon murres may arrive at their breeding rocks in December or January, certainly by mid-spring. They tend to return with the same mate to the same little niche on the same breeding rock, year after year, throughout their lifetime, which could be more than twenty years. There they stand, like little penguins, almost shoulder to shoulder, tens of thousands of them packed together in colonies covering the tops of rocky monoliths. The timing of their egg laying is closely linked to the availability of food. When the water at the sea surface starts to cool, generally in late May or early June, that means there will be more food available. To any parent, that seems like a good time to start having kids.

Or a *kid*. The female murre lays but a single egg—always just one—in what passes for a nest: a small depression on a narrow, bare rock ledge, for instance, or a rock platform next to a cliff wall. The egg, longer than a large chicken egg by about a finger's width, is distinctly narrower at one end, like an avocado: a critical design element for a bird that nests without a nest. Should a murre egg get bumped, it will roll in a tight semicircle. Each little family occupies just enough space for two adults to stand front to back or side by side—and no more.

For the next month, both mother and father murre take turns sitting on the egg; while one sits, one is away on the sea, feeding. One day, a crack appears in the egg, and over the next couple of days, the chick peeps and pecks its way out, finally emerging, downy and gawky like a cartoon bird with its big feet and long legs. Now there's a chick to feed, and the parental tag-team continues. Three to five times a day, one or the other parent will return from foraging at sea with a single fish in its mouth. Shielding the prey from her close neighbors, the mother murre—or the father—passes it to the chick, who gulps it down, bite by bite.

The chicks—there may be thousands of them by this time on a single rock—are no more than twenty or twenty-five days old when the colony, as a group, starts preparing to depart in mid-July or early August. Why wait? Getting the chicks onto the water and foraging for themselves saves the already feverishly flying parents a lot of energy. Following a genetically encoded internal timetable, the adult murres of the colony begin congregating at the cliff edges and calling excitedly, and the chicks start stretching their wings and moving away from the only home they've known. Within about forty-eight hours, at dusk, pairs of common murres—father and chick—start moving toward the water, the father softly crowing his encouragement, the chick answering with a high *wee-wee-wee*. The chick jumps or tumbles thirty or forty or fifty feet into the water, followed immediately by dad—unless it's dad who's gone first, flying down to the water and calling up to his chick to join him. If the chick survives the drop without smashing onto the rocks below or being picked off by a hungry gull, it paddles off with its father, in the company of all the other fathers and chicks, to begin its education, and its life, at sea; flight lessons come later. Mother, meanwhile, lingers on the breeding rock for a couple more weeks, giving her swimming partner and offspring a head start, before following by air with the rest of the colony's females.

In flight, murres flap their wings fast, furiously, unceasingly, because they have to. Gulls soar. Cormorants beat their wings with a slow, measured rhythm. Murres fly like they're driven by some inner need, and they are: by an almost insatiable quest for calories, to fuel an almost absurdly inefficient flying mechanism. One thing about wings: they can fly you through the air, or they can fly you through the water, but they can't do both well. Wings are built to soar, like an albatross, or dive, like a duck, but not both. That stubby murre body won't stay aloft for long unless wings better suited to swimming than soaring are in constant motion.

Without much fat on their bodies and burning calories like crazy when they fly, murres have tremendous appetites. It's like a crazy treadmill they can't get off: flapping so hard, they work up a fierce appetite, but to eat, they have to fly, and dive, more. An adult murre eats 10 to 30 percent of its body mass daily, or ninety to three hundred fish. Picture eating an entire Thanksgiving dinner yourself—the whole turkey, the stuffing and the mashed potatoes, a green bean casserole and the entire pumpkin pie, running laps between courses, and then doing it again the next day. Welcome to the murre's world of eating without ceasing.

Sitting on the ocean's surface, a murre will suddenly tilt forward, open its wings, and disappear underwater, heading for the ocean bottom, usually in waters at least a hundred feet deep, searching for small fish, crustaceans, and squid. Nearing the ocean bottom, it starts hunting, flapping its wings to glide through the water, swimming about as fast as we walk, capturing prey in its bill as it dives sixty, a hundred, two hundred, even five hundred feet deep, to the ocean floor or just above it, usually staying down a minute and a half, sometimes as long as three minutes. Underwater, a murre moves as easily as a fish, propelling itself with quick wingbeats, diving deep and darting through the black water, snatching prey. A murre typically eats what it catches immediately, even before surfacing, swallowing its prey headfirst and finishing it off in short bites: sand lance, rockfish, Pacific tomcod, whitebait smelt, northern anchovy, speckled sanddab, Pacific herring, market squid, crab larvae, and little shrimp-like krill.

Murres often forage in mixed-species flocks: murres, pelicans, gulls, cormorants, and other birds all working a fish-rich patch of ocean together, complementing rather than competing thanks to distinctly different foraging strategies. One bird species hovers, then plunges at a passing fish; another spies its prey from the air, settles on the sea, and then dives; another skims and dips. A whale or dolphin, capitalizing on the same bounty, can aid the birds by grabbing a mouthful of a fish and stirring up the school in the process.

Though seabirds are among the longest-living birds, up to twenty-six years for murres, they are vulnerable, too, to predators, accidents, or disease. Bald eagles and other raptors sometimes attack murres in flight— more often these days, with bald eagles reproducing more successfully along the Oregon coast. Diving for their food, murres sometimes dive into fishing nets, become entangled, and die. Childhood is the chanciest time of life for murres, as for many of us. Periodic infestations of parasites are harder on a colony's chicks than on the adults. Gulls and ravens may grab eggs and chicks, especially if the parents are scared off the nest. Chicks that wander too far from a parent may fall off a rock ledge or may perish on their inaugural plunge with daddy. Once at sea, the flightless chicks are easy pickings for sea lions and seals.

Oil spills hit murre populations hard. The birds live relatively close to shore, often close to or within shipping channels, where ships tend to wreck. Murres then pick up spilled oil as they rest or forage on the water. The oil coats their feathers, robbing them of their natural insulation so that they die of hypothermia; or they die of malnutrition after ingesting oil while preening their oiled feathers—the oil damages their liver and other internal organs. An estimated 350,000 seabirds, most of them common murres, died as a result of the *Exxon Valdez* oil spill in March 1989, and many murres die every year from other oil spills that never make it into the headlines. Millions of dollars have been spent cleaning oil-soaked birds—it makes for heart-warming photo opportunities—but few of the "rehabilitated" birds live more than a week or two after their release.

But oil spills, devastating as they may be, aren't routine events. The big killer of murres, summer after summer, is starvation. On the Oregon coast, murres' well-being, their very survival prospects, are closely tied to the *upwelling*, a complex ocean phenomenon involving wind and current and, along the coast, the Coriolus effect and the Ekman effect and various other effects familiar to physicists. When winter's sou'westers give way to summer's prevailing northwest winds along the Oregon coast, the warm water on the surface of the sea close to shore starts to move west, offshore, and is replaced by much colder, much saltier, and much more nutritious water burbling up from deep below, as much as six hundred feet deep, from the bottom of the continental shelf. This water is full of decomposed plants and animals from the sea floor: truly, the bottom of the food chain. The blessings of the upwelling then reverberate up through the food chain, from the smallest to the largest creatures that dwell in or on the sea. As the cold water moves up, traveling as fast as sixty feet a day, it becomes food for zooplankton, the smallest animals in the ocean. The zooplankton grow and multiply and feed larger creatures, from small fish and crustaceans to whales, and those little fish feed bigger fish and other whales and seals and birds, including—winging through the water and grabbing prey like underwater falcons—common murres. That's why murres wait to mate until the sea's surface starts to cool. To a murre, cold water means life.

Except sometimes the wind is late, or light, and the ocean upwelling doesn't occur quite on schedule, or something else goes haywire in this finely tuned system of marine checks and balances. When the upwelling is late, murres—whose biological clock is attuned to the chilling of the sea—delay their nesting, or fewer birds lay eggs. Or, sensing the start of a promising upwelling, they lay their eggs and hatch their chicks, nurture their chicks, and head to sea with their chicks—and starve, the chicks in particular, if the upwelling fails to pan out.

Even when everything works like clockwork—the wind blows, the cold water rises, the zooplankton are fruitful and multiply—big die-offs of adult murres in the summer are not unusual. Nature seems to consider murres expendable, a safety valve in the trophic system. Most years, more murres are added to the population than the ocean's resources can support. Some years, a lot more.

YEAR-ROUND, IT'S NOT UNUSUAL for one or two dead adult murres to show up in the wrack line on any given mile of Oregon beach, even more from June through August or, for young murres, through October. Pink-footed shearwaters, black-footed albatrosses, green-winged teals don't show up on the beach so often. But dead white-winged scoters, with their telltale white wingtips and stout duck's bill, are fairly common on Oregon beaches in late winter and early spring. And if you don't find a dead northern fulmar on the beach in Oregon in November or December, you're just not looking.

It's all in Bob Loeffel's records, filling a corner file cabinet in his home office south of Newport. I had read about Loeffel in a CoastWatch newsletter after he found a sooty shearwater with a scientist's metal band around one leg. He'd been looking for dead birds on a 4.6-mile stretch of beach near his home every week or so for nearly thirty years. I gave him a call, and he invited me to drop by; if the timing was right, we could walk the beach together. But the day I arrived at his house, tucked in the woods east of the highway, his wife, Shirley—now his birding partner—was a little under the weather. We talked instead in his home office, the better to access his records. In his late seventies, soft-spoken and deferential, dressed in jeans and a plaid shirt, he moved with the youthful grace of an athlete.

Fish, not birds, were what led Loeffel to Newport in mid-career back in 1970. Trained in fish biology and fisheries management at the University of Washington, he was sent by the Oregon Fish Commission to head a new field office at the marine science center on Yaquina Bay. His title was marine research manager, but there wasn't much research involved; mainly he kept tabs on the harvest of clams and crabs and marine fish— bottom fish, tuna, everything but salmon, which were managed by other agencies. He soon found, however, that whenever people found a bird on the beach on the central Oregon coast—a dead bird, or a wounded live bird—and felt compelled to report it to someone or even to bring it in, they tended to look around for some sort of official government agency on the coast, something to do with wild creatures. Back then, his agency was it.

In July 1977, the Portland office started getting reports of a high number of dead penguin-like birds on the beach. Naturally, the Portland office called Loeffel to ask what was going on. He had no idea. But he headed down to the beach and, indeed, there were a whole lot of dead birds—dead common murre chicks, specifically. He made a rough count per mile, then returned to the office and called in his report. Yep, lots of dead murre chicks, he said, but he had no idea why. He didn't even know if it was something to be concerned about.

The summer drew to a close, and reports of the dead birds on the beach tapered off. But his interest had been piqued. He regularly ran on the beach for exercise, and now his eyes were drawn to any damp clump of feathers on the sand; usually they were the same species, over and over. But late that year he found several birds he couldn't find in his Little Golden Book, the only bird field guide he owned. He asked some friends, who keyed them out and told him what they were.

"Then," he recalls, "I thought, why don't I monitor what's going on here?" So he did, tapping his resource-management training and his own penchant for order to keep careful records and slowly getting to know the various species most likely to appear. He let his exercise routine— how much of the beach he was likely to cover in at least one round-trip run every week or ten days—set the boundaries of his survey. The 4.6-mile stretch from Beaver Creek to Lost Creek seemed doable. He kept up the survey by himself for the first six years, and then one friend or another joined him, and in 1993, his wife. In recent years it had become a foursome: Bob and Shirley walked a 2.85-mile stretch, and another retired fisheries biologist and his wife covered the remaining 1.75 miles. To avoid counting the same bird twice, Loeffel got in the habit of tossing his finds into the dunes, above the high-tide line. Rarely does he now find a bird he can't identify off the cuff; in the year before I went to visit him, his records contained only one "unknown." Year after year, most are murres.

His purpose, he said, had never been to determine the cause of death; he leaves that to the researchers to whom he now turns over his data, researchers who have relied on his dead bird counts for at least three scientific papers, he says. His records were pivotal in the $4 million settlement that resulted from a spill of more than seventy thousand gallons of oil from the *New Carissa,* a wood-chip freighter that ran aground off the mouth of Coos Bay on February 4, 1999. Its bow section broke off during attempted salvage operations and drifted north to Waldport, just ten miles south of Bob's survey beach, spreading oil and death all along Oregon's central coast. "It came down to marbled murrelets," Loeffel explained. An endangered species and a close relative of the common murre but half its size, the marbled murrelet feeds at sea but nests inland, high on the mossy branches of ancient western hemlock, Sitka spruce, and Douglas fir trees. "There were a number of them found oiled and dead on the beach," he explained—262 of them, to be exact. "The question was, was that a normal thing? The only information they had, the defenders and the prosecutors, was this information," he added, waving an arm at the file cabinet in the corner. "We had twenty-one or twenty-two years of observations on a nearly weekly basis in this area for the months of February and March on what comes in on the beach at that time. And there were no marbled murrelets! Virtually none; we had two this past year, but no one could argue that the numbers they had seen had any reason to be normal. And the data that we collected is the thing that it swung by."

Only a handful of the thousands of dead birds he'd found in nearly thirty years of looking were banded: marked with a metal band on one leg, attached by researchers hoping to track its whereabouts. Most of the banded birds were cormorants. So he was particularly surprised to find a banded sooty shearwater one day in late May 2004. The beach that day had been covered with wrack. A strong west wind, Bob had learned, usually brings in the more interesting finds, such as glass floats and—in his sphere of interest—a few carcasses of pelagic birds, birds that live and often die far out at sea. And that was the case this day: five albatrosses, two fulmars, and five sooty shearwaters, one of which had a thin stainless-steel band around one leg, stamped with "Z 36524" and instructions about where in New Zealand to send a report. He took it to a friend at the U.S. Fish & Wildlife office at Newport's Hatfield Marine Science Center, who got on the Internet and found that it had been banded as an adult bird in 1997 on Tuhawaiki Island, off the south coast of New Zealand's South Island. White New Zealanders call them muttonbirds; the Maori, who harvest the birds as a traditional food source, call them *titi*. The research project behind the bird's banding was a collaboration among the Maori and scientists at the University of Otago, both of whom had an interest in better understanding the birds' behavior and boosting its survival prospects. The name of their project: *Kia Mau Te Titi Mo Ake Tinu Atue,* or "Keep the Titi Forever." Funding for the work came from a settlement following a 1998 spill from the oil tanker *Command* off San Francisco and San Mateo County, a patch of ocean sooty shearwaters use as a staging area prior to winging back to New Zealand, where they nest. As many as fifteen thousand of the shearwaters died as a result of that spill.

You could say that find sparked Loeffel's fifteen minutes of fame; it generated headlines from Portland (*The Oregonian* newspaper) to Dunedin, New Zealand, where he was featured in the project's *Titi Times*. But the banded shearwater wasn't his most memorable find. That had occurred way back in 1981, just three years into his nearly three-decade-long survey, when he stumbled across a seabird of uncertain species while jogging on the beach. Curious, he picked it up and took it to a friend at the science center, who suggested it was a gadfly petrel, a category that includes more than two dozen species of seabirds, among them shearwaters. The friend, also uncertain, sent the dead bird to another researcher, this one at the Oregon Institute of Marine Biology in Charleston, who tentatively pegged it as a Solander's petrel—a rare find on the Oregon coast, if that's what it was. But he wasn't sure either, so he prepped it for preservation and sent the "skin mount"—wings and body feathers, stripped of flesh and bones, dried for indefinite preservation— to the American Museum of Natural History in Washington, D.C. Before long Loeffel received a letter in the mail from Dr. George Watson, curator of the Division of Birds. The gadfly petrel, he said, was a Murphy's petrel, a little-known native of the South Pacific. It turned out to be the first recorded find of a carcass of a Murphy's anywhere on the North American continent. If you find mention of Murphy's petrel in a field guide of birds found in western North America—such as my Peterson's field guide, which classifies it as a "rare" or "accidental" species, "recorded in California, Oregon"—that's Loeffel's bird they're referring to. The carcass is now part of the museum's permanent collection. A few years later, on a visit to Washington, the Loeffels visited the bird, entombed in a drawer at the museum. "It is," he says modestly, "the single recovery of a bird that has been that outstanding, or that different."

But finding the rare bird, the bird no one else has found, isn't why he keeps walking the beach, he insists with a slight smile. "I'm not one that clamors to get something written up. Overall, it's more a matter of monitoring change than it is finding something unusual." Just surveying the same mile of beach, week after week for decades, makes Loeffel himself a rarity—unique, perhaps, in western North America.

"It's just something that isn't that easy," he says simply. "You've got to be of the right ilk, and you've got to be in the right location, and you've got to have time available, and be tolerant of the weather." You've also got to be a little bit compulsive about keeping records—and be good at it, he said.

"The other thing that became apparent, once I started doing it," he said, "was that I had a tiger by the tail.

"I started doing something that had merit, and I couldn't let go of it."

IT WAS AN OIL SPILL that turned University of Washington biologist Julia Parrish's attention to murres back in the summer of 1991. Then a post-doctoral student in zoology, Parrish was in the middle of her second summer camped out on uninhabited Tatoosh Island, twenty treeless acres of salmonberry and thimbleberry and fireweed and rock owned by the Makah Indian Reservation and located one-half mile off the tip of Cape Flattery, the northwesternmost point of land in the contiguous United States. Parrish had a particular interest in animals that live in groups: pods of whales, colonies of penguins, prides of lions. Group living has obvious advantages: all for one and one for all, and all that. But she was also interested in the personal and group costs of living so cozily, the risks incurred by close clustering. Pollution, for instance: if a neighborhood becomes fouled and everyone in a big extended family lives there, the whole family is harmed. She had already spent several years studying schooling fish and was looking for a new research subject.

Limpets fit the bill. Close relatives of snails, limpets live inside shells shaped like little conical hats and thrive by grazing on the coralline algae that grow encrusted on rocks along the shoreline. On Tatoosh

Island, large aggregations of limpets live high in the intertidal zone—the area uncovered by the ebbing tide twice every day. One of Parrish's professors had for years been running a research project focused on the rocky intertidal ecology of Tatoosh, and he invited her to join the project. She jumped at the opportunity and, in the summer of 1990, began commuting by boat from the dock at Neah Bay to Tatoosh with other members of the research team, camping out for days at a time in a rustic, wind-raked hut.

Now and then she'd take a break from marking limpet shells and recording changes in the mollusk colony at her feet to stretch her back, gazing up at the colony of common murres braying noisily on the cliffs overhead. Clearly, this was another animal that was big on togetherness. Tatoosh was rich with wildlife of all kinds, and Parrish would watch as bald eagles and peregrine falcons buzzed the murre colony, especially early in the nesting season. One advantage of group living, Parrish knew, was its potential for defense against predators: the bigger the group, the smaller your chances of being eaten by a predator, or so went the theory. A big group would be less likely to get uniformly flustered by one attacking predator than would a small group; while a small group might be scattered by an attacker, only a small part of a large group was likely to flee at a predator's approach.

The thing was, the murres on Tatoosh didn't appear to have read the same scientific literature Parrish had been reading. She'd watch a bald eagle fly over the colony—not even attack, just fly by—and the entire colony, two thousand or more birds, would levitate off the rock and wing away, in some cases leaving their incubating eggs unprotected and exposed. It was a spectacle she found impossible to ignore—and, as a zoologist, absolutely compelling.

In late July of her second year on Tatoosh, while she was on a break on the mainland, Parrish heard the news: a Chinese freighter had collided with the Japanese fishing vessel *Tenyo Maru* twenty miles miles west of Cape Flattery, and the fishing vessel, loaded with some 475,000 gallons of oil, had quickly sunk in ninety fathoms of water. She and the rest of the team quickly figured out just where the oil was headed. It wouldn't be pretty—and they needed to be there to witness it. They packed the boat with supplies and headed back to the island.

The weather on the day the oil slick arrived, pushed south and east by wind and ocean currents, was typical of late July and early August on Tatoosh Island. A kind of bright fog hung low over the water, backlit by sun that strained to break through the low, evanescent cloud, and where the cloud was especially thin, tendrils of mist fingered the shoreline. With fog obscuring her view of the water, Parrish, working on the shoreline, heard the oiled murres even before she saw them. It was a sound she had never heard before and one she would never forget: the slow, irregular flapping of hundreds of pairs of wings as murres that could neither fly nor swim, murres coated with thick, black fuel oil, moved toward the shore with a kind of awkward, halting butterfly stroke. Some birds made it to the beach before dying; others died at sea and floated to shore. In the end, some 4,300 dead birds were collected on beaches from Vancouver Island to northern Oregon following the spill and thrown into bags for later identification. Nearly three-quarters of them turned out to be common murres.

That's a lot of dead murres.

Or, Parrish found herself wondering, is it? Dead murres aren't uncommon on Northwest beaches in late summer. So how many is a lot? What's normal? How many more died as a result of the *Tenyo Maru* oil spill than might have died in the normal scheme of things? In fact, no one really knew. There were no baseline data for this part of the coast. No one—no official government agency, at any rate—had bothered to count dead seabirds on the beach in a normal year. "That kind of shocked me, when I really thought about it, and got me thinking about these large mortality events," Parrish said to me, speaking quickly, in a voice that seemed fired as much by a sense of urgency as by her own enthusiasm for the work. I had met her in her office in the glass-and-concrete Fishery Sciences building near the shore of Lake Union at the University of Washington in Seattle. "The cost of the clean-up for the *Tenyo Maru*, just the sort of normal, day-to-day stuff, nothing special, was a little over $5 million. I mean, that's a lot of money. And there was a settlement with the spiller, and they paid some $9 million, and immediately half of that evaporated as costs already spent. How is it that we can be spending all this money, collecting all these carcasses, and we have no idea whether this is a big thing or not a big thing, with respect to these species, these populations?"

Oil spills are common enough, it turns out, that there is a standard "cost recovery schedule" used to determine the dollar value of damaged natural resources—the price of an oil-suffocated limpet versus an oiled sea otter. Insurance companies add up the number of a particular species believed to have died as a result of a spill, multiply it by its predetermined value, add that to the value of other dead organisms also found to have expired in that event, and the case is closed. "You just do the math," Parrish said.

"I mean, it makes sense to me, and I understand you have to have this starting place," she said of the dollars-and-cents side of oil-spill response, "but you know, a murre in northern Washington is much more valuable than a murre in Oregon."

"If a thousand murres die in Oregon, it's a small percentage of the murres that are breeding there. If a thousand murres die in Washington"— where, with more sandy beaches and fewer offshore rocks, murres are much less common—"you could wipe out a colony or do some serious harm to the overall population." What was missing, Parrish realized, was a clear understanding of seabird mortality under normal conditions, in specific locations, year to year—as she put it, "the standard patterns of death on the beach."

"It kind of drove me nuts," she continued. "I had all this information, just really detailed information about what was going on with the murres on Tatoosh. I could tell you what they eat, I could tell you when the eggs are laid. I could tell you who eats the eggs. I could tell you where it's safe to feed, and on and on and on, I could tell you *everything* about the murres on Tatoosh, but that's just *one* place. And I know the murres move around. So it kind of drove me nuts that I had no way to census the larger population of birds. Selfishly, I wanted to know what the patterns were. And so I thought, I've got to do something about this."

It was the *Tenyo Maru* spill itself, its wake of oiled seabirds, that finally offered up a solution: Why not count dead birds? It was so obvious, it was brilliant.

"The great thing about dead birds," the zoologist said, "is that you don't have to sneak up on them." If you're looking, you can find them. You can examine them closely, even positively identify them if you know what you're doing—not always easy with a bird on the wing at a hundred yards.

What she'd need, she realized, were techniques to help the average non-scientifically trained person-on-the-beach identify commonly beached birds. And she'd need a way to mark the birds, to ensure that they weren't being counted twice and to allow researchers to track how long dead birds of different species persist on the beach. She spent several seasons trying out her ideas on Tatoosh, using the island as her laboratory.

What evolved in the late 1990s was a unique citizen science project she dubbed COASST, for Coastal Observation and Seabird Survey Team. The plan was to train volunteers to comprehensively survey perhaps twenty-five individual stretches of beach on Washington's outer coast, counting the dead birds that appeared each month and sending the data to Parrish's lab at the University of Washington for confirmation and collation. Monthly walks on the same stretch of beach, making observations following fairly rigorous protocols: COASST asked a lot of its volunteers. But somehow, Parrish struck a chord with the beach-loving public. COASST started in 1998 with twelve volunteers in Ocean Shores, Washington. By fall 2007, the project had more than four hundred volunteers doing monthly monitoring of beaches from Eureka, California, to Alaska's Pribilof Islands, in the middle of the Bering Sea.

Beached Birds: A COASST Field Guide, published in 2000, is one of the keys to the project's success. Regular bird field guides, Parrish found, are useless to volunteers faced with a heap of feathers and bones clumped in a line of wrack. Field guides typically express bird size in the measurement from bill tip to tail tip, and they rely on pictures— paintings or photographs—of birds in action, adding descriptions of the bird's behavior and voice as keys to its uniqueness. But a dead bird has no behavior, no voice. The plumage may survive, but often the bird is in pieces, missing body parts or, at best, disheveled. So Parrish and colleague Todd Hass began to rethink bird ID and construct an entirely new paradigm specifically for dead birds.

"Once we realized that the standard way that birders have taught themselves to identify live birds just doesn't work for dead birds, we realized we had to go back to square one and ask the question, what body parts last the longest?" Parrish recalls. "So we did a little study on Tatoosh, and then at Ocean Shores, and it turned out that feet last longest, followed by wings." So that's where *Beached Birds* starts: with an easy-to-follow dichotomous key—a branching series of paired questions, yes or no, leading progressively toward an identification—of feet characteristics, followed by a "wing table" based on the size and color of the wing. The field guide focuses solely on those sixty-five bird species commonly found dead on Oregon and Washington beaches.

The other key to the program's success is the trainings COASST staff hold for volunteers. Once they understand that the field guide for dead birds works differently from the field guides they're used to, once they've had a chance to handle some birds and practice keying out the feet and the wings, they're hooked. "There are a lot of people who come to trainings, especially on the outer coast, and they say, 'We've walked the beach for a long time and we never see dead birds,'" Parrish said. "When we did a training in Florence, Oregon, we went out on the beach for a little test run. We only had to walk fifteen feet, and there was a dead murre, and another, and another." It was an August weekend, the peak of the summer vacation season and the peak of the annual murre die-off, she said, "and the beach was completely covered with people who were flying kites and building sand castles and playing their radios and running around and going swimming, and there were dead birds *everywhere,* and it was quite clear they didn't see any of them.

"But take the training," she said, smiling smugly, "and I guarantee you, you will see dead birds *everywhere."*

THE SKY WAS STEEL GRAY, THE COLOR OF COLD, as I headed north to Bellingham, Washington, for a day of COASST training. Bare-limbed trees lined the freeway through the Skagit Valley, then blue-gray lumps of hills, and then hillsides dusted with late-February snow and, finally, sharp mountain peaks covered with snow, nearly disappearing against the white sky. There were no signs of the tulips that would be blooming here in a couple months; just the flatness of winter fields, brown-gray and muted with frost. A dozen Canada geese in formation caught my eye, transiting the sky ahead, and then a pair of long-necked swans angled across the freeway directly over the car. A flock of gulls dispersed in the sky off to my right; below them, a flooded field was dotted with ducks. I stopped at a freeway rest area and counted forty or more crows milling about the lawn and hopping among the alders and cedars.

Once you start to look, it's hard to *not* see birds.

The training was held in the conference room at the RE Store, a rough collection of re-purposed buildings built on top of the Holly Street landfill in Bellingham's Old Town, where Whatcom Creek tumbles into Bellingham Bay north of the mouth of Puget Sound. The RE Store is run by RE Sources, north Puget Sound's grassroots environmental-education organization, and its conference room was what you'd expect of a meeting room in a recycled building supply center: mismatched utility tables jammed together to create one big conference table, surrounded by a collection of secondhand chairs of every description. The dozen or so of us assembled there matched the demographics of Audubon Society chapter meetings I'd attended: a few men but mostly women, mostly retirees but a few folks in their fifties and, here and there, a college-age or just-post-college person. A bit past 10 a.m. Wendy Steffensen, wearing an enthusiastic smile and a baggy olive green sweater that appeared to have been re-sourced itself, introduced herself as the North Sound Baykeeper and told us what that meant: she worked full-time for RE Sources as an "educator and advocate and watchdog for our marine resources."

"Our presenters might be a little late," she cautioned, between descriptions of other environmental stewardship efforts we were also welcome to join.

A half-hour later, the COASST team swept in, loaded with laptop and projector and large plastic boxes and apologies. On their way from Seattle that morning, Jane Dolliver from COASST and two student interns had had not one but two flat tires. In one extended burst of enthusiasm, Jane simultaneously introduced herself and her helpers and opened her laptop and hooked up the InFocus projector and found outlets and people to find extension cords.

Jane had started working for COASST as an undergraduate intern; now, with a master's degree in zoology and biology, she worked for the program full time. "COASST is one of my passions—and seabirds as well," she said, smiling broadly. Meanwhile, the interns passed out COASST field guides and toolkits: large plastic bags each with a bundle of one hundred or more multicolored plastic cable ties—I knew them as *zip strips*—as well as a toenail clipper, a five-inch fixed-point divider (used like calipers to measure), a six-inch white plastic ruler, a COASST-branded retractable 150-cm tape measure, another ruler with 15 centimeters counted out in bold black and yellow bars, a piece of blackboard the same length and half as wide with the yellow-and-black centimeter bars on top and blank space below, and a white piece of chalk. Completing the toolkit were a handful of data sheets, a COASST volunteer contract, a thirty-seven-page instruction booklet, a volunteer profile form, a checklist of beach characteristics, and COASST's most recent twenty-eight-page annual report.

COASST volunteers look for a lot of things, Jane explained as she passed out our gear, but mainly dead birds. "Why document dead birds?" she posed rhetorically, now following her PowerPoint presentation and summarizing the answer in five short declarative sentences. "There are a lot of them. They were once alive. They died of something. They can be identified by anyone. They can be thoroughly examined and can provide a lot of valuable information."

Seabirds, she said, are "upper trophic"—top-o'-the-food chain. Seabirds die because the food they eat—fish, mainly—disappears, and the fish disappear when there's a change in the ocean. Scientists can learn a lot about the ocean's condition and the health of a range of marine systems simply by following patterns of seabird die-offs. "People *really* love whales," she said with an ironic grin. "But there are a lot more birds." Besides, she added, people like birds. They like to watch them—live ones especially, but dead ones, too, it turns out.

And after a little practice, COASST volunteers get really good at identifying the dead birds they find. They can determine the family a bird or parts of a bird belong to 93 percent of the time, and four out of five times they can even name the species.

The key, Jane said, is getting familiar with the *Beached Birds* field guide, one created, she explained, "because we realized there really was no guide we could give volunteers that wasn't filled with jargon and scientific hoopla." And unlike other bird books, *Beached Birds* does not include all the songbirds and the raptors, the woodpeckers and the kingfishers. It includes only those species that typically wash up dead on the inner and outer coast of the Pacific Northwest, on Puget Sound and the ocean beaches. They are mainly marine birds, especially the seabirds, which spend their lives on the ocean, along with some migratory shorebirds and a few land species commonly found at the beach—the American crow, for example.

The last thing to rot away or be eaten is the foot, so that's where *Beached Birds* begins, grouping birds by foot type. Is the foot *free* with little individual claws like outstretched fingers, or *lobed* with very fat fingers, or *webbed?* Big lobed toes mean it's a grebe, usually a western grebe, though there are a couple of other options. Otherwise it's more complicated. Free feet could mean anything from a little three-toed shorebird like a sanderling to a big four-toed perching bird like a crow. Webbed feet can be partial or complete, small or large, have three toes or four, and that fourth toe could be lobed or webbed or free. The guide, Jane explained, walks you through this process of elimination with large, simple drawings and yes-or-no decision points.

"We like to call it *Dead Birds for Dummies*"

From the feet, the book proceeds to bill length. Each entry in the book includes an outline of that species' head, so you can actually lay the dead bird's head on the water-resistant pages to compare the shape. Then you look at the plumage, which helps clarify the difference between, say, a common murre, with its uniformly dark, stubby wings, and a pigeon guillemot, with a white patch atop otherwise dark, stubby wings. Finally, a look at the bar graph shows relative seasonal abundance. Black bars indicate how likely it is this particular bird species will appear, dead, on either the Oregon or Washington coast any given month. The graphs, Parrish had told me, were best guesses, based on the only databases available at the time the book was published: several years of observations by a birdwatcher on the southern Washington coast, and for Oregon, Bob Loeffel's nearly three-decade record.

To be a "COASST bird"—that is to say, to be worthy of mention in the data sheets on a volunteer's monthly survey—the dead bird's remains must include at least one part that is measurable: a foot, a head, or a wing. Jane demonstrated how to use the fixed-point dividers to precisely measure the length of the bill, from the tip to the top of the mandible; the wing chord, from the tip of the longest feather to the "elbow," where the wing bends; and the tarsus, or the long bone connecting what might be called, in human terms, the bird's ankle and knee.

One of the interns began circulating around the table, a dead bird cradled in two purple nitrile-gloved hands, demonstrating what Jane was describing.The other intern dropped a black bird wing on the table in front of each of us and directed us to pull on the gloves COASST provided. "We use gloves," Jane said simply, "because we're touching dead things." We did so, then gingerly picked up our wings—normally stored in a freezer at the lab but thawed by now and each labeled with a number on a string —and began measuring them. The wings brought a faint odor into the room, of death and the sea. Grains of sand still clung to the feathers, black and brown on top and mottled white underneath. I pulled gently on my wing; it unfolded easily, like a fan.

It turned out we'd all been handed wings from common murres— naturally, given their abundance. "They're our first species in the guide," Jane pointed out.

Then she passed out feet. The feet were a little less smelly. The webbed murre foot I got was collapsed into itself; the toenails, curved and sharp, curled like an arthritic hand, black and scaly and reptilian. Above the ankle joint, downy tan feathers were still attached to the leg, just above where it had broken off, bone and sinew sticking out.

I had already bought the *Beached Birds* field guide and had tried, unsuccessfully, to use it—but in my usual fashion, without reading any of the introductory material. Now, being led through it, its plain-spoken descriptions and step-by-step, process-of-elimination logic seemed simple and straightforward and eminently understandable. Every piece of information one would need was there, every clue clearly laid out in color photographs and stats and simple drawings, just the way you needed it. It even had its own simple shorthand for the birds included: jam together the first two letters of the first and second parts of the common name, or if it's a one-word name, take the first four letters of that. So sanderling becomes simply SAND, western grebe WEGR, and common murre COMU.

One of Jane's slides showed a sinusoidal curve—illustrating how we were to walk the beach, snaking up and down, catching both the upper and lower beach and, ideally, everything in between. Especially on the broad outer-coast beaches, you can't just walk in a straight line and expect to find much, Jane said. "Birds can be hiding in wrack, so poke the piles of seaweed. If there are dead birds, often that's where you find them."

A little past 2 p.m., Jane and the interns began dumping whole birds and bird parts—feet and wings and bills—on the long tables in front of us. I picked up a small black bird, cold to the touch, still a little frozen from the lab freezer but its feathers downy soft. The head flopped as I turned it, cradled, in my hand, and the shiny black wings yielded willingly to my manipulations. The foot was webbed, with three toes—an alcid. But too small to be a COMU—unless it was a juvenile? The white breast was dappled with pale gray. I paged through *Beached Birds,* a little half-heartedly: it had been a long day of sitting, with a lot of new information. I was finding it harder and less compelling to distinguish one small black or charcoal gray bird from another.

"How many millimeters in a centimeter?" one woman asked. I wasn't the only one starting to get a little punchy.

A moving shadow in the corner of the room caught my eye. Out of nowhere, a slender black cat had appeared—drawn, no doubt, by its native interest in the subject, the increasingly pungent dead-bird smell filling the room. Slowly, with the calculated gait of the hunter, it closed in on a large opaque white plastic box, lid askew, sitting on the conference room floor. Standing on hind legs with its forepaws propped on the upper edge of the box, it peered inside, sizing up its pre-packaged prey, its black tail flicking.

"THE WAY THE TRAINERS TALK, two people should do it, but no way!" Mary Lou Letson asserted, standing in the Baker Beach trailhead parking lot north of Florence in a light rain and, like everyone, pulling on serious rain gear. "We find that six is wonderful!" It was the first Friday of October 2006, the start of the thirteenth consecutive monthly beached-bird survey of Baker Beach. Val Knox, another CoastWatch volunteer, had issued an open invitation for me to join the group on their monthly survey whenever our schedules meshed. A former plant-nursery owner and Bureau of Land Management botanist now living in Mapleton, she had taken the COASST training in Florence in 2005, where she met the rest of what became the Baker Beach COASST team. Mary Lou lived south of Eugene but had a beach house in Florence. Her daughter and son-in-law, Diane and David Bilderback, had driven up from their home in Bandon; Anne Caples and Cindy Burns were from Florence.

The group's first survey the previous fall had nearly done them in. They'd hit the beach a little after 9 a.m. that day and immediately spied their first dead bird. Slowly and carefully, they keyed it out with the *Beached Birds* field guide, confidently identifying it as a common murre. They recorded the required stats, photographed it, tagged it, and moved down the beach to find another dead bird, and then another, and another. More common murres, a couple of dead songbirds, a glaucous-winged gull, a pelagic cormorant, three Canada geese, an auklet they tentatively identified as a Cassin's, and two birds, or collections of bird parts, they couldn't identify. That first day on that one mile they found forty-seven dead birds, thirty-seven of them common murres—almost twice as many as they would find on any other dead-bird survey over the next year. Did I mention that the weather was lousy? They straggled off the beach about 3 o'clock to hot baths, cold beers, and easy chairs.

Trudging over the dunes to the beach, rain pants swish-swishing, we headed north, toward the mouth of Berry Creek, until Val, holding a GPS device, raised a hand already gloved in white nitrile and called a stop: "This is our starting point, ladies!" Dave, the group's sole gentleman, had already wandered off to the south, his attention drawn by a big orange plastic float resting on the hard sand. The rest of the group fanned out behind him, randomly canvassing the broad beach from the wet sand to the foot of the foredune—anywhere a wave could deposit a dead bird.

"It's amazing how different it looks each month," Mary Lou chirped, tramping down the beach in her oversized brown rain gear and wearing a broad smile. "It just blows you away!"

0912: Val called out the first find, and the team merged on the spot. It was a member of the alcid family—Val could see that right away from the foot type—and it had been dead for some time. The sheath was gone from the bill and the eye from the socket. Cindy pulled out the measuring tape while Val scrawled "454"—this dead bird's COASST ID number—on the little blackboard and posed it next to the bird. As Val called out measurements for the tattered wing, the tarsus with its folded, sand-flecked feet, Mary Lou filled in the blanks on the survey sheet. She had adopted the role of team scribe for herself and, months earlier, had fashioned a customized clipboard with binder clips and rubber bands after a heavy wind had swept a day's worth of data sheets out of her hands and scattered them down the beach. The contraption now hung around her neck, under her rain parka, making her look a bit—her words—"like Sponge Bob." As Val clipped out the numbers, the identity of the ravaged carcass became obvious: COMU in COASST shorthand. Anne arrived and snapped a photo with her digital camera. Val pulled out the colored zip strips and attached them, green-blue-green for 4-5-4, to the leg. Then she threw her supplies back in the bucket and started walking. 0919: seven minutes, start to finish.

"If it's raining, let me tell you, it's a lot harder!" Mary Lou said, still smiling. "If it's raining, it's a real pain!"

Actually, it *was* raining, but not much, not like it could be, not like it had on some of their survey days. As I strolled south with Anne, she told me about going to Dutch Harbor, Alaska, on the first ferry of the spring to watch whiskered auklets. Just ahead, Val, Cindy, and Mary Lou clustered around a gray lump on the sand. We arrived, and Anne pulled out her camera, glancing at Val.

"Murre?"

"Murre."

Cindy, a biologist who worked for the Forest Service monitoring the local population of federally protected snowy plovers, had flipped the bird around to give the camera a better view of the underside of one wing and the topside of another, stretching the neck back in the process and causing the beak to open in a silent cry. One wing looked like the end of a chicken dinner, picked clean at the joint, but at the wingtips the feathers were still intact: white and dark brown, ruffled out of alignment by the passing teeth of some scavenger. The feet were akimbo. The bill on this bird was intact; black, with black feathers at the upper base of the bill. Measuring, recording, photographing, and tagging this bird took four minutes.

"It used to take us so long, 'cause we had to look everything up," Mary Lou declared. "It took us twenty minutes a bird, and that adds up."

Dave called out from a bowl of wind-sculpted sand on the upper beach. We walked that way, past drifts of green feather boa algae, escaped crab pots, and iridescent black-blue mussel shells, hinged like pairs of wings and bristling with hairy hold-fasts. Dave was already gone by the time Anne, Val, and I arrived.

It was a "re-find"—a ratty bird with one yellow and two green tags cinched on a spindly dark gray leg. Wind had hollowed out the transverse dune, scooping out sand and leaving a collection of drift: brown and gray and tan-striped logs; brittle purple, white, and salmon-colored razor clam shells; a scattering of butter clam shells; humps of yellow beach grass; a small, sandy nest of bright aqua-colored rope, frayed to a tangle; and a scattering of tiny shell fragments, polished smooth. Mixed with the shell bits were millions of minute pieces of white and green and blue plastic—a little like beach glass, but not as pretty.

Cindy called from behind a nearby drift of sand: "We have somewhat of a bird up here. In parts."

We found Cindy in another dune cirque, sifting her hands through the moist sand and coming up with palms full of fluffy feathers. "It's just kind of in a big heap," she said. "We've got a leg, we've sort of got a head, and we've sort of got some wingy-dings." What remained of the bird's head had a short, stout bill attached—like a rhinoceros auklet's, only white, not orange as in the field guide. But like the faded, once-orange plastic fishing floats that turn up on the beach, I imagine a dead bird's orange bill would eventually bleach to white.

"Nothing's attached to anything," Val observed. "I don't think we should count it."

"We've got a bill and a foot," said Mary Lou. "Let's do that."

Cindy cradled the disembodied bird head in her white-gloved right hand, measuring the bill with her left.

"24 millimeters."

"24 millimeters," Mary Lou echoed, scribbling. Cindy fingered a scraggly wing.

"24 millimeters for the tarsus."

Val laced three colored cable ties through the bones enclosing the orbit at the top of the skull. She turned her attention to the leg: three webbed toes dangled from one end. "I'm thinking Cassin's auklet."

"We were thinking rhinoceros auklet," Cindy countered.

They held the bird's head up against the auklet profiles in the COASST field guide. The consensus: juvenile rhinoceros auklet.

Glancing up, Cindy spotted Diane twenty yards to the west, standing on the hard, wet sand where the surf ran out, waving her arms over her head. "Western grebe!" Cindy announced when we arrived.

Even I could see that. If the previous find—a handful of scavenged, disassembled bird parts, barely enough for a speculative identification—was one end of the spectrum of countable dead, beached birds, this grebe was the other. The duck-like diving bird, a close cousin of the loon, appeared to be merely sleeping: "A perfect death pose," Val mused with quiet reverence. The slender, swan-like neck was doubled back on its rounded football of a body: white ventral feathers and narrow yellow bill stood out starkly against the soft charcoal-gray of its back. Sand flecked the grebe's gray legs and webbed feet, arranged in a neat plié. Its red eyes were like glass beads, clear and unclouded.

"He looks like he came ashore alive," Cindy observed.

The sand around the grebe was disturbed slightly, seeming to tell a story, of a grebe floating in on a wave, ailing but upright, then shuffling a bit before assembling itself in a posture of repose and resigning itself to death. It seemed a shame to disturb it for measurements. Val attached cable ties to the grebe's leg. Anne snapped a picture.

A few yards to the west, a lone herring gull stood on the beach, eyeing us warily. To the south, a hundred or more sanderlings skittered in their start-and-stop foraging dance at the edge of the waves, seemingly oblivious to us. Small, pale gray sandpipers, they winter in Oregon or pass through on their way as far south as California; by late April they'd be heading back north to breeding grounds high in the Arctic.

We, meanwhile, drifted south, dispersing across the beach. I fell in with Dave, a retired botany professor, and Diane. Three years earlier they'd moved from Missoula, when both retired from jobs at the University of Montana, to Charleston, a small port town on Coos Bay, where Dave's late father—who survived a career as a Coast Guard rescue pilot to retire there—had left them a house. They now lived a few miles farther down the coast in Bandon, where they had quickly woven themselves into the fabric of community environmental activists, volunteering for the Marine Mammal Stranding Network, adopting a mile for CoastWatch, and surveying not only Baker Beach for COASST but two more miles of beach closer to their home.

To the south, down the beach ahead of us, bits of moving color contrasted brightly against the gray shoreline: Diane's rust parka, Cindy's sky-blue jacket, Val's red supply bucket. Shortly, they met up with us. Val's GPS device had called an end to the mile and to the day's survey, and they were heading back.

"It's amazing how, with a foot and a wing and a beak, you can identify almost anything," biologist Cindy mused as we walked north, following the tide line. "I guess I *knew* that, but it's just so much more obvious."

Eight birds, at least four of them COMUs—this was a modest death count for a day in October. The previous October they'd found forty-two birds, and last month they'd found nineteen. Clearly, the low numbers were not for lack of looking.

However, the October 2006 beached-bird survey of Mile 175, Baker Beach, was not quite finished. In the wrack line we were following, scribed in scraps of green algae and eelgrass tangled with gray and white feathers, bleached mole crab carcasses, small gray twigs, broken shells, and tangled beach grass, Val spotted a little black lump of feathers, not four inches long. It wasn't among the species detailed in *Beached Birds;* there was nothing that small in the book.

But biologist Cindy recognized it immediately: a ruby-crowned kinglet. A "birdlet," as my *Western Birds* field guide describes the little songbird. The kinglet spends its summers in conifer forests in the far north, in Alaska and Canada, and journeys south as far as Guatemala for the winter.

Val, still nitrile-gloved, took its measurements: bill 8 millimeters, wing chord 5.5 centimeters, tarsus 2 millimeters. Nine centimeters, tip to tail—smaller than a sparrow. Cindy gazed down at the nest of bright green eelgrass where Val had laid the little bird—pert and chubby and olive-gray in life, but now inert, dark, and waterlogged. "It was just trying to migrate," Cindy said, half to herself, in a voice of genuine regret.

"I don't think we'll see that again," Mary Lou mused.

Then Cindy's head jerked up. "Oh, there they go!" We all looked up to see the big flock of sanderlings rise at once, then turn in the air, their white wings catching the day's feeble sun like mirrors. They circled as one body, a tight formation fanning across the sky, turning south and winging down the coastline. She smiled, watching them disappear down the beach. "Be careful!" she yelled after them.

WHO KNOWS WHAT KILLED THE KINGLET, much less why it had washed in on the tide; such songbirds tend to migrate inland, not over the ocean. But there was little mystery to the day's common murre deaths, nor to those Jack and I had found a year earlier on Mile 157. One early result of the COASST surveys, Parrish said, was a better sense of the natural ebb and flow of the Northwest's murre population, including the standard patterns of death.

"We now know that, in Oregon, July is a standard time in which lots and lots of birds wash up on the beach," Parrish explained. "And that's because breeding has largely finished in the Oregon colonies and there are lots of chicks that are going to wash up on the beach. So, when we have an elevated number of murres washing up on the beaches in July in Oregon, that's normal, and we don't get alarmed." Not so on the northern Washington coast, where murres start their breeding cycle some six to eight weeks later. "If we see that in Washington in July, we start to get alarmed, because that's too early."

In Oregon, the annual spike in murre death tends to start in July and radiate north, as the Oregon birds disperse north to more productive feeding grounds and the Washington birds begin leaving the breeding rocks. "So, in a really good year, in which everybody has a kid, and every kid fledges, what you get is a lot more chicks on the water, and when you get more chicks on the water, you get more chicks on the beach"—a "high chick signal," as Parrish and her colleagues call a big breeding year.

"When you get a really high chick signal, that actually tells you it was a good year on the colony. You might be seeing a lot of dead birds, but that's just basically the ineptitude of youth." It's not the raw numbers of dead murres that's most telling, she explained, but the ratio of dead adults to dead chicks. "If we see a high total number, but they're fifty-fifty chicks and adults, or even more chicks than adults, that tells us it's been a good breeding year." But if most of the dead murres are adults, she said, "that tells us it's been a really tough fall"—tough, meaning, not enough food. It gets more complicated, naturally. Take September 2005, the month we stumbled upon all those dead birds. High murre deaths raised alarm bells up and down the coast, prompting the front-page story I'd read in

The Oregonian that August—triggered, perhaps, by heightened anxiety about global climate change. But the high number of murre deaths in Oregon hadn't alarmed Parrish and her colleagues; it was all the early-season dead murres in Washington that indicated something was astray. "We think that's because your murres"—she said, meaning those that nest on the Oregon coast—"abandoned their colonies, swam north to the Columbia River plume, tried to get something to eat, and a bunch of them died." Then, there's also the influence of seasonal currents and wind direction—a bunch of starved birds may be floating offshore, but if the wind's blowing offshore, back toward the sea, those dead birds are not going to wind up on the beach. Wind direction also influences the timing of the upwelling, which affects whether birds thrive or starve. It's just the sort of ever-more-complicated picture that Parrish, with help from a small paid staff and a growing cadre of eager volunteer surveyors, relishes teasing apart.

"So, it's this cool interaction between how stressed are you when you're on the colony, where you go as a live bird, what attracts you, where the big feeding stations are, and once you're there, once you die and you become a drifter, what happens to you," she said, eyes shining. "All those pieces go together."

THE BIGGEST COMMON MURRE BREEDING COLONY in Oregon is at Three Arch Rocks, on the north coast, but it's too far offshore for good viewing. For that, I learned, you go to Yaquina Head, north of Newport. I headed there early on a bright, windy spring day. But I'd forgotten about the lighthouse restoration project under way on the headland. The 93-foot-tall lighthouse was swathed in protective wrapping and surrounded by scaffolding, and fencing blocked access to the seaward viewing platform overlooking the largest nesting site, atop Colony Rock. So I headed to the smaller Sentinel Rocks off the headland's southern shoulder: tall, craggy basalt monoliths, their tops about at eyelevel for humans on the headland. I raised my binoculars for a better look at the dark and light shapes atop the near rock. At first I thought I was seeing simply the play of light and shadow on gray rock. But as I focused, I realized it was the black heads and white breasts of hundreds of murres, blanketing the top of the rock.

Black long-necked cormorants were flying wads of seaweed to niches on the rock's sides, building their nests. Here and there, a tall cormorant head stuck out above the sea of black murre heads bunched on the top of the rock. Along the edges of the colony, a gull or two milled nervously, and I watched as a pair of brown pelicans glided up from the south, pausing briefly to hang in the air over the colony before continuing north with slow, languid flaps. Otherwise, nothing but murres filled my binoculars' lenses: murres standing, all facing the same direction. The air was filled with the sound of their calls—the guttural, staccato braying of birds greeting their mate or keeping their neighbor off their immediate family's little piece of real estate. Periodically, a murre would raise its sharply bent wings and take a hop to the south, into the wind, launching itself and circling out to sea, wings pumping. The sky around the breeding rocks was alive with birds, most of them common murres. Returning to the rock, a murre would hover, flapping crazily, feet dangling, before settling; some arriving murres would hover like that for a while, above the dense colony, then wing away again, seeming to have given up on finding a landing spot.

Far below the gray storm-roiled sea undulated, waves rolling in and smashing at the base of the rock. On a ledge just above the water, I spotted a silvery baby seal, squirming like a clumsy kitten toward its reclining mother, nuzzling her. It was late May; the murres, too, might already have begun breeding, laying their pear-shaped eggs on ancestral rock niches. Soon, the crowded Sentinel Rocks that didn't seem to have an inch to spare would find room for almost half again as many murres, as the downy chicks pecked their way out of their shells to start their lives in the colony.

It's sentimental, I know. But I couldn't help but wish them luck.

Chapter Three: Havoc, Size 11

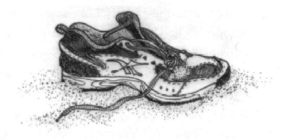

THERE'S NO MAGICAL BEST TIME to comb the beach, no perfect month or season, but some seasons are more likely than others to yield treasures from faraway places. "Winter, especially late winter, is the preferred time for beachcombing during a statistically 'normal' year," according to Walt Pich's *Beachcombers Guide to the Northwest.* Stormy winter weather, with its strong winds, tends to drive flotsam—debris that floats on the surface of the sea—onto the shore. West winds, particularly in March through May, also tend to make spring a fruitful season for Pacific Northwest beachcombers. But summer, as the *Beachcombers Guide* puts it, "customarily means poor pickings for the tide-line treasure hunter."

Which made the discovery of two good-as-new athletic shoes, a Reebok and a Converse, on Labor Day 2000 even more of a surprise. I'd actually found a shoe on a visit to Mile 157 four months earlier, in mid-May. It was also a Converse, size 11. I'd left it on the beach, even though seven months earlier I had attended a CoastWatch-sponsored talk by Cannon Beach artist and beach scavenger Steve McLeod about finding athletic shoes and other consumer goods that had spilled off container ships in the North Pacific. He'd explained how athletic shoes could be tracked by means of the manufacturer's code printed on a label on the shoe's tongue. "If made in China," I had scribbled in cryptic shorthand on a scrap of paper, "has code of #s—when, tells all." Sounded simple enough. McLeod, I learned, was part of a network of a dozen or more correspondents scattered along the United States coastline and beyond, in Japan and the Netherlands, for *Beachcombers' Alert,* a quarterly newsletter updating subscribers on what's washing up on the world's beaches, from "sea beans"—seeds from tropical trees and vines— to Japanese survey stakes and hagfish traps. It was the first I'd heard of Seattle oceanographer Curtis Ebbesmeyer, the newsletter's publisher. By this time he had been written up in a dozen or more magazines ranging from *Scientific American* to *Boys' Life* and even *People* for his efforts in tracking debris across the ocean and, in the process, helping broaden understanding both about ocean currents and the tons and tons of garbage that they carry.

Wouldn't it be cool, I had mused with my sister after telling her about finding the Converse, to write a book based on the stories of things I found on just one mile of beach?

"If the shoe's still there next time you go," she said brightly, "it's a sign that you should write the book!" A charming thought, and I know she meant well. But nothing is ever "still there" on the beach, no flotsam anyway, not three months later. The tide comes in, the tide goes out, new things are deposited, once-living things decompose, some things are picked up and washed somewhere else. It's the nature of the beach. At least I was off the hook. A book would have been a lot of work.

And I was right—the size 11 Converse was gone when we returned on Labor Day, following an early-season storm. But in its place were two other shoes, a size 11 Reebok and a different Converse, this one size 12. They were just as Steve McLeod had described shoes spilled from a container ship, as opposed to shoes someone might have kicked off on a visit to the beach and failed to retrieve. The soles showed no signs of wear, but even more telling were the laces. On both shoes, they were threaded through the bottom two holes, crossed in a big X and rethreaded through the top holes on either side of the upper and finished off with a loose overhand knot. I'd seen this type of lacing on shoes still in the box at sporting-goods stores; no one would wear a shoe laced that way. Both knot wads had been colonized by gooseneck barnacles, close cousins of the barnacles that cluster on rocks along the shore but larger and ocean-going; they're at home when attached to a log or glass bottle or other floating object. The Reebok had more such barnacles clinging to the mesh lining inside the heel. Otherwise, both shoes were in pristine condition, bright white and blue, showing no signs of wear, unfaded, a little sandy but barely soiled. Run them through the washing machine, give them some fresh laces, and they'd be as good as new.

This time I picked up the shoes and carried them back to the car. It would be nearly four years before I picked up the shoes' story again, and two more before I was able to trace just one shoe's journey from beginning to end.

FOR FOUR YEARS THE IDEA OF TRACKING the shoes' journey nagged at me. Then one day in 2004 I caught a snippet of a radio interview with Richard Pollak, author of *The Columbo Bay,* the nonfiction account of Pollak's five-week voyage from Hong Kong to New York aboard the container vessel *Columbo Bay* in 2001. Many times I'd stood at the south jetty, at the mouth of the Columbia River, or on the nearby Astoria waterfront where the shipping channel hugs the wide river's south bank, and watched container vessels glide by. Most of the big sea-going ships in the Columbia are bulk cargo carriers transporting wheat; expediting shipment of wheat to England was the Port of Portland's first purpose, and it remains the third-largest center for wheat export in the world. Portland's port actually handles relatively few shipping containers; terminals in Seattle and Tacoma together see nearly twenty times the number of containers that Portland does, and Los Angeles handles nearly thirty times that. But once every day or two, on average, a container vessel heads up the Columbia, its deck packed with rectangular orange and blue and gray and green and red steel boxes stacked one atop the other like super-sized children's blocks. I bought Pollack's book and read it in one sitting, engrossed by his accounts of the day-to-day workings of these vessels in and out of port. He described perils at sea, past and present, from piracy—yes, still today—to killer storms that tossed ships like rubber duckies in a bathub, even ships the size of the *Columbo Bay*, which was the length of three football fields and carried 3,500 containers. The statistics were numbing: 90 percent of the world's trade moves on these ships, delivering—at that time—six million containers a year to the United States alone. And sometimes, when an unexpected storm arises or the captain's efforts to outrun a storm fail, some of those containers fall off. That was the case, Pollack mentioned in an aside, when a vessel called the *APL China,* loaded with containers full of consumer goods for the Christmas season, ran into high seas and winds of up to a hundred knots—fallout from Typhoon Babs, which had ripped through southeastern China, Taiwan, and the Philippines. The *APL China* had survived the storm to limp, two days late, into Seattle, but not before spilling more than four hundred containers into the North Pacific and damaging perhaps twice that number. The date of its tangle with the typhoon: October 26, 1998, roughly two years before I found the two shoes.

Inspired, I set out to track down Curtis Ebbesmeyer and *Beachcombers' Alert,* e-mailing him the shoes' serial numbers and asking if he could give me any leads for tracing the origins of either or both shoes.

"There are clues here," he responded. "The shoes, being made in China, were probably lost en route from there to here. You will have to do what I do, that is, find someone in the transportation departments of these shoe companies and ask for the latitude and longitude and date where these shoes were lost. With Point A, and your find's Point B on the Oregon coast, you have the beginning." I shared with him my theory: that both shoes had been among the consumer goods that spilled from the *APL China* in 1998.

"*APL China* is a good bet," he responded. "Now, if you can just get through to the transportation departments …"

I got on the Internet and found telephone numbers and e-mail addresses and mailing addresses for Reebok's and Converse's headquarters. I left phone messages, I sent e-mails; no response. Finally, I wrote letters to both companies asking when and at which factory, in what part of China, a shoe with that serial number would have been made. As a bonus, I said, I'd appreciate learning from which port it was shipped and what might have occurred to cause it to end up in the ocean.

I never heard a word from Converse. Two weeks later, however, I received a canned response from Reebok. "Thank you for your interest in the Reebok brand," it began. "Unfortunately, the product(s) you are inquiring about, the Havoc, style #41646, is from a discontinued line." Obviously, since I found it four years earlier—much longer than the life cycle of the shoe styles I found in sporting goods stores. Did they think I wanted to buy a pair? Someone in Customer Service must have just pushed a button to generate this unhelpful missive.

"The Havoc was manufactured in July 1998 and was a running shoe with Ultra Hexalite technology," the letter went on. "Ultra Hexalite is a honeycomb cushioning in the heel, which provides a lightweight cushioning. The style #41646 was a men's shoe in the colorway of Jet Blue/Tech Gold/Black ..."

Wait: July 1998? Three months before the *APL China* disaster? It was a start.

"We are committed to your complete satisfaction," the letter from Reebok continued, providing a customer service number I was invited to call, Monday through Friday between 9 a.m. and 5 p.m. Eastern Standard Time.

I reached for the phone.

TO GET TO THE SHANGRI-LA HOTEL in Shenzhen, China, from Hong Kong, it's wise to board the KCR East Rail Train at its origin, at Tsim Sha Tsui station on the Kowloon side of Hong Kong, to ensure you'll get a seat for the forty-minute trip to Lo Wu, the rail station at Shenzhen on the Chinese border. Shenzhen is a popular day-trip destination for Hong Kong residents; everything's cheaper there, from dental work and massages to the consumer goods, many of them knock-offs, filling the five-story Luo Ho Commercial City mall adjacent to the train station. The express train from Kowloon starts underground but soon emerges to grant views of roads and buildings and tropical vegetation and, in the distance, green hills obscured this July day by thick rain clouds. Now and then another rapid train would pass in a blur of blue or red.

At Lo Wu—the end of the line—you disembark and take a long walk through a maze of buildings holding customs and immigration to cross over into China proper. Hong Kong became a part of China in 1997 but was allowed to retain its social and legal systems as well as its free-market economy for fifty years. The differences between Hong Kong and the rest of China become immediately apparent at Lo Wu. On Hong Kong's KCR train, among the signs advertising glamorous stores and schools for learning English were signs threatening modest fines for littering. Passing through customs and immigration at Lo Wu, signs on the walls in both Chinese and English repeatedly threatened prison terms for any deviation from order: No waiting. No lingering. No U-turn. No photo. No refluence. (*Refluence?*)

Less than a half-century ago, Shenzhen was just a sleepy fishing village. Political and economic "reform and opening" following the Cultural Revolution led to Shenzhen's designation as a "special economic zone"— China's first—in 1980. Fueled by foreign investment, it's since become a sprawling manufacturing hub, with tens of thousands of factories, including the hundreds of shoe factories that have made China the world's leader in shoemaking. A wall used to enclose the Shenzhen city center, limiting Chinese citizens' movement in and out, but the zone's explosive growth couldn't be contained so easily. Now Shenzhen spreads over hundreds of square miles, having absorbed dozens of villages that have since become part of the metropolis. For decades it's been the fastest-growing part of China, with an official population of about nine million in 2005 but an unofficial total probably closer to seventeen million in the entire metropolitan area. The most prosperous corner of China, it has the highest per-capita income—and highest spending. Consequently, it's a magnet for young people from rural villages throughout China seeking employment and adventure. Some return home, with money in their pockets, to get married or start businesses. Others—increasing numbers of young Chinese—never go back. The Chinese government calls Shenzhen its "window to the world." Chinese people have another term for it: the "overnight city."

I was early for my rendezvous at the Shangri-La Hotel, so I explored a short radius from the train station. The weather was clearing, and tall, skinny skyscrapers pierced the blue sky. Unlike Hong Kong, where everyone seemed perpetually in a hurry, I saw lots of people simply standing or squatting, waiting for something. I passed a fancy shopping mall with a grand escalator leading from the sidewalk up to the front entrance, one level up, but the escalator wasn't working. I wandered back to the Shangri-La, across a wide plaza from the train station entrance, and entered the lobby; an electronic readerboard welcomed the day's conference attendees with a greeting in English—upside-down. I thought back to a passage describing Shenzhen in a book I'd been reading by an American author, a collection of short stories set in and around Hong Kong called *The Train to Lo Wu*: "I turned to the east and looked up at the skyline, or what little of it I could see through the smog: a jumble of tall spires and cylinders and shining glass tower blocks, some of them copies of buildings in Hong Kong, others probably copied from buildings elsewhere in the world. *Why is it that Shenzhen doesn't look quite right, I wondered. Why does it seem like such a mirage, as if I might come back next week and find it gone?*"

A young man in neat khaki pants and a plaid pastel cotton shirt entered the lobby, darting glances at me, then finally approached: "Are you … Reebok?" he asked. He escorted me to a minivan parked at the hotel's entrance, and we headed out. He maneuvered onto a five-lane, one-way surface road leading out of town, passing more gleaming skyscrapers thirty or forty stories tall and crumbling concrete apartment buildings, gleaming motorcoaches and bicycles with bamboo panniers, one laden with fruit, another with plastic brooms. The road turned into a freeway cutting through a tunnel of green hills, past more tenement buildings and rock quarries gouged into hillsides of orange rock fringed with green. Power lines marched across the landscape, one after another, crisscrossing the countryside, and the freeway in both directions was filled with container trucks: flatbeds each carrying a single standard-issue forty-foot-long steel shipping container.

Twenty minutes into the drive, we exited at a sign for Longgang—one of those villages that had been absorbed by the Shenzhen metropolis. We joined another freeway, and we began seeing more factories, many belching smoke, scattered across a green geometry of farmers' fields.

All those shoes, those computer parts and Tickle Me Elmo dolls, made in these factories popping up in what had been, a generation ago, agricultural land. It suddenly felt as if the land itself, the orange rock and the trees and verdant fields, was being transformed into plastic toys, running shoes, Nintendos, DVDs, umbrellas, shin guards, carburetors.

In another twenty minutes we left the freeway, pulling onto a broad, traffic-choked boulevard lined with trees and new or newish buildings, none more than ten stories tall, one of them with a grand sign in English: "World Trade Center." Right behind them were construction cranes, at work on the next row of buildings. "Longgang?" I asked the driver. He smiled, nodded vigorously: "Longgang!" We crept through heavy traffic for another ten or fifteen minutes, then pulled up at a gate in front of a walled compound with a big overhead sign in English: "Kong Tai Shoes Manufacturing."

A combination of persistence and plain luck had led me to the factory where the Reebok shoe I had found on Labor Day 2000 had been made in 1998. Six months earlier, after receiving the canned letter from Reebok, I had called the company's customer service number and started asking questions about the Havoc. When was it manufactured? From which port did it ship out? Not the sorts of questions Customer Service is accustomed to fielding. But instead of stonewalling me, as I'd frankly expected, the woman I spoke with passed me up to a supervisor, who passed me up again to someone who gave me the name and phone number of someone else who she thought might have the information I sought.

That right person, when we finally connected, was a font of information, though it took a few phone calls over several days to piece it all together. The Havoc was made by Kong Tai Shoes and had been shipped out of Hong Kong in multiple shipments. Three vessels had carried Havocs to North America, departing Hong Kong mid-April through June 1998: the *Munkebo Maersk*, the *Sealand Pacific,* and the *Dragoer Maersk*— contrary to my theory, the *APL China* was not among them. My contact told me a lot more, including details about her personal and work life that one doesn't normally share with a stranger over the telephone. Only later did I put it together: I happened to have called on the very day that the acquisition of Reebok International Ltd. by German shoe giant Adidas-Salomon AG for $3.8 billion had been finalized. The Reebok staff was still in shock, and some—including my new telephone friend, who'd worked at Reebok for more than twenty-five years—weren't certain how much longer they'd have a job, or what job it might be.

I found a phone number in Hong Kong for Kong Tai Shoes; by this time I had begun researching flights to Hong Kong and visas for travel into China. "Factory visits?" asked a woman in clipped Chinese-accented English. "Oh, you'll have to talk to Leo," she explained briskly, giving me his number at the KTS factory in Shenzhen.

"How did you find me?" Leo Leung asked, laughing, after I introduced myself over the phone. Leo was the product development manager for KTS, which operated the Shenzhen factory in partnership with Reebok. He'd love to show me around the factory, he said, but he'd need approval from Reebok. At his suggestion, I reiterated my request in an e-mail, pushed send, and in a leap of faith, lined up an airline ticket to Asia. Then I waited. A month passed before an e-mail arrived from Reebok granting me permission to visit; my request had gone to company headquarters in Massachusetts, where an Internet search of my credentials had revealed a benign interest in "nature, hiking, etc. … I would say she is probably not digging for anything that would concern us," according to an e-mail buried at the end of a string of e-mails with input from a half-dozen Reebok officials on two continents.

The next day—one day before I'd arranged to fly to Hong Kong via Japan—I got another e-mail. "We are informed by the supplier that the timing of this visit does not suit them and therefore we can not arrange access for you." More e-mails, more waiting—by this time I was in Japan, checking my e-mail in Internet cafes there. Finally, with no particular explanation, a tentative green light from Reebok: permission to visit the factory, located in Longgang, with the possibility, still to be confirmed, of touring one of its production units. "I suggest you meet our driver in the lobby of Shangri-La, which is in front of China Customs (about two hundred meter walk)," Leo wrote. "Our driver will hold a REEBOK sign while searching for you in the lobby."

KONG TAI SHOES MANUFACTURING is a compound of white- and blue-tiled, four-story buildings isolated from the rest of rapidly developing Longgang by a tall stone wall. Four mirror-image production buildings stand at the front of the compound along with an administrative building housing a management suite and shoe sample-making facility; toward the back of the compound are dormitory buildings. It's a small- to mid-sized factory, as Chinese shoe factories go, and other than some machinery updates it has changed little since 1990, when the KTP Group—a publicly owned company started by investors from Hong Kong and Taiwan—built it. The location seemed ideal: close enough to company headquarters in Hong Kong to visit easily, and close to the Port of Hong Kong, facilitating not only shipment out of finished products but shipment in of shoe-making materials, almost all of which had to be imported from outside of China in the early days. And Longgang was outside of the heavily controlled center of Shenzhen, which made it easier to recruit workers. Longgang was just a little farming community when the KTS factory was built, surrounded by undeveloped open fields, though by 1998 it no longer stood alone; more factories had edged out the farmers, and something of a modern town center was beginning to take shape. KTS had five thousand workers when it opened, slightly more than it does now, a result of manufacturing efficiencies. It was outfitted with technology from Taiwan, an Asian manufacturing hub until China entered the game with cheaper labor. From the beginning, it was a "white shoe" company—industry lingo for athletic shoes, as opposed to a "brown shoe" producer of dress shoes and hiking boots and the like, typically requiring an entirely different manufacturing process. And from the beginning, it was dedicated almost exclusively to making shoes for Reebok.

The Havoc I had found actually began life in late 1996 or early 1997 in the mind of a shoe designer at Reebok headquarters, then located in Stoton, Massachusetts. It was positioned as a men's running shoe, intended to get into stores in the third quarter of 1998. Today many of the materials used to create athletic shoes in Chinese factories are made in China as well, but back in 1998 no such domestic supply chain existed. Nearly every one of the Havoc's almost three dozen components was imported: the compression-molded foam midsole and solid rubber outsole (Japan), the tough imitation leather "Benecke" that comprised most of the shoe's upper portion (Germany), the white "Merry Mesh" lining the tongue and the jet-blue nylon heel pull tab with reflective accents (Taiwan), the Hexalite cushioning the heel (United States). Every component arrived in container trucks through the front gate and was unloaded into warehouses on site before it was distributed to one or another of the four production buildings; the empty steel container was then sent back to the Port of Hong Kong and stacked, with other containers, to await its next assignment.

My Havoc took shape in the hands of young women in blue hairnets and pink aprons in one of those production buildings. The women were scattered at workstations on three floors of the four-story building, in assembly lines carefully designed by industrial engineers for maximum efficiency. Nearly all of the employees, including management, lived in dorms at the factory; in 1998, there wasn't much temporary housing in Longgang outside the factory, and for a young single woman from rural Sichuan arriving in what was essentially an economic frontier town, the factory's locked gates provided security and an alternative to an otherwise hard-knock education in city life. ("We have to teach them to look both ways before crossing the street," a Reebok manager told me.) The workday started at 7:30 a.m. and usually ended by 4 p.m., six days a week, with an hour off at midday, though the work went longer at crunch times. In March, when the first batch of Havocs was being assembled, it would have been pleasant enough on the factory floor, but by July there was no denying the heat, even with the overhead fans circulating air from the big windows on three sides of the large room.

The Havoc was built with strobel construction, typical of athletic shoes. Unlike dress shoes, characterized by an upper stitched to a rigid sole, strobel-built athletic shoes generally have three sole components:

a flexible inner sole and a molded midsole and outsole. The midsole and outsole are glued together, the upper is stitched to the inner sole, and the two halves are then glued together to complete the shoe.

To craft the Havoc's upper, stacks of a dozen or so sheets of faux leather Benecke were laid out on large tables on the production building's cutting and pre-assembly floor. It was the job of several young women to cut the eight different pieces made of Benecke; others skived the edges to a taper, and still others traced faint stitching lines by hand in silver-colored ink on the tough white fabric. Elsewhere on the floor, more teams of young women, overseen by slightly older women and men, cut and pre-assembled the rest of the components of the upper, including all six pieces that composed the shoe's tongue. These pre-assembled parts—the tongue, the vamp and vamp underlay, the eyestay and its reinforcement, the toe box and toe cap, everything but the midsole and outsole—were dropped into blue plastic crates, three shoes to a crate, and sent to an elevator that carried them to another floor for final assembly.

That floor was a sea of humming, whirring Brother and Pfaff sewing machines: four assembly lines of stitching, each one employing some forty seamstresses. At the start of the assembly line was a metal detector, there to detect pieces of stray sewing-machine needles that might have broken during pre-assembly and lodged somewhere in the shoe. Here the Havoc's insole was stitched to the shoe's pre-assembled upper and tongue, then a worker inserted a *last*—a foot-shaped piece of, in this case, aqua-colored plastic—into the evolving shoe, and its laces were pulled tight, helping conform the shoe to what stood in for the eventual customer's foot. A conveyor belt carried this upper-insole combination through a heat setter, conforming it even more closely to the last. As the upper emerged from the heat setter, one worker grabbed it and painted the insole with primer while another picked up a matching shoe bottom of the same size—the midsole and outsole, which had already been joined on another assembly line—and painted the top of the midsole with primer as well. Both parts of what was now a two-part shoe went onto a conveyor belt, which slowly moved them through a dryer. Upon emerging, both parts got a coating of cement with soft toothbrush-like brushes wielded by more young women in blue hairnets, and both went briefly into another dryer. As the two halves emerged on the conveyor belt, their cement primed for optimal adherence, workers picked them up and slapped them together. Now the Havoc was complete, from its diagonally grooved heel to the extension of hard black rubber outsole wrapping its toe.

Next came a ride on a perforated metal tray that spun around, like the Wave Swinger at a carnival, cooling and setting the cement in the factory's ambient air for a minute or so. Then the Havoc was carried into a chiller set just a few degrees above freezing to cool the last, still snug inside the shoe; the chilling hardened the last, readying it for service inside the next same-size shoe.

More workers applied the finishing touches. One pulled out the last, tossing it into a box that was filling up with other disembodied aqua-colored feet. One inserted a sock liner. One coaxed out any remaining wrinkles in the midsole with a hand-held heater. Another stuffed tissue into the toe of the shoe to help it hold its shape through the weeks it would take to cross the Pacific, travel overland to a distribution center, and arrive at its final destination. All this was for the purpose of connecting it with a shopper who would pull out the wad of tissue and slip it tentatively on a stockinged foot. Finally, the Havoc was laid on another piece of tissue paper, wrapped, set inside a cardboard box, and placed on an elevator tray headed to the second-floor shipping room.

All told, it took dozens of hands about one hour to cut, stitch, assemble, glue, and pack one pair of Havocs.

In the shipping room, my now-finished and boxed Havoc and its mate would have been piled with more size 11 Havocs, then packed into a carton of twelve boxes, already labeled with the shoes' destination. That carton and twenty-three others like it was stacked on a wooden pallet and set aside as more and more Havocs rolled off the assembly line. Ten thousand pairs, twenty thousand shoes: that's how many typically fit inside one standard 40-by-8-by-8-foot steel shipping container, characterized as two TEUS, or twenty-foot equivalents, in shipping lingo. When the order was complete, a container truck would have been ordered from the Port of Hong Kong. It would have backed up

to the bottom of the blue tin chute angling down to the ground from
the second-floor storage room door. One carton after another, as many
as four hundred of them, would be shoved out the door and down the
chute to the waiting container, where more workers would stack the
cartons tightly inside the long steel box. Finally the rear doors would
have been closed and secured. A "seal," like a stout bicycle-cable lock,
would be attached to the doors. Once sealed, it could not be opened by
anyone but customs officials until it reached its destination overseas.
Then the big truck would have maneuvered through the courtyard and
out the factory gates, winding among the other trucks and cars and
bicycles crowding the streets of Longgang and onto the G 107 freeway,
one of hundreds of container trucks leaving factories all over Shenzhen
that day and headed south to the Port of Hong Kong.

"WE ARE VERY SURPRISED TO GET YOUR E-MAIL!" said KTS general
manager Steve Yeh with a wide grin. The entire KTS-Reebok joint
management team had assembled in the air-conditioned administrative
suite to greet me: Hong Kong-born, twenty-something Leo, plus middle-
aged Steve from Taiwan; the facilities and production managers, both
from the Philippines; and Mike Napolitan, Bostonian by birth, the lone
American in the group and a twenty-one-year Reebok veteran with nearly
twelve years in Asia. The team had even gone to the KTS archives and
pulled out a white-and-blue Havoc, identical to the shoe in the snapshot
I had brought with me, taken on the Oregon beach.

"Nobody knows where that shoe is from; maybe somebody puts it on
the ocean!" Steve suggested, chuckling.

I was quite certain it fell off a container ship and had circulated in the
ocean for awhile, I explained: the lack of wear on the sole, the way it was
laced, the marine life colonizing it. One big mystery remained: when and
where did it fall into the ocean, and off what vessel? All three of the ships

that had carried the Havoc, according to my source at Reebok, had set sail in the spring, before the typhoon season typically kicked into high gear. I had searched the Internet for news of container spills and found some, but none from these ships in this time period, though the list I found was probably not comprehensive, given overseas manufacturers' and shippers' reluctance to share bad news about their contributions to ocean debris. I had e-mailed Maersk's U.S. headquarters to ask if there had been any spills from any of these three vessels. The terse reply came from the manager of external communications: "We decline to comment on this at this time." I'd even run into Curtis Ebbesmeyer again at the Beachcomber Fun Fair in Ocean Shores, Washington, a couple of months earlier; I had updated him on my progress and asked if he had any more ideas.

"You're on a difficult quest," he had said gravely—an appropriate tone from the oracle of beach trash. To date, the only company that had been willing to share information with him about container losses, effectively turning their losses into a vehicle to help promote scientific understanding of ocean systems, was Nike. "The information is out there," he said, "but to get it—*firewall* doesn't begin to describe it," he said of the reluctance of most shoe companies—most manufacturers, period—to part with information about losses at sea. He sent me off with a few more suggestions and wished me success. "And then we'll all benefit," he had said, "because we'll have followed a second 'species.'"

"I know we lost a couple containers one time," Mike Napolitan mused. "They fell overboard during one of the storms in the Pacific. I don't know if we have any shipping records that go back that far." He paused, frowning. "How long will you be in Hong Kong?"

"Until Friday."

"Maybe Mike Collier could tell you—Mike is our logistics person in our Hong Kong office," he said. "I do remember hearing a story that there was a vessel that lost some containers, and some of them were Reebok. I'll send Mike a note and see if he can talk to you and give you some information."

That would be most helpful, I assured him.

"This is very interesting!" Steve exclaimed, grinning broadly.

"Do you think you could send us a copy of the book when it comes out?" Leo asked. "Because this is the first time we have had an author visit!"

That's when it struck me: I'm their Havoc. Other than the occasional human rights monitor, Kong Tai Shoes Manufacturing in Longgang, China, doesn't get many visitors, foreign or otherwise. I'm like a piece of unexplained flotsam myself, a curiosity from a distant shore whose function isn't entirely clear, deposited at their feet.

Back in Hong Kong, I spent the next couple of days obsessively checking my e-mail, hoping for a message from Mike Collier, but no word came. Finally, the morning of the day before I was scheduled to leave Hong Kong, I ventured a phone call.

"I'm leaving on holiday myself tomorrow, and I'm heading to a meeting shortly," he said brightly, "but I have some time right now ..." I filled him in, giving him the shoe's serial numbers. I could hear the tap of fingers hitting the keyboard. Long pause.

"Is this shoe called the Havoc?" he asked. That's the one, I told him.

Another pause; more tapping. "We produced only four orders ..." Four?

"Here's one," he said after another pause. "The *Munkebo Maersk;* it sailed April 27."

"Right, I know about that shipment."

"Here's another one: The *Sealand Pacific,* sailed on the third of May from Hong Kong."

"Yep ..."

"Next one is the *Dragoer Maersk;* that sailed on the 31st of May. That was a small shipment, probably LCL"—less than a container load, he explained.

A longer pause, as his fingers clackety-clacked on the keyboard. Then—

"Ah, *here's* your shoe," he said.

"There was one order made in September, the largest order, really. This one shipped on the 11th of October, 7,068 pairs. There's a notation here—says 'typhoon China.' Because it went overboard, they don't have full information."

Typhoon China—in October 1998! "Does it say what vessel it shipped on?" I asked in a rush. I could hear him scrutinizing the screen. Reebok contracts with various carriers and uses a freight forwarding company—Maersk Logistics—to arrange shipping, he explained. He didn't see the vessel noted by name, he said, but apparently it was not shipped on a Maersk vessel as the three previous container loads were. "Actually," he said, "this was on an American Presidents Line vessel."

APL—the *APL China*?

He dove back into Reebok's database. Eight years and one big typhoon later, few details of this fourth shipment of Havocs remained on the books, and he couldn't be sure. The same was true at American Presidents Line, whom Mike later queried. Too much time had passed, and no one could confirm that this final container load of Havocs had actually shipped aboard the *APL China* or any other specific vessel. Mike didn't even know for certain which port the container of Havocs had shipped from.

But it was probably Hong Kong, according to Leo, who said that, in 1998, KTS had not yet switched to shipping out of Shenzhen's own port of Yantian, as it does today. The *APL China* had departed not from Hong Kong but from Kaohsiung, Taiwan, just a couple of days after the Havocs had left their port of origin, according to Reebok records. But then as now, it was not unusual for feeder ships to ferry cargo from Hong Kong to Kaohsiung, where within a day or two it would be transferred to a large container vessel for the journey to North America. Three other container ships reportedly lost cargo in the same storm, including another APL vessel, the *President Adams,* bound from Yantian to Los Angeles.

In the end, I couldn't confirm that the container of Havocs had sailed on the *APL China.* But it seemed to add up. And the more I learned about container shipping in the North Pacific, and about what happens when some of those containers are accidentally separated from those ships, the more certain I was.

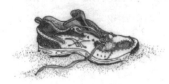

TOBACCO, VITAMINS, PLASTIC CUTLERY, fine china, toys, car parts, silk lingerie, shoes: regardless of the commodity, if it needed to be shipped from one place on the Earth to another, the same painstaking process had been used, essentially unchanged for centuries, until the middle of the twentieth century. Burly men would pick up and carry the boxes, drums, barrels, and other containers full of assorted goods, load by load. Eventually, cranes came to their aid, but even then longshoremen still did much of the heavy lifting or positioning of small lots of goods. At every transition, whether from wagon to ship or ship to railcar, the routine was the same: load and unload, bundle by bundle. No wonder the introduction in the 1960s of standard-size steel shipping containers—containers that could be transported over land, on trucks or rail cars, and on sea without having their contents unpacked and repacked at each juncture—launched, in author Richard Pollack's words, "the greatest revolution in the international transport of goods since the coming of steam propulsion." Shipping became cheaper and easier. Large, expensive inventories were replaced by just-in-time delivery. Consumer goods could be manufactured overseas, where labor costs were a fraction of those in the United States, and shipped at a cost that set the retail price within reach of millions more consumers. That single innovation—containerization—was primarily responsible for Wal-Mart, Target, and every other American big-box store and the corresponding worldwide lust for inexpensive consumer goods.

In 1998, Hong Kong was home to the world's busiest container port, with an average of more than one hundred vessels arriving every day of the year, unloading China-bound wheat, soybeans, rice, lumber, plywood, computer components, and Benecke and Merry Mesh to make athletic shoes, and taking on outbound products from the factories that were springing up seemingly overnight in the countryside of China's Guangdong province. The truck carrying my Havoc would have been met by a tall gantry crane, which would have plucked the forty-foot container off the truck's flat bed and, moving with smooth deliberation, dropped it with a clang atop a growing stack of like-size containers, piled like building blocks around the periphery of the port. There it would have remained for a few hours or days until more giant cranes placed it on a feeder vessel for the short hop across the Taiwan Strait to Kaohsiung, on Taiwan's southwestern shore, where more cranes would have maneuvered it into its predetermined spot on the *APL China*, the vessel's sleek black hull riding a little lower in the water with every two-TEU steel container it took on. Some would have been dropped into bays in the vessel's watertight holds below deck. Others would have been stacked on the outside deck, as high as six containers tall. The first three layers on a container vessel are lashed in place with steel rods. All the containers in a stack, above and below deck, are attached to one another at their corners with latching interbox connectors. Nearly all, anyway. Sometimes the longshoremen who secure the containers in place don't like to climb that high on the outside stacks; then all that holds those top containers in place is gravity. The box holding the Havocs must have been set high on the deck stack; shippers sometimes pay extra to get their container last on, and thus first off, the vessel.

The *APL China* was capable of carrying 5,316 TEUs, or 2,658 forty-foot containers like the one full of Havocs. It was early October, the cusp of the North American Christmas buying frenzy, and much of the merchandise stuffed into the containers stacked on the vessel's decks would have been destined for holiday merchandise displays in stores in the Midwest and West: Huffy bicycles, Gap jeans, shoes, clothing and accessories and electronics and sports equipment from factories scattered throughout Asia.

It's more than six thousand miles from Hong Kong to Seattle as the crow flies, a quarter of the way around the world. But crows don't cross the Pacific Ocean, and if they did, they wouldn't make a beeline to the east any more than albatrosses or shearwaters do. They'd follow the currents of air flowing in a great clockwise pattern above the sea, currents that would get them to their destination with the least effort, just as whales and fish follow great rivers within the ocean to reach their destinations.

Ships prefer to follow those currents too. Container vessels bound for Los Angeles from ports in southern China and Taiwan, such as the *President Adams,* follow a fairly direct route to the northeast, cutting through the Hawaiian Islands. But vessels leaving Kaohsiung and headed to Seattle or Vancouver go east by first heading north up the west coast of Taiwan, then dropping into the Kuroshio Current, one such river-in-the-sea in the far western Pacific Ocean that begins just off the eastern coast of Taiwan. Nearing the waters off Japan back in October 1998, the *APL China* would have made a turn to the northeast, leaving the Kuroshio Current and entering the North Pacific Current, a river of warm water running east between 40 and 50 degrees north latitude, south of the Gulf of Alaska toward southern Canada. That eastbound current forms in the ocean just off Tokyo, where the northbound Kuroshio Current collides with the southbound Oyashio Current. Approaching the British Columbia coast, that eastbound current merges with the southbound California Current; there, the Seattle-bound *APL China* would have pulled out of the current, continuing east into the Strait of Juan de Fuca and toward the opening of Puget Sound.

But the currents don't stop. The California Current continues on, flowing south along the coast of North America to the southern end of Baja California. There it runs into the westbound North Equatorial Current, triggered by the eastward rotation of the Earth. That current crosses the wide middle of the Pacific north of the equator to meld with the Kuroshio Current off the east coast of Taiwan. Put them all together, and you have what oceanographers call the North Pacific Gyre, an immense circular current running clockwise in the northern basin of the Pacific Ocean.

To retailers, early October is the build-up to the holiday shopping season. But early October has a different significance to mariners in the North Pacific: it's the last of the big typhoon months. Typhoons can appear any week of the year, but they peak from July through October. Typhoons—they're called hurricanes in the Atlantic and on the west coast of North America—are the most violent form of tropical cyclones: seasonal storms with winds that rotate around an area of low air pressure. By definition, they're limited to the tropics, and they begin over the ocean. To give birth to such a storm, the water must be warm (at least 79 degrees Fahrenheit) and at least two hundred feet deep for several hundred square miles. The western North Pacific is a regular cyclone factory, producing an average of twenty-five such storms a year. Three-quarters of them evolve into typhoons, which are defined as cyclones that have winds exceeding 64 knots.

A couple days after the *APL China* departed Hong Kong, meteorologists observed a tropical depression forming in the ocean hundreds of miles east of the Philippines. By the next day they'd given it a name: Tropical Storm Babs. Over the next few days, it wandered west without gaining much strength, until October 19, when it quickly grew in intensity, spouting 140-mph winds. Now *Typhoon* Babs, it raged across the Philippines, triggering mudslides and flash floods that killed more than two hundred people. Hundreds of boats were wrecked, tens of thousands of houses flattened, before Typhoon Babs lost her punch and dissipated in the South China Sea west of Taiwan.

The typhoon drama was playing out far from the *APL China*; by the time Babs was running amok through the Philippines, the vessel was thousands of miles to the north, near the Aleutian Islands and approaching the International Date Line. But the typhoon had more tricks up its sleeve. It had spun off a fast-moving type of extratropical cyclone that meteorologists call a "bomb." Unlike typhoons, extratropical cyclones have no warm, clear "eye" around which the storm swirls. Rather, they're spread out, sometimes covering vast tracts of ocean as much as three thousand miles across, and they can last for days. With sustained high winds blowing over a broad area of the ocean, extratropical cyclones can quickly produce very large waves and, as a result, dangerous seas. It was just this sort of storm that followed the *APL China* across the North Pacific in October 1998. The captains of the *APL China* and several other vessels had apparently tried to outrun the cyclone or skirt its edge, but this storm was too fast to outrun.

When it hit late on the evening of October 26, the cyclone brought winds reportedly as high as one hundred knots that whipped the ocean into 40- to 75-foot swells, battering the 905-foot-long vessel for twelve hours with confused, violent seas reaching as high as the bridge and pounding the stacks of containers on the deck. The ship began to roll 35 to 40 degrees—even to 50 degrees, by one account, far more than the 20 to 25 degrees anticipated by the ship's designers. When a large container vessel, with its widely flaring bow and stern designed to maximize deck space, is caught in heavy seas where the length of the ship is about equal to the distance between wave crests, the rolling that results can quickly get out of control as the vessel crests one wave and drops into the trough of another. Engineers call this *head-sea parametric rolling,* and it occurs when the speed and length of the vessel and the frequency of the waves prevent the vessel from ever quite reaching equilibrium after a roll. The rolls become larger and larger, requiring a drastic maneuver—a turn, or a change of speed—to break the cycle. It was a phenomenon that had plagued smaller vessels but not been expected to affect huge "post-Panamax" ships such as the *APL China*—ships too big to fit in the Panama Canal. This storm was rewriting the modern mariners' handbook.

A ship at sea can move in six directions at once, pitching and rolling, yawing and heaving, and stressing the ship, the container stacks on deck, and the containers themselves. On board the ship that night, it was "as if the devil had taken control" of the vessel, as the captain was reported to have described it. Huge waves slammed the ship all night long, and water breeched the Number 1 hold, filling it with sixteen feet of water. Through air vents, water breeched the emergency generator room, cutting power to the vessel. Wallowing in heavy seas for twenty minutes until power was restored, the ship was essentially at the cyclone's mercy. Gangways, sidelights, and a stern light were all ripped away by the waves.

And then the containers started to go. Shipping containers sitting on the deck of a vessel weathering a storm at sea can fail in a variety of ways. Compression from the ship slamming through violent waves can cause one wall of a container at the bottom of a stack to crumble, and soon the whole stack starts to lean. Waves of what mariners call "green water"—solid walls of water, as opposed to mere spray—pummeling the stack can smash open the sides of containers where they stand, particularly containers weakened by being knocked around during loading and unloading. But the *APL China*'s violent rolling is probably what did the most damage. Some containers fell onto the vessel's deck, rearranging themselves, crushing other containers and burying the ship's stern lines and mooring winches. Others pitched directly into the sea, where they would have bobbed like malevolent bathtub toys, temporarily buoyant, until seawater seeping in or rushing in displaced enough air to send the container and its contents to the bottom of the ocean, more than three miles down.

Perhaps the container holding my Havoc floated for a while, buoyed by air trapped in the foam soles, in the cardboard boxes, the air at the top of the container not-quite-filled with cartons of shoes, until torque from the storm waves pried open a seam. Perhaps it was an older container, its corner posts already stressed from too-heavy loads or too many hard falls from the gantry crane, and it came apart while still in the stack, writhing with the ship. Maybe a sharp roll simply pitched the weakened container two or three hundred feet down to the sea's surface, where it split open on impact: an explosion of corrugated-cardboard cartons and flimsy cardboard boxes and sturdy shoes, the white of their Benecke uppers dulled to pale gray in that moonless night. Havocs freed from their boxes might have landed on their soles, but soon the uppers would have become top heavy with rain and seawater, and the shoes would have heeled over until only the soles were visible, floating just above the sea's surface, black footprints spreading out across a night-black ocean. The wads of tissue that had been hand-stuffed into each toe would become soaked like little sponges, and the two white shoelace ends would be dangling from the knot wad, drifting just below the surface and waving slightly, like jellyfish tentacles.

CURTIS EBBESMEYER AND HIS FRIEND and colleague Jim Ingraham learned about the container spill from the *APL China* the same way everyone else did. "Rough trip across Pacific," read the headline over the photograph in the November 1, 1998, *Seattle Times* the day after the ship limped into the Port of Seattle, two days behind schedule and looking like it had suffered a direct assault by Poseidon himself. What had left Kaohsiung as neat phalanxes of stacked containers had become ragged, teetering rows with big gaps, capped in places with crumpled containers or containers lying crosswise, even dangling over the gunwales. At the stern, a dozen rows of containers stacked six tall were all leaning hard to port, still attached to one another, except for the topmost containers on the port side, which were gone. The storm had overtaken a half-dozen container vessels, and four of them had lost cargo, none more than the *APL China*. A total of 406 containers had fallen off that vessel alone, and at least that many had been damaged, with the losses set at more than $100 million, twice the value of the ship itself. It was the worst loss from a single ship since the beginnings of containerization in the 1960s.

As attorneys for APL, Ltd., insurers, and manufacturers of the goods lost at sea began gathering evidence for their day in court, Ebbesmeyer and Ingraham headed to the computer. Back in the 1970s, Ingraham—then a scientist with the resource ecology and fisheries management division of the Alaska Fisheries Science Center, part of the National Oceanic & Atmospheric Administration—had been involved in developing an innovative research tool dubbed OSCURS, for Ocean Surface Current Simulations. The idea was to investigate how ocean surface currents might have influenced the movement of fish populations in the North Pacific Ocean and Bering Sea over time. Fish eggs, larvae, plankton, and other small organisms that drift near the surface move at the whim of sea surface currents anywhere from ten to fifty meters deep; even mammals and such fish as salmon are affected by changes in sea surface movements. Unlike the steady, circular flow of the deep rivers within the ocean that power the North Pacific Gyre, whose waters take about six years to make a complete circuit of the northern ocean, sea surface currents change with shifts in the strength and direction of the wind and can move things along much more quickly; things drifting at or just below the surface can make a round-trip in the gyre in three years or less. Those wind changes are determined in large part by changes in sea-level atmospheric pressure. As air heats and cools across the ocean and land, that air expands and contracts, creating high- and low-pressure areas. Nature abhors a vacuum, and air rushes in to fill those low-pressure areas, creating wind.

The North Pacific Ocean is vast, unimaginably so. Ingraham and his colleagues seeking to better understand its surface dynamics knew that it would be impossible to comprehensively monitor and track actual changes in wind and sea surface currents across its breadth. Instead, they tapped into the atmospheric sea-level pressure measurements that had been recorded daily since 1946 by buoys scattered in a grid at sea, compiled by the U.S. Navy Fleet Numerical Meteorology and Oceanography Center, and, these days, by hundreds of ships at sea reporting air pressure readings every six hours. Additional data from the National Center for Atmospheric Research allowed them to calculate sea surface movements as far back as 1901. All those data points became OSCURS' proxies for surface current changes across the broad sweep of the Pacific. With OSCURS, they began unraveling such mysteries as the timing of the return of sockeye salmon to Canada's Fraser River from year to year and the survival prospects of juvenile walleye pollock, one of the most commercially important fish species in the Bering Sea.

But it was OSCURS' use in tracking debris that caught the world's attention, presenting Ingraham with unprecedented opportunities to fine-tune the model. Scientists studying ocean drift—the movement of things on or just below the surface of the sea—have launched drift bottles stuffed with contact information, a few hundred at a time, and waited to see when and where they washed up. If they were lucky, they might recover 1 to 2 percent of the bottles—not more than three or four bottles from a launch of two hundred. Then in May 1990 an event Ebbesmeyer termed "accidental, but fortuitous" occurred that ultimately changed his life's direction. Hundreds of brand-new Nike shoes and boots in a narrow range of styles had begun washing up on Northwest beaches. Newspaper reports described beachcombers holding swap meets, matching beach-salvaged right and left shoes of the same size and type.

"Isn't that what you do?" Ebbesmeyer recalls his mother asking him at the time, pointing to an article about the spill.

"Well, not exactly," he replied. What he actually did at the time was measure and analyze ocean currents for the small oceanographic consulting firm of Evans-Hamilton, Inc., tracking oil slicks such as one from the *Exxon Valdez* and helping municipalities figure out the least-harmful sites for sewage-treatment plants and their outfall.

"But I'll look into it," he told his mom. This shipping disaster, he began to realize, had the potential to become a windfall for science. He started tracking down Oregon beachcombers who had found the Nikes, recording how many shoes they had found and where they'd found them. Then he managed to make contact with someone in the marine transport division at Nike, who gave him particulars of the spill: twenty-one containers, five of them holding eighty thousand Nike shoes, had been swept off the deck of the vessel *Hansa Carrier* on its way from Korea to Tacoma. From shipping lawyers he learned exactly where and when the spill had occurred.

From Nike he also learned about the code numbers found inside each shoe, numbers unique to each shipment or production run: "messages in a bottle, " or MIBs, Ebbesmeyer began calling them. If and when a beachcomber found a Nike on the beach, Ebbesmeyer could confirm it was from this particular spill by means of the MIB. A comparison of the codes he received from Nike and the codes on the shoes that were washing up indicated that only four of the five containers of Nike shoes had been breeched, putting the total number of shoes liberated in mid-ocean at a little more than sixty thousand.

Then he naturally thought of Jim Ingraham, with whom he'd been friends since their graduate-school days at the University of Washington, and Jim's OSCURS computer model. If Jim plugged in the coordinates of the spill—Point A—and the coordinates of the beaches where individual shoes had been found—Points B_1, B_2, etc.—and ran the model, they'd have a field test of OSCURS the likes of which no NOAA-funded grant could possibly match, neatly proving the efficacy of OSCURS and fine-tuning it in the process. With intelligence gathered by Ebbesmeyer, Ingraham was able to accurately track the bulk of objects in a debris plume and estimate, almost to the day, when and where they were likely to wash ashore. More spills and more tests for OSCURS followed, including a 1994 spill of thousands of buoyant hockey gloves that Ebbesmeyer and Ingraham followed for months—by computer—to the shores of British Columbia.

"One Thursday or Friday I said, 'Curt, hey, the gloves are going to be here next week,'" Ingraham recalls smugly. "And Monday we got a call from Canada: fifteen hockey gloves found on the beach!"

But as ocean-drift research subjects, nothing could compete with actual tub toys. In January 1992, some twenty-nine thousand little plastic yellow duckies, green frogs, blue turtles, and red beavers fell off a container ship and into the big, cold bathtub of the North Pacific. Unlike most of the Nikes, which were swept clockwise with the North Pacific Gyre, the tub toys got pulled into the Pacific Subarctic Gyre, circling counterclockwise in the Gulf of Alaska and Bering Sea. On a map of ocean currents, the two gyres look like the number eight, the top gyre smaller and flatter than the bottom one. Within seven months of the spill, Ebbesmeyer began receiving reports of toys washing up near Sitka, Alaska. Years later, most of them were probably still spinning around the gyre, according to OSCURS. But as time passed, the floating toy cohort began to disperse. After making one complete three-year circuit in the Subarctic Gyre, some peeled south into the North Pacific Gyre and wound up on beaches in Oregon and Washington, even Hawaii; OSCURS indicates others may have made it to the coasts of China and Japan, though no findings of the toys have been reported there. Still others escaped north through the Bering Straight into the Arctic. There OSCURS reached the limit of its prognostications; it worked only with the currents of the North Pacific and Bering Sea. But Ingraham's knowledge of other ocean currents allowed him to estimate the toys' track through the Arctic Ocean and into the North Atlantic. He knew it would take about five years for the toys to make it through the seasonally frozen Arctic and into the North Atlantic and start washing up in Iceland, Britain, and Norway. The first reports of beach-stranded tub toys in the Atlantic actually came from beachcombers in New England in 2000. And in 2003 a vacationer in the Hebrides in northwest Scotland came back from a walk talking about a curious little green plastic frog she'd seen on the beach.

But with hundreds of containers lost overboard and potentially millions of drifters riding the sea's surface currents, the *APL China* disaster had even more potential as a test for OSCURS than any previous spill. Ebbesmeyer didn't know exactly what was in all the containers that spilled, but only so many consumer goods—shoes, hockey gloves, bathtub toys, umbrella handles—would float and would still be floating after months at sea. He spread the word among Northwest beachcombers to watch for debris—in no great hurry; it would be a year or better before anything showed up—and he obtained the coordinates of the spill: 176.6 degrees east longitude, 40.867 north latitude, about halfway between the Midway Islands and the Aleutian Islands. Now Ingraham could start tracking the path of the debris plume, adjusting it according to data gleaned from the Nike shoes and hockey gloves, the plastic duckies, a shipment of peeled Douglas fir logs, and everything else the pair had tracked in the previous eight years.

Debris floating on the sea's surface doesn't move at quite the same speed as fish eggs entirely suspended in the water. Wind catches whatever portion of the debris is sticking out of the water, pushing it faster and at a different angle to the wind. Through trial and error, Ingraham had developed drift coefficients for common ocean debris: 1.2 for athletic shoes, or 20 percent faster than the speed of water. Hockey gloves have a drift coefficient of 1.4, and plastic bathtub toys, bobbing high above the water, are 1.6. In addition, the larger the object, the more surface area it exposes to the wind, the more its direction will deviate from the direction of the ocean surface current. Asked to track the drift of a thirty-eight-foot sloop after its sailor perished in a storm off the California coast, Ingraham plotted the boat's last three known locations—where it was when the storm hit, and two later sightings by ocean-going ships—and was able to determine that this particular boat drifted 5.5 times faster than surface water and veered 60 degrees to the right of the wind.

Riding the gyre, nudged by ocean surface currents, pushed by the wind blowing across the sea, the Havocs began their eastward drift. Ingraham and Ebbesmeyer, meanwhile, were adding daily data points to a computer model tracking the likely path of the debris plume from the spill. For three months the plume appeared to be moving steadily to the east, heading toward the Oregon coast. Then, in February, the data indicated a change in direction, a slight shift to the southeast. For two months or more the plume of debris was apparently drifting toward Baja California. Then it shifted again, back toward the Northwest coast. Sometime in July 1999, still well offshore, the red path of the trajectory that had been creeping across Ingraham's computer screen took a turn to the south. It twisted back on itself briefly, but by the fall of that year there was no doubt about where it was going. No need to mobilize Ebbesmeyer's network of beachcombers; clearly, there would be no shoe tide on the beaches of the Pacific Northwest, no beachcombers' bonanza, no swap meets, not from this spill. Most of what had fallen off the *APL China* in October 1998 and was still afloat a year later seemed to be drifting right into the heart of the Eastern Garbage Patch.

THE PATCH—THE TERM WAS COINED in the mid-nineties at an international marine-debris conference—lies in the middle of the North Pacific Gyre between about 30 and 35 degrees north latitudes. It's a calm area of high atmospheric pressure, twice the size of Texas and centered roughly halfway between Honolulu and Seattle, though its precise location is constantly shifting. It's like a huge eddy in the middle of the Pacific Ocean; flotsam that's pushed into the Patch by wind and current tends to spiral toward its center and can stay there for decades. That's where the sailboat Ingraham was asked to track headed as well; it's not been seen since. That's probably where any debris from the *President Adams* went, and much more quickly than the *China*-spilled goods. Now and then, strong winds from the southwest push the Patch north and east and it releases some of its floating treasures—escaped fishing gear, athletic shoes, old Japanese glass fishing floats—onto West Coast beaches, particularly in Oregon and Washington. Those are heady days for beachcombers—days, they say, when the biggest, rarest glass floats, the kind fishermen haven't used for decades, roll onto the beach, along with every other kind of flotsam. These days, most of that flotsam is plastic.

Few humans have actually seen the debris-strewn Patch firsthand. Most of its contents float right at or just below the surface, and are too small to be seen from a plane or a satellite. Observers at the rails of ocean-going vessels cutting across the Patch wouldn't see much either; they're too far above the water. Fishermen avoid the Patch; the fishing's poor. Sailors navigate around the windless Patch. A friend of a friend told me about sailing a forty-six-foot catamaran from Hawaii to Santa Barbara back in the mid-1960s; partway back, the novice teenage navigator and crew of five found themselves becalmed on a sea as smooth as a mirror and bobbing with glass floats of all sizes and colors, as far as they could see. They began grabbing at them, gathering as many of the biggest and brightest as they could stash in their living quarters or in nets suspended between hulls, especially the golden yellow floats three feet in diameter that they came across by the hundreds. After two days of floating through glass ball heaven, the winds picked up, and the floats were gone.

These days there's a lot more than glass floats in the Patch. In the past, as recently as the mid-twentieth century, nearly anything caught in the Patch besides glass floats—those can bob for decades, maybe for hundreds of years—would eventually have decomposed and biodegraded. But the worldwide proliferation of plastic, running parallel to the development of container shipping, changed all that. "I don't remember seeing any shoes," the catamaran sailor had mused as we talked about his sail through the Patch in the sixties. Of course not: container shipping was still in its infancy, and athletic shoes as we know them today had not yet been invented, much less mass-produced overseas.

Over time, plastic photodegrades, breaking down into smaller and smaller pieces that continue to float, many of them trapped in the Patch. Some particles get scooped up by fulmars and albatrosses and other seabirds skimming the waves, feeding on the surface of the ocean. The smallest pieces, resembling microscopic zooplankton, are eaten by jellyfish, which are in turn eaten by larger sea creatures and thus become part of the marine food chain.

"Trash never disappears," as Ebbesmeyer puts it, "but just goes somewhere else."

Captain Charles Moore had an inkling of what he'd find when, on a whim, he steered his catamaran research vessel *Alguita* (equipped with two auxiliary diesel engines) through the middle of the Patch on his way back to California from Hawaii in 1997. He'd spent his life at sea—

as a deckhand, an able seaman, and eventually as captain of his own ship—and had witnessed the increase in plastic debris on the ocean. But Moore's shortcut, through what would eventually become known as the Eastern Garbage Patch, still stunned him. Gazing at the surface of "what ought to have been a pristine ocean," he wrote in *Natural History* in 2003, "I was confronted, as far as the eye could see, with the sight of plastic."

"It seemed unbelievable," he continues, "but I never found a clear spot. In the week it took to cross the subtropical high, no matter what time of day I looked, plastic debris was floating everywhere: bottles, bottle caps, wrappers, fragments." He returned with a crew of oceanographers in 1998 to sample the surface waters of the Patch. They collected six times as much plastic, by weight, as zooplankton. Oregon beachcomber Steve McLeod joined Moore in summer 1999 on a three-week voyage aimed, in part, at tracking down the *APL China* debris plume. They weren't able to find that particular congregation of flotsam—the Patch is vast. But they found plenty of other junk. Even the guts of the fish they caught for dinner was full of plastic bits.

"Most oceans probably have a garbage patch like this," Ebbesmeyer remarked in an event I attended at the Beachcombers' Fun Fair in Ocean Shores, "but this is the only one that's been well documented. I'll bet you there's a dozen abandoned yachts out there in the Patch. It's archaeology of the ocean—just a wide-open field."

Ebbesmeyer is an entertaining speaker—articulate, knowledgeable, funny, as you'd expect of a guy who posed naked (from the waist up, along with his friend Ingraham) in a bathtub full of toy ducks for *People* magazine in 1995. And his passion for his favorite topic is infectious. "It's sort of a poor man's oceanography," he told the magazine. "To me, if science isn't fun, then it's really drudgery and it's probably not good science," Ebbesmeyer later remarked. "I always try to tell kids, it doesn't matter what you keep track of, if you keep track of it long enough, it's awesome stuff." But behind the zeal and sense of wonder are some undeniable and sobering facts. "People ask me all the time, how do we clean this up?" he said to the standing-room-only Fun Fair crowd. "I honestly don't know. My view is that plastic is eventually going to end humanity."

BY NOVEMBER 1999, INGRAHAM could see that the plume of debris from the *APL China* would not make landfall like the Nikes from the *Hansa Carrier* had done back in 1990. The largest spill in the history of container shipping was eddying out in the middle of the Pacific Ocean. It was likely to swirl around the Patch for years, for decades. And the observations of Ebbesmeyer's corps of West Coast beachcombers bore him out; no windfall of debris had followed the *APL China* disaster. Once it appeared that the debris was headed right into the Patch, Ingraham and Ebbesmeyer stopped tracking it. There wasn't much point. Anyway, there would be other spills.

But somehow, like the duckies that beached in Hawaii and Maine, my Havoc had exited the main plume of debris.

"I was wracking my brain over that one for a long time," Ingraham said of the fate of the flotsam from the *APL China*. "It was a big story, from the fact that there were so many containers lost. But we just had to let it go."

I had sought out Ingraham at his house on Camano Island, north of Seattle, to examine his computer models and solicit his best guesses about the path of the Reebok Havoc, which almost certainly fell off the *China* but had somehow diverged from the rest of that spill's flotsam plume. Ingraham, retired in 2004 after forty-one years as a scientist with NOAA in Seattle, and his wife had moved to a large house overlooking Puget Sound's Saratoga Passage and, beyond it, forested Whidbey Island, shrouded that day in a pale veil of mist, and the snow-capped Olympic Range. Upstairs is an adult care home, the Ingrahams' retirement business. Downstairs are their living quarters and Jim's computers, tucked in a couple of windowless rooms, humming. They're key to Ingraham's passion and his second retirement business, Driftbusters. Unlike shoe manufacturers, who might prefer Ingraham not track and therefore publicize spills of their merchandise cluttering the world's oceans, private parties and governments sometimes seek out Ingraham's help to solve mysteries involving things floating on the sea, such as the family of the sailor who died at sea and whose boat and belongings, at least, they hope someday to find. Once Ingraham was flown to Hawaii to help investigate the case of a corpse that had been found drifting in a survival suit. "He was a one-armed man, draped with lots of gold," Ingraham recalled. As far as he knows, the man was never identified. Ingraham and his wife suspect drugs were involved, but at that point, he said, the case moved a little out of his area of expertise.

My report to him about the Havoc I had found and its likely link to the *APL China* had sent him back to the computer-simulated track of the debris plume from that spill that he had created in 1998 and eventually abandoned. Any way you looked at it—and he had looked at it from every possible angle—most of the stuff must have headed into the Patch. Most of it never got close enough to the West Coast to get blown onto the beach.

But OSCURS isn't a homing system. It doesn't precisely track individual pieces of debris. It simply makes predictions about the direction the bulk of the objects in a drift plume will go. Once freed from the tightly packed confines of the steel container, shoes and other flotsam begin to spread out across the sea's surface—"like smoke rings in the air," Curtis Ebbesmeyer had written in *Beachcomber's Alert*. All of it begins by flowing in the general direction of the current, but turbulence on the sea surface starts to disperse the objects, more broadly as time goes by, and wind disperses it further. Ebbesmeyer described a shipment of 350 telephone poles destined for Oman that had fallen off a ship eight hundred miles southeast of Bermuda. Over 113 days the poles dispersed until they had spread over an area seventy miles across—roughly one pole per ten square miles of ocean—consistent with the rate projected by oceanographic drift experiments of shorter duration. At that rate, Ebbesmeyer figured, the poles would eventually be spread over about forty-nine thousand square nautical miles—an area more than half the size of Oregon. A container load of Havocs would no doubt disperse in a similar manner.

Theoretically, objects at the fringe of the plume may get caught in other currents. But this particular debris plume had begun floating right in the middle of the North Pacific Current. Based on years of experience observing oceanic trash, Ingraham expected that most of the objects in this plume would have stayed clumped together long enough to land in the Patch before they started appreciably dispersing.

The plume had been a good 250 miles offshore when it turned south and headed toward the Patch. Four years later, in spring 2002, OSCURS indicated that strong winds had pushed the Patch to the northeast, depositing some of its contents—probably including flotsam from the *APL China*—on Pacific Northwest beaches. That computer prediction was borne out by beachcombers; spring 2002 was one of those bonanza seasons. But that was two years after I'd found my Havoc on the beach.

So exactly how did the Havoc reach Mile 157? "There are all kinds of possibilities," Ingraham said. One of them: this shoe, and possibly others—possibly the Converse I found with the Havoc, even the Converse I'd found four months earlier—may have indeed been driven by water and wind to the outer edge of the plume and been snagged, sometime in the winter of 1999-2000, by nearshore currents off California, currents such as the Davidson Current, a northbound "countercurrent" that tends to run November through March off the West Coast of the U.S. Another possibility: it may have been drawn to shore far to the north of Oregon, then blown to the south in summer 2000, when the prevailing winds begin blowing from the northwest.

Then he posed another possible scenario. With containers dislodged from their fasteners and teetering on the gunwales of the battered vessel, the container holding the Havocs may have survived the storm's lashing but finally fallen into the sea in the four days it took for the *APL China* to limp into the Port of Seattle, which would have given the Havocs an entirely different Point A. In that case, the shoes could have washed onto a Washington or British Columbian beach well before September 2000, later washing off and floating north and south for months, according to seasonal changes in wind direction and nearshore currents, before finally landing on Mile 157. This third scenario was less likely, however, since it would have put scores more Havocs onto Northwest beaches.

"It's just another idea," Ingraham said. But he was reluctant to speculate further. It was OSCURS' scientific rigor that had made it such a useful tool to fisheries biologists. Many more what-ifs, and we would quickly find ourselves moving "out of our science area," as he put it.

What about the rest of the Havocs in that container, the other 14,135 shoes? After I contacted Ingraham in fall 2006, he revived the drift trajectories he'd started back in 1998, filling in the atmospheric pressure-generated data points for the subsequent days, months, years. Once they reached the Patch, the shoes would have dispersed further. Some of them are probably still floating upside down in the Patch, and some may have been spit out of the Patch and onto an Oregon or Washington beach in 2002. And some that failed to make landfall in 2002 probably drifted south again, swinging to the southwest somewhere off Baja and getting caught up in the westbound North Equatorial Current. Early in 2004, they would have floated past the Big Island of Hawaii. According to the drift trajectory outlined in red on the computer screen in Ingraham's basement, the shoes' path would have made a dogleg north around the outside of Taiwan and then west again, approaching the Chinese mainland at about Fuzhou. From there, the path turns south, down the Chinese coastline. It wouldn't surprise Ingraham if some Havocs floated right past the port of Hong Kong in about January 2006.

Like very slow salmon, migrating home.

Chapter Four: Flight of the Minke

JACK AND I HAD BEEN WALKING NORTH on the beach when we first saw it, maybe a quarter-mile away. A log? No. A dead sea lion? (We'd found one of those before.) No, it was a whale, an actual whale on the beach. A small one as whales go, but still big—a good seven paces long. Certainly not as big as an adult gray whale—it must be a baby gray, we figured. It clearly wasn't an orca, unmistakable with its tall dorsal fin jutting three to six feet tall, and the only other whale I'd heard of on the Oregon coast was the gray whale.

The whale we found *was* gray—mostly gray, anyway. It lay on its belly, mired in the sand. The back was dark gray. So were the flippers, but for a pale stripe; was this something baby gray whales outgrew? The whale was fairly intact: there were just some puncture marks, an odd squarish bite out of its back, and some damage to its upper jaw, where half the baleen had been ripped away. Dead, presumably, or—glimpsing a fluttering of the white fibers at the edge of the remaining baleen—could that be its breath? But it was only the breeze, dancing through the cavernous beaked mouth. (The fact that whales breathe not through their mouths but through blowholes—whale nostrils—at the tops of their heads did not occur to me at the moment.)

Back at home I called the number CoastWatch had provided for the Oregon Marine Mammal Stranding Network. The whale didn't actually seem merely *stranded,* it seemed *dead.* Nevertheless, it seemed like an occurrence that should be reported to someone. But the woman who answered the phone said mine was not the first call about the whale; she'd already been out to see it, in fact, seven days earlier.

And it wasn't a gray whale, Tamara McGuire explained; it was a young minke whale, the smallest member of the rorqual whale family, whose best-known member is the humpback whale. Like gray whales, rorquals are baleen whales. They feed not on large prey as, say, orcas and sperm whales and other toothed whales do, but on small schooling fish and even smaller animals—zooplankton—by scooping up vast quantities of sea water in their mouths, then filtering and trapping the small prey with a comb-like baleen consisting of hundreds of thin, closely packed plates made of keratin—like fingernails, or horses' hooves—that hang down from the upper jaw in lieu of teeth. Minkes are dark gray above but white underneath, with a white band across each flipper; grays are all gray (even the babies) but for the barnacles and whale lice that tend to pock their skin. Minkes have a curved dorsal fin about a foot tall and about two-thirds of the way down the back; grays have a dorsal *hump* but no fin. Unique to rorquals, minkes are characterized by the long, furrow-like grooves, or ventral pleats, at the throat, starting under the jaw and stretching back behind the flippers—nearly half the animal's length—allowing the throat to expand like a pelican's during feeding, accordion-like. And minkes are small: as adults, they're a bit bigger than orcas, but just two-thirds the length and a quarter the weight of full-grown gray whales. A yearling gray whale might be about the size of the minke we found. In other words, it would be easy to mistake a minke for a small gray whale it if were lying on its belly, and if you didn't know a thing about either one.

But it *was* stranded, even if it was dead. According to the stranding network, any whale or dolphin found on the beach, dead or alive, in any condition, is classified as a stranded marine mammal. It's out of its element, outside of its survival envelope; by definition, stuck. There are rare exceptions. Orcas have been known to snatch seals off beaches, then wriggle back out to sea, and bottlenose dolphins may ride waves all the way to shore, even chase fish onto muddy banks, and turn around without harm. A live seal on the beach, on the other hand, is considered stranded only if it's injured, or ill, or weak and can't get back to the water. Unlike whales, pinnipeds such as seals, sea lions, and elephant seals can walk on their flippers; they typically spend part of their day hauled out on rocks or beaches, even leaving their babies beached for hours at a time while they forage for food. That's where things sometimes get sketchy between wildlife and humans. A baby harbor seal left on the beach by its mother is *not*, by definition, stranded. But try telling that to the beachcomber who comes upon the liquid-eyed, kitten-soft animal, mewing plaintively, sounding like nothing so much as a hungry, cold human baby. I had come upon a seal pup once myself, early one morning at Porter Point north of Lincoln City. Another beach walker was in a tizzy over the pup, proposing to rescue the poor thing and carry it off the beach in her large striped canvas bag. I pointed toward the water, where a sleek, dark, cat-like head was bobbing in the waves, staring at us and—if harbor seals can pace—anxiously pacing the breakers. But a whale on the beach, dead or alive, generally cannot get off the beach on its own and rarely even with help. To the stranding network, that's about as stranded as you can get.

Tamara didn't know much about minkes herself. She had done her doctoral research on the Amazon river dolphins of northern Peru— "because they're weird," she explained later with an wry smile. Gray-pink in color with beady little eyes, river dolphins look funny, and they make a sort of snorting sound when they surface. Like that of other dolphins, their mouth line curves up in the corners like a smile, but in river dolphins it's a slightly crazed, sneaky-looking smirk, not the Mona Lisa smile that's made ocean dolphins a New Agey icon. Which is exactly what Tamara—a slight, brainy brunette who wore her jeans and bulky sweaters baggy—liked about them. She had been coordinator of the Oregon stranding network for only about a year and had seen lots of different marine mammal species in that year—"unfortunately, most of them dead"—but no minke whales. Nearly two hundred pinnipeds had stranded on the beach in Oregon in that time, plus five dolphins and three whales, one of them a gray whale and the other two unidentifiable. (Sometimes just the head—or the headless body—of a decomposing whale or other long-dead marine mammal is thrown ashore after a storm.) Certainly, gray whales are more likely to wind up on the beach in Oregon than any other whale species; there were only seven known minke strandings on the Oregon coast from 1930 to 2003, and for each of those, eight gray whales were beached, nearly one a year. Tamara had never actually seen a minke whale, alive or dead, except for the

articulated skeleton suspended over the walkway outside her office at
Hatfield Marine Science Center in Newport. She knew better than to
make any assumptions about a whale's ID until she'd seen it herself.

The first call about the dead minke—Tamara had reconstructed every
detail of the stranding on a tracking sheet—was actually to the Reedsport
headquarters of Oregon Dunes National Recreation Area. It was 9:30 on
Thursday morning, March 4, 2004. A woman reported that her husband,
standing on the viewing platform at Dunes Overlook, had seen a whale
on the beach, more than a half-mile away. He thought it might be alive,
the woman told Janine at the Dunes headquarters. Janine called the
Oregon State Police dispatcher—twelve years after establishment of
the Oregon stranding network, staff at local police and wildlife offices
still didn't necessarily know whom to call to report a stranded whale.
The state trooper called the Oregon Department of Fish & Wildlife field
office in the port town of Charleston, thirty miles south of Reedsport.
Heidi, in the field office, called Tamara in Newport.

By now it was nearly noon. Tamara called Janine in Reedsport to gather
more details of the purportedly stranded whale. One thing Tamara had
learned in her year on the job was to not rush out at the first report of a
dead whale on the beach. Among the cautionary tales she had heard when
she arrived at the marine science center was one about an orca reportedly
stranded in the mouth of a creek in Tillamook County, a couple of hours'
drive to the north. Volunteers had hopped in the network's truck and
sped to the site, only to find that the "orca" was actually a cow—black
and white, like an orca, but one of the thousands of Holstein cows that
furnish the Tillamook County Creamery Association with milk. Now she
asks questions before rushing out—questions, she says with a grin, like,
"Does it have hooves?" Oddly, not every call to the Marine Mammal
Stranding Network concerns a *marine* mammal. Just a day after the first
report of the minke, Tamara heard from a woman in Bandon, on the
south coast, who wanted to report a "dead cow, dead cat, and two dead
sea gulls" in front of her house at the south jetty. (Tamara referred her
to the proper authorities.) A couple of weeks later a minor panic would
ensue when a woman called in about a baby gray whale entangled in
fishing gear that had been rescued and was being towed into Charleston

harbor at that very moment; she had seen it on the television news. Tamara and some science center colleagues quickly began making calls to the Coast Guard and other agencies; no one had heard anything about a whale being brought into Coos Bay. Then another colleague wondered aloud—correctly, it turned out—if it might have been not Charleston, Oregon, but Charleston, *South Carolina.* Her favorite story was about the irate tourist from Georgia who called about a sea lion seemingly in the final throes of dying on Agate Beach just north of Newport. "I thought Oregon was the state with death with dignity!" she fumed as she described the large animal's tortured bellowing, its swollen snout dripping snot, and the patches of hairy skin sloughing off its humped back. Tamara knew right away what was going on: it was an elephant seal, not a sea lion, and it was merely shedding its fur, as all pinnipeds so, usually once a year. But while seals and sea lions molt gradually, hair by hair, elephant seals go through what scientists call a "catastrophic molt," shedding hair in huge sheets, fasting in the process, and getting understandably cranky. With his almost grotesque proportions, a male elephant seal even in the peak of health looks a little out of sorts; his annual molt couldn't be pretty. Tamara did her best to reassure the caller that the animal wasn't in pain, much less dying. Apparently the woman hadn't seen the sign posted seasonally at the edge of the beach, right behind the elephant seal, stating that visitors should not be alarmed if they happen to see molting marine mammals.

In the matter of the dead minke whale, the couple who had made the original report about the whale were long gone, and Janine didn't have any more details. She urged Tamara to contact Mike Northrup, a fisheries biologist with the Forest Service's Mapleton Ranger District office in Florence; she'd need his authorization to drive south on the beach via gated Waxmyrtle Road to reach the whale. She'd also need his key to the gate. Tamara called Mike; it happened to be a slow day for Mike, and he said he'd be happy to drive down and take a look with a colleague. It would have taken Tamara more than an hour to drive south to Waxmyrtle Road—a long way to go for what might be nothing more than a resting sea lion, or a tree stump—but from Mike's office in Florence it was only about a ten-minute drive. At this point Tamara doubted the whale was alive, if it was a whale at all. A live stranded whale that's not dying for another reason can live for a while, breathing air like any mammal, but without the buoyancy of the sea, its lungs will soon collapse, suffocating it. She also knew that dead whales can look alive—especially from a distance of a half-mile—when they're moving in the surf.

At about 2 p.m. Tamara got a call from the Mapleton Ranger District receptionist. Mike had radioed in to report that it was indeed a whale, a dead one: a minke, he guessed. An hour later Mike, back from the beach, called Tamara himself from the ranger station. He estimated the whale's length at twenty to twenty-five feet, and it hadn't been dead for long; it had only a "faint whiff of decay," he told her. He e-mailed her some digital snapshots he'd taken of the whale; definitely a minke, she confirmed, consulting her Audubon Society *Guide to Marine Mammals of the World.* There wasn't really enough daylight left for Tamara to get to the site, examine the whale, and collect tissue samples, and Mike was hoping to collect the baleen and keep it for display in the ranger station. They agreed to meet in Florence the next day and go out together.

Tamara arrived at mid-morning, but they had to wait a few hours for the tide to ebb before they could drive down the beach to the whale. Tamara had been having trouble with her truck—funding for the stranding network was always slim—and she didn't have much experience driving on the beach; she was happy to let Mike do the driving. He borrowed the district snowy plover biologist's seafoam-green Forest Service pickup truck, its tires slightly deflated for driving on sand, and they headed south.

They found the whale at the high tide line, west and a bit south of the Dunes Overlook. Tamara looked it over: a male, a young one, she figured. She paced off the length: twenty feet. Adult male minkes run to about thirty-two feet, females to thirty-five feet. Judging by his size, he was probably about two years old. Then she looked him over for evidence of parasites, or gunshot, or collision with a boat, or net entanglement, or starvation, or bite marks, or other obvious causes of stranding. All of the stranded young gray whales Tamara had seen in her work with marine mammals had become entangled in crab pots and the ropes that suspend them. On some, the crab pot was still attached to the tail; the animal had starved while swimming around dragging the huge trap. On others, ropes had eaten into the animal's flesh, leaving obvious scars. Predation by orcas is a common cause of mortality among Antarctic minkes but not those in the Northeast Pacific; in any case, this minke had no chunks missing, no scarring from the raking of a predator's teeth. It had no significant scars of any kind other than what looked like gunshot wounds, but they were just peck marks left by scavenging birds, holes that had enlarged as the flesh had decomposed. Its ribs weren't evident, as they would be if the animal had starved, and Tamara saw no sign of parasites. She had no way of knowing for certain whether it had even been alive or dead when it stranded.

Not that her job as coordinator of the stranding network required Tamara to determine, or even speculate about, the cause of the stranding. The form she filled out simply asked if there were signs of human interaction, and if so, to check one: "boat collision," "shot," "fishery interaction," or "other human." It also had boxes to check for "other causes": yes, no, or "could not be determined." She left the boxes blank.

Few whales survive stranding, with or without human intervention. Scientists and others have long puzzled over why seemingly healthy whales get stranded. Some may be sick, in less-than-obvious ways; damage to their brains or simple weakness may have led them unwittingly down the path of self-destruction. There is good evidence that military sonar activity may cause some strandings, though exactly *how* remains uncertain. But the likely cause of many more strandings may be celestial, not human, disturbance. The sun goes through cycles of more or less radiation-producing activity. Scientists in Britain analyzed ninety-seven sperm whale strandings in the North Sea between 1712 and 2003 and found that eighty-seven occurred in periods of lower solar activity, when the magnetic field is disrupted. It's been well established that pigeons, which navigate with the help of a magnetic sense housed in small crystals of magnetite found in certain cells, can get confused and go astray in times of high solar activity. So, it seems, may whales a hundred thousand times the size of the little birds.

The external inspection completed, Mike set about removing the baleen from the minke's upper jaw. The baleen is like a comb, but with thin, hard, flexible plates stacked closely together—325 per side, each up to six inches long, in the case of this whale. To Mike, it looked just like a car's air filter and felt like plastic. The outside edge of each plate is smooth and sharp, like a slender letter-opener, but inside the edges are frayed into fine hairs. The frayed edge of each plate meshes with those on either side, creating a thick, fibrous mat like a coir doormat through which the whale strains a mouthful of water to get a meal. Since the baleen is made of keratin, it preserves well; Mike thought it would make a nice addition to the natural history display in the ranger station lobby, next to the baleen plate from a ninety-ton bowhead whale leaning against the wall, fine strands of keratin curling off the thin, rigid, charcoal gray plate like horsehair from a violin bow. That single plate of bowhead whale baleen was almost a foot wide at the base and stood ten feet tall.

High tide had maneuvered the minke onto its right side, pointed north, mouth agape and half-filled with sand, its pink-gray tongue flaccid and flecked with foam, its tail flukes half-buried. While Mike worked at the whale's exposed left gum line, separating the baleen from the jaw with a filet knife, Tamara cut a square plug of skin and blubber from the whale's back. She took a sample of blubber and muscle from the abdomen as well, slitting the abdomen in the process. If you don't slit the abdomen of a dead whale, Tamara knew, not only might it refloat at high tide and wind up on another beach, but it would swell and possibly explode from the pressure of decomposition gasses. Which is exactly what had happened five weeks earlier in southern Taiwan's Tainan City, where a fifty-ton male sperm whale had stranded alive but died soon after. Nine days later, as it was being transported on a flatbed trailer to a research station for necropsy—what scientists call an autopsy on an animal other than a human—it exploded, showering shops and cars and people with rotten entrails and blood. While it was still on the beach, intact, the corpse had reportedly drawn hundreds of onlookers, many of them men interested in "experiencing"—as a *Taipei Times* reporter put it—the 56-foot-long whale's proportionately large penis, about five feet long.

Mike managed to sever the baleen from the left side of the jaw, craning his head out of the mouth every so often for a gulp of fresh air; "bad breath" doesn't begin to describe the smell inside a decomposing whale's mouth. But to cut the baleen off the right side of the jaw, you'd have to actually crawl inside the whale's mouth. Which is what Tamara did. Her long brown hair captured in a ponytail, clad in standard whale-biologist necropsy garb—a blue rain slicker and rain pants, yellow dishwashing gloves—she shimmied into the mouth of the whale up to her hip and, resting on the leviathan's tongue, worked to separate the rest of the baleen from the jaw. She managed to pry away part of it, but she couldn't get a knife around to the rear section, embedded in the sand with the weight of the head resting on it. The two of them tried to roll the head—a futile gesture; judging from its length, the whale probably weighed ten tons. Even the tongue was too heavy to move. Tamara had hoped to get a chunk of the baleen herself to take back to the lab at Newport, as well as samples of the kidney and the liver. But the south wind was fierce that day, blowing sand into their mouths and eyes as they worked close to the ground collecting samples from the rotting whale, and they were starting to lose daylight. With half a baleen in Mike's hands and a six-inch chunk for Tamara, plus photos, measurements, and a few tissue samples, they called it a day.

Tamara headed back to Newport with both pieces of baleen; the necropsy lab there was a better place to finish whittling away any remaining gum tissue than was the parking lot at the ranger station in Florence. Mike planned to join her at the science center in a week or so, to finish cleaning the baleen and to pick up a copy of the letter Tamara would write to the National Marine Fisheries Service in Seattle authorizing transfer of "325 contiguous baleen plates" from specimen number HMSC04-C5 to the Mapleton Ranger District office. Without such permission in writing, possession of the baleen or any part of a stranded marine mammal could land Mike in jail.

Hatfield Marine Science Center, a cluster of low buildings with gray pebbly aggregate walls and long, sloping shingled roofs, sits on a peninsula of land jutting out from the south shore of Yaquina Bay across the water from Newport's bay front, where tourist shops and cafes stand cheek-by-jowl with working fish-processing plants. Tamara's office looked out onto an interior courtyard piled with crab pots and green fiberglass aquaculture tanks; inside, the office was crowded with plants and memorabilia from her travels, many of them from Peru: photographs of river dolphins, and a crude wooden carving of a dolphin painted a slightly brighter pink than nature painted the actual animal.

But her first stop was the necropsy lab, where she ditched her rain slicker and pants. The necropsy lab opened onto a concrete courtyard with doors large enough to accommodate a small whale. In it were stainless steel gurneys up to eight feet long and, against the wall, collapsible stretchers and steel halibut gaffs used to pick up and transport large dead marine mammals. She cleaned her filet knives and stored them, with the rest of her collection, in a cupboard against the wall of the bone room. When she'd arrived at Hatfield she'd found it well equipped with raincoats and rubber boots and filet knives, but most were large, sized for men, despite the fact that most of the marine mammal specialists at Hatfield were women. One of the first tasks she assigned herself was equipping the lab with smaller boots and medium-size rain gear.

The bone room was, among other things, a holding area for every skull and bone and other odds and ends salvaged from a marine mammal that didn't have another home; they were things that might be useful someday in research or for teaching but apparently weren't valuable enough to be catalogued and archivally stored. Bones of every description, some classified and tagged and some not, were piled on a jumble of mismatched tables and metal carts. It stank faintly—not a bad smell, really, but a distinct, musty smell of old things, formerly alive. High on one shelf was the lower jaw of a sperm whale. A baby seal lay curled in a jar of formalin. A couple of small bones, each about five inches long, lay on a shelf apart from the piles—seal penis bones, each labeled with black ink in a scientist's precise hand. It was not unusual for stranding network volunteers to find the penis of a dead pinniped missing by the time they arrived, Tamara had learned. In fact, the harp seal's penis bone—a supposed aphrodisiac, a quality apparently found mainly in rare or endangered animal parts—has reportedly become even more valuable on the black market than the seal's pelt.

Tamara left the pieces of baleen on a metal table in the necropsy lab for the moment, then walked down the corridor to the science center's walk-in freezer to stash the tissue samples, twisting the dials on the freezer door's padlock to open it. The thermometer above the door read 8 degrees Fahrenheit. Inside, on shelves to the right and left, were stacks and stacks, in no apparent order, of animal parts sealed in plastic Ziploc bags and even whole marine mammals, some of them piled on the floor as well. Chunks of baleen and heads of whales. Entire intact dolphins, including a seven-foot-long striped dolphin stuffed into a black plastic garbage bag, its gray tail flukes sticking out the top. Baby seal pups, mottled gray or snow white with black spots, were stacked in one corner like kindling, their bodies hard as rocks but their fur still downy-soft. They had been removed from the beach, in most cases, by a stranding network volunteer after someone made a fuss about leaving the dead pup to decompose on the beach.

Tamara had sealed the blubber and other tissue samples from the minke whale in clear Ziploc bags, labeled with their origin. An analysis of the blubber might someday reveal whether environmental toxins—lead, cadmium, heavy metals, pesticides—could have accumulated in the whale's body and been a factor in its stranding. But that would have to wait until someone could thaw out some funding. She laid the bags on a shelf and closed the freezer door.

SOME EIGHTEEN THOUSAND GRAY WHALES inhabit the eastern North Pacific Ocean, making one of the world's longest migrations from mating and calving lagoons off Baja California to summer feeding grounds in the Bering and Chukchi seas off Alaska. Tourists line Oregon's headlands in March and December, straining for a glimpse of a gray whale's blow or, luckier yet, breech during the animals' spring and winter migrations. In recent years some two hundred grays have split from the migration to spend all summer off the Northwest coast between southern Oregon and central British Columbia. Off the central Oregon town of Depoe Bay, they feed at the edge of the kelp beds, sandwiched between the whale-watchers lining the seawall on shore and those lining the rails of tour boats that have motored out to the open water to the west. When volunteers set themselves up at viewpoints in winter and spring to help visitors spot whale spouts among the whitecaps, posting signs reading "Whale Watching Spoken Here," everyone knows it's all about gray whales.

The people who pay closer attention to whales are well aware of the variety of cetaceans in the waters off Oregon, if only from stranding records. At least a dozen different species of whales (including orcas and false killer whales, both of which are technically in the family of ocean dolphins) have been stranded on Oregon beaches since 1930. Bruce Mate, director of Oregon State University's marine mammal program based at Hatfield Marine Science Center, had prepared a whale-watching flier that I once found in the lobby of an Oregon coast motel showing the profiles of seven whales exhibiting three types of behavior: beginning the dive (look for the size and shape of the dorsal fin or hump), diving (some just sink out of sight; others flash their tail flukes), and surfacing and blowing (the height, shape, and even angle of the blow is unique to each species). Conspicuously absent from the flier was the minke whale.

But it's out there, off the Oregon coast and beyond; worldwide, there may be more minkes than any other kind of whale. They're most numerous in the oceans of the southern hemisphere, where two separate species dwell: the southern minke and the dwarf minke. Off Antarctica, where Japanese factory ships still prowl in defiance of the International

Whaling Commission, minkes number at least a half-million, perhaps even a million or more.

A single minke species inhabits the oceans of the northern hemisphere. At least 120,000 minkes—possibly as many as 192,000—inhabit the North Atlantic. And at least three distinct populations of minkes inhabit the North Pacific. The most numerous group of these, around 47,000, occupies the waters in the Sea of Japan, Yellow Sea, and, further north, the Sea of Okhotsk. Of the remaining two groups of North Pacific minkes, one is found off Alaska and a second one off Washington, Oregon, and California.

Scientists estimate the size of that group, to which the minke I found belonged, at just six hundred or so animals, much fewer than the number of blue or humpback whales, both of which are federally protected as endangered species. No wonder so few minkes have stranded here, despite their preference for waters less than fifty fathoms—three hundred feet—deep. That puts them fairly close to shore; off Oregon, the continental shelf is roughly fifty miles wide. Sperm whales lurk where it drops off, diving deep to feed on the likes of giant squid.

Minkes may swim close to shore, but they're almost impossible to spot. They blow, of course—every mammal has to breathe air—through paired blowholes, but it's a low, vaporous blow, virtually invisible. When they rise for air, they barely break the surface; there's a sliver of black in the ocean's black chop, and they're gone. No one knows exactly when and where they migrate, though like most whales they seem to spend summers feeding at high latitudes and head to warmer waters to mate and calve. They probably migrate some distance to their calving grounds, actively foraging along the way, unlike other baleen whales. Minke socializing and courting are still mysterious. They tend to travel alone or in pairs of one male and one slightly larger female, not in sociable schools or pods. Orcas and gray whales have few secrets anymore; they've been studied intensively for many years. Every orca in pods J, K, and L, moving among Washington's San Juan Islands, is known to researchers by pet names; their movements are tracked by a large cadre of orca researchers investigating every aspect of their life history. Put a radio tag on a gray whale in Scammon's Lagoon, off Baja, and stick a receiver in your Honda Civic and you can track that whale's northern migration for hundreds of miles just by driving up the coast highway; with gray whales, it's all about getting from point A to point B. Although minkes sometimes move that way, maintaining the same direction and surfacing at regular intervals, they're also known to dart and dash, at speeds up to twenty mph. Because it's hard to know just where they'll turn up next, radio tagging doesn't work well with minkes.

A 1958 text, perhaps the era's most authoritative work on whales, makes dismissive reference to the minke whale under another of its common names. "The little piked whale," wrote E. J. Slijper, "is of no interest to what is called the big whaling industry." There were whalers going after minkes back then, from South Africa to Korea, but they were small, local operations. Hunting these small, fast animals wasn't worth the trouble for the big guys. That changed dramatically in the 1970s, when bigger whales got harder to find and new pelagic whaling techniques evolved, paving the way for industrial-scale hunts. Today, the minke is the only whale species in the world that is still extensively hunted: by Norwegian ships and, since 2006, by Icelandic whalers, which both tend to use small whaling operations close to shore, and by Japanese factory ships, which hunt for minkes in the Antarctic for supposedly scientific purposes. (The research method still employed with impunity by Japanese researchers aboard whaling vessels involves killing the animal, dissecting it in the name of science, and sending the meat to restaurants in Tokyo, where it is served braised with mustard sauce, smoked like bacon, or presented between buns as whale burger.) All three countries are operating in defiance of the International Whaling Commission, which banned commercial whale hunts in 1986 but whose edicts are not legally binding. Whalers in Norway and Japan had been taking about a thousand minkes a year, though in 2005 Japan announced its intention to double its annual hunt, which could bring the total above fifteen hundred.

When I looked for current information on minke whales, two names kept coming up. Tamara remembered a professor of hers, a minke specialist, Jonathan Stern, from Texas A&M, where she received her doctorate in wildlife biology in 2002; she Googled him and found he'd written a book on minkes with Rus Hoelzel. Jon Stern also figured prominently in a *National Geographic* article I found about the status of minke whales worldwide; apparently he had done research on minkes in northwestern Washington's San Juan Islands. I called a friend, sea kayak outfitter Clark Casebolt, to ask if he ever saw minkes on his paddling trips in the San Juans. Yes, but not often, he said. He checked with someone at Friday Harbor's Whale Museum—a sort of clearinghouse for all things cetacean in the San Juans—and learned that Rus Hoelzel of northern England's Durham University would be back in the area that summer, 2005, returning to the minke whale studies he and Jon Stern had helped to pioneer in the early 1980s. They used a benign, non-lethal research technique, unlike the Japanese. Jon's and Rus's research depended not on penthrite harpoons but on a Nikon camera with a 300-mm lens. By photographing the whales when they surfaced, identifying them by slight differences in fin shape, pigmentation, and scars, and closely tracking their movements over time and space, they were slowly unlocking secrets to minke whale population structure, ecology, and behavior.

I tracked down an e-mail address for Rus Hoelzel and got this reply:

> *Hi Bonnie. Both Jon Stern and I will be in the San Juans working with minke whales this summer—I'll be there from August 9th to 18th, Jon for longer. I think it would be fine for you to come out with us one day during that time, but let us know closer to the time when you can be there so we'll have room for you in the boat (and note that we'll probably put you to work!). Best, Rus Hoelzel.*

IT'S AN HOUR-LONG FERRY RIDE from Anacortes, north of Seattle, to Friday Harbor on San Juan Island, through closely clustered islands green with Douglas firs and pines and shot through with ochre from the bark of madrone trees, thriving here in the rain shadow of the Olympic Mountains. I arrived late on a warm Sunday afternoon in mid-August: the sky was cloudless, a slight breeze was stirring the sailboats jamming the harbor, and there were long lines out the ice cream shop as vacationers killed time waiting for the ferry. Two blocks up Spring Street was Kings Market, where I met my friend Clark, gathering dinner ingredients. He wintered in Seattle but spent summers running his sea kayak business on San Juan Island; his island home was a primitive yurt he'd erected on a grassy hillside, where he'd invited me to crash for the night. Before heading to the yurt, however, we stopped to pick up a friend of his who was joining us for dinner, someone he thought I'd like to meet.

Alison Gill was still fighting jet lag after flying in from Africa two days before. With her master's degree in marine and fisheries science from the University of Aberdeen—she'd grown up outside of London—she had a job working six-week stints monitoring whale activity from aboard an oil-exploration vessel off the coast of Angola, where humpback whales breed. The ship used seismic air guns to explore the geology of the sea bed, searching for underwater oil fields. Military sonar was known to kill marine animals, she said, and while there was no proof that seismic guns harmed whales in any way, oil companies—under the scrutiny of environmental groups—were being cautious. Her job as monitor was to watch for whales; when one swam near the ship, she'd notify the crew to hold off on firing the guns until the whale swam away.

But her passion, it turned out, was another rorqual whale: the minke. Prior to starting her current job, she had spent several years as a naturalist aboard whale-watching boats in the Inner Hebrides, off Scotland's northwest coast.

"'Minkes are *boring,*' people say," she said, drawing out the *orrrr* in that particular English way that makes it seem even *more* boring. "People say, *our* minkes don't *do* that 'round here," she added, meaning they don't spy hop—rising vertically out of the water to take a look around—like orcas, or bow ride—surfing the pressure wave that forms just ahead of a moving boat—like dolphins. She'd heard that from people in Scotland and in the San Juans as well. "But they *do,*" she insisted. "You've got to focus on them. You've got to give them time. They're not at all boring. They spy hop, they love flashing their bellies at you. If you read a book about minkes, they say minkes don't bow ride. But they do." She suspected that minkes find one another in the wide ocean by singing, as do their fellow rorquals, humpbacks and dwarf minkes. Only recently had researchers determined that a two-and-a-half second mechanical *boing* sound heard and recorded in the North Pacific since the 1950s was actually a minke whale vocalization. She had once heard about a live stranding of a minke that was reportedly making lots of sounds before it died, but no one had recorded it, to her great frustration.

We sat in chairs on a wooden deck below the yurt, facing south with a view down the rocky hillside, August-yellow with dead grass, to a green valley and forested ridge and, beyond, the Strait of Juan de Fuca and the Olympic Mountains, in hazy silhouette. A fat half-moon hung in the southern sky. Bats darted in the twilight, sparing us a few mosquito bites. Tall and slender with long strawberry blonde hair, in jeans and a slouchy black knit top, Alison's manner was deferential, shy even, until she started talking about minke whales. Not only did she know them well, but she obviously had great personal affection for them. Her Web site, www.projectminke.com, she said, "has got only a fraction of what I want to say."

Her initial interest in whales had actually been piqued on a visit to the San Juans ten years earlier. She had returned to England, got her master's degree, and started up with the Scottish tour boats. Once she started working on oil-exploration vessels, with long stretches on duty and equally long breaks, she realized she could actually live anywhere in the world. Four months before I met her, she had rented an apartment on the outskirts of Friday Harbor.

Alison hadn't deliberately chosen minkes as her research subject in grad school; she had been offered a project involving minkes, which she happily accepted. "People would say, 'Humpbacks are so cool; why do you want to study *minkes?*" she said. "But I was glad I was offered a species that not many people had studied." The project involved photo identification of minkes in the Hebrides, and was similar to the work Jon and Rus had done in the San Juans. She became intimately familiar with the two men's work and that of their mentor, Ellie Dorsey. "They were really the three minke people who led the way," Ali said. She had corresponded with all three over the years (Jon Stern's enthusiastic reply to her initial e-mail: "Welcome to the Minke Club!"), but she had never met any of them. When she learned of Dorsey's death at age fifty-one in 2000, Alison says, she grieved as if Dorsey had been a close friend and mentor. In a way, she had been. She wrote a letter to Dorsey's parents, who wrote back and even visited Ali in Scotland, giving her some of Dorsey's personal mementoes as gifts.

Now that Rus Hoelzel and Jon Stern were also on San Juan Island at the same time as she, Ali intended to meet them—as soon as she returned from a planned trip to Seattle the next day. That meant she wouldn't be going out on the boat with us the next day. But she did have a word of advice among us "ladies": "Take a bucket!" No telling how late Rus and Jon would stay out if the minke-spotting was going well.

FRIDAY HARBOR LABORATORIES is the University of Washington's marine science outpost, a campus of cabins, laboratories, and offices scattered among the Douglas firs on a low, forested bluff slanting down to the water just around the point from the busy public marina and ferry landing. I was to meet Rus and Jon at the laboratory's marina at 8 a.m.— or later, if the recent pattern of thick morning fog persisted. The sky was clear as I left Clark's hillside yurt, but the shoreline, as predicted, was enveloped in a dense gray cloud. Shortly a smiling middle-aged man with a fringe of gray hair and a pale brown beard appeared on the wooden walkway. Rus Hoelzel extended his hand, confirming that our departure would be delayed. With his neat tan khakis, crewneck sweater, and bulky knit cap and his guardedly polite manner, he seemed as English as his e-mail address, but his accent was all-American. Turns out he grew up in the upper Midwest, attended Reed College in Portland, and wound up at Cambridge for graduate school. There he met an English girl, and he'd lived in England ever since. He'd give me a call on my cell phone when the conditions improved.

I grabbed a muffin and a cup of coffee in town and returned to the marina to wait and watch the science center greet the new day. The tide was out, and the rocky shoreline slanting into the bay was strewn with green and brown seaweed. From my perch on the marina's upper dock I watched as a woman, her jeans rolled up to mid-calf, prowled the rocks a hundred yards down the shore, now and then bending to pick up something and drop it into a white bucket. Near her, another woman, her jeans tucked into rubber boots, was scrutinizing an old concrete structure, colonized by a mosaic of intertidal flora and fauna. The fog was thinning, the sun a strengthening presence in the haze, when a couple of young women appeared on the dock below and began measuring a small, flaccid porpoise laid out on a stainless steel tray. It looked like a newborn, or maybe a near-term fetus. It had been in a freezer on Lopez Island for a year, I heard one explain.

At 9:45 a.m. my phone rang. "We're going out; want us to make you a sandwich?" Jon Stern asked without preamble.

Soon Rus reappeared, carrying a bag of groceries—our lunch—and cases of gear. With him was a bigger man in slouchy olive-green cargo pants and an oversized red T-shirt, with a neat white beard and long white hair under a purple cap with the words "Gulf Coast Ammonia Producers Conference" in yellow writing. A slender silver feather dangled from one ear, and dark Ray-Bans obscured his eyes. He greeted me by way of a sideways smile and slight nod. A formal introduction, at that point, seemed superfluous.

Jon climbed into the right-hand driver's seat of an eighteen-foot skiff, part of the laboratories' fleet, assigned to Jon and Rus for the duration. Rus settled in next to him, and I climbed into the rear-facing seat behind Rus. As Jon pointed the boat out of the harbor, Rus explained his system of recording whale sightings. When we started seeing whales, he said, Jon would be driving and he, Rus, would be busy looking for more whale surfacings; they'd need me to record details of the sightings. He had a stopwatch and a GPS device; I was to note the time, to the second, and exact location of every whale encounter, from a breech ("B" for short) to an "SS"—simple surfacing.

It was sunny when we pulled away from the dock at 10:30 a.m. but still socked in on the Strait of Juan de Fuca—usually the last patch of water to clear up, Rus explained—so Jon pointed the boat north, toward Waldron Island. I asked to take a look at their navigation chart, attempting to get my bearings. They both laughed as Rus tossed me a roll of laminated paper secured with a rubber band. It was a placemat, the kind of thing you might find in a family seafood restaurant: a yellow-and-black navigational chart of the San Juan Islands, shrunk to fit a table setting. They were still chuckling when Jon pointed out the fine print: *Not intended for navigation.*

Rus smiled apologetically. "We've been here a long time."

It started back in 1980. Jon was about to graduate from Sonoma State University with a bachelor's degree in biology when he heard about a researcher named Ellie Dorsey who needed volunteers to help with a minke whale photo-identification project she was launching in the San Juan Islands. The day after graduation, Jon headed north to Friday Harbor to sign on. Rus, in Portland, had just graduated as well and was hoping to get involved in some orca research in the San Juans. In Friday Harbor both men and a handful of other eager volunteers met with Dorsey to hear more about the project. She intended to identify individual minke whales by photographing them and scrutinizing the photos for minute distinctions. Since their seemingly erratic travel patterns all but ruled out radio tagging, identifying and tracking the movements of individual whales might reveal new information about population size and movement over time and space.

The project got off to a slow start. Dorsey had arranged for a boat to be delivered from Vancouver Island, but delivery was delayed. One by one, the other volunteers drifted away from the project, but Rus and Jon stuck around, finding ways to help. Finally, they arranged to charter a salmon troller to take them out to look for whales. It was from that fishing boat that they captured their first photos of individually identifiable minkes. "We took the photos still dripping wet out of the darkroom and slapped them on the wall of the Whale Museum, and it was obvious," Jon recalled, smiling broadly at the memory of that moment twenty-five years earlier. "Bingo!"

"People used to tell us, oh, they're impossible because they're hard to follow, and one looks like another," Rus added. He smiled smugly. "But they don't."

A half-inch notch near the tip of a dorsal fin here; a blush of pink on an otherwise slate-gray back there. In the lab that summer and for the next several summers, Jon and Rus carefully scrutinized the day's photos to determine whether they'd seen one whale or several, in the same spot or elsewhere, minutes earlier or another day or even another year. The differences tended to be pretty subtle from one minke to another, Rus said. "Having said that," he added, "there are some we can tell a mile off." Each whale gets a name, one that may say as much about the namers as about the individual whales. Jackie (Onassis), in her day the darling of the paparazzi, was the name given to their most frequently photographed whale in the eighties. Jon, who was never not listening to music while working at the computer, called one whale Johnny Rotten and another Joan. ("For Joni Mitchell," he explained. "You know *The Circle Game?* This whale kept swimming in circles. It was either that or Billy Preston's *Will It Go Round In Circles.* But I thought that would be too arcane.") Jon had been scandalized to learn that Rus's assistant the previous summer had named one of the minkes they'd photographed Scarlet, and another Snowflake. *("Snowflake."* He spat the name out when he found it in the photo archives. "That's just *wrong."*)

When Ellie Dorsey moved on to work with right whales off Argentina in 1981, Jon and Rus temporarily picked up leadership of the Minke Project, spending every summer through 1984 in the San Juans, both of them parlaying their research into Ph.D.s and university professorships. In that period they identified about thirty individual whales, some of which had appeared year after year. Prior to their research, Jon said, "I think you could count the number of minke papers on your fingers. And it was all about killing them."

Rus's research had evolved into studies of population and evolutionary genetics: in the case of minkes, the differences and similarities between those found in different parts of the world's oceans. Jon, meanwhile, had been shanghaied in the late 1990s by something called random walk theory and its cousin, Lévy's flight theory: ways of analyzing animals' behavior using tools from physics. The Navy had used similar search theories as a basis for strategies to hunt for enemy submarines (the Navy has challenges a minke doesn't provide: these submariners are, simultaneously, trying not to be found). Esoteric stuff for a marine biologist, but the more Jon learned, the more sense it made as a tool to analyze minke whale foraging behavior, and the more compelling the research became.

The pair returned to the San Juans in the late 1990s for more research, then Rus came back in 2004 to duplicate the work they had done in the eighties, funded by a foundation established after Ellie Dorsey's death, to see how things had changed in twenty years. Among the minke unknowns is the animal's average lifespan, thought to be in the twenty- to forty-year range. If so, it was conceivable that they might see some of the same whales that they'd seen in the eighties.

But things had changed. The area we were headed toward, racing a half-hour north up choppy San Juan Channel, was a broad patch of open water six miles wide bounded by Speiden, John, and Stuart islands to the southwest, Waldron Island to the east, and on the other side of Boundary Pass, the Southern Canadian Gulf Islands. Ellie Dorsey had named it Minke Lake. "There used to be tons of minkes here," Jon explained. When colleagues, friends, or family visited them in the San Juans, hoping to see minke whales, they'd pile them into the skiff and head to Minke Lake, and *voila.* "It was so predictable," Jon said, "we were almost annoying."

That was then. So far, in 2004 and the first few days of minke-watching in 2005, they hadn't seen a single minke in Minke Lake—nor off Yellow Island, nor in Haro Strait, nor in Griffin Bay, nor anywhere in San Juan Channel between San Juan and Orcas islands—nowhere, in fact, but at Hein Bank and Salmon Bank in the Strait of Juan de Fuca, off San Juan Island's southern tip. But they hadn't given up; they were still taking the time to check all the old haunts, when conditions permitted.

We slipped between Flattop and Speiden islands and, quite suddenly, the chop was gone. The water was flat, so flat you could practically water ski. No, you *could* water ski if you didn't mind the occasional floating log. Jon steered the boat into the middle of Minke Lake and cut the engine. The air was utterly still, and hot. We tore off the jackets we'd put on to break the wind during the brisk boat ride.

Jon rolled up his pant legs and stretched in the driver's seat, sunning his bare feet. (Students at Texas A&M used to joke about his habit of going barefoot during lectures or wearing flip-flops year-round, he said, even while attired in academic robes during commencement ceremonies.) Rus, standing, circled slowly, around and around again, binoculars glued to his face. A couple of rhinocerous auklets flapped furiously by. A black-and-white common murre dropped onto the water's surface and bobbed there. The dorsal fin of a harbor porpoise sliced the water's surface off the starboard bow; Rus made a note on the clipboard. The air was fresh, clean-smelling, without the briny tang of the intertidal close to shore. Three miles north, a constant parade of ships—container vessels, sailboats, motor yachts—moved slowly through Boundary Pass.

"Just flat as a pancake," Jon said, with a wide smile. "The thing that's really cool," he added: "People find waiting boring. But there's this anticipation that at any moment something really cool could happen."

We lingered for a half-hour or so, drifting, scanning, before giving up on Minke Lake and starting a long, bumpy run down the west side of San Juan Island, fighting an incoming tide. Approaching the strait, we could see that the fog had diminished to a haze. The water was rough, however: black waves scalloping the steel blue sea. We slammed through the swells, heading to Hein Bank. When the tidal flow hits the shallow sea surface at underwater banks such as this, the water and nutrients it carries are forced up, inviting whales and others to the feast.

Then suddenly, "Bad news," Jon said ominously. He had spotted a clutch of tour boats not far ahead: orca-watching tour boats. I wondered what the problem was; maybe they disturbed the minkes? No, nothing like that, he said. It was just that their presence here in our path, clustering and gawking, was harshing Jon's mellow. As we approached, we could see what had drawn them here; a tall charcoal dorsal fin appeared, knifing through the water in a smooth arc and disappearing just as quickly—a three-second glimpse at most.

"L Pod," Rus said off-handedly. "Male, relatively young guy."

We lingered in the vicinity of the tour boats for a few minutes, watching orcas appear and disappear out of the gray water, then Jon restarted the motor and we continued in the direction of Hein Bank, banging through swells that steepened as we ventured farther into the strait, until Rus pointed out, perhaps a quarter-mile away, a dark gray inflatable boat with four figures in red survival suits. "It's the fecal sampling people," Jon said with glee, turning the boat and racing in their direction, then idling when we got to within fifty or a hundred yards. By then Jon and Rus were both chuckling and grabbing for the Nikon. I had to ask: were they really collecting whale poop?

Indeed, Jon confirmed: they dissected it, looking for the likes of fish scales and squid beaks, to see what the whales had been eating. We inched closer; one crew member was perched on a metal platform elevated above the inflatable's bow. He was holding the long handle of what looked like a pool-cleaning net. Ahead of the boat, traveling north, were three orcas, surfacing and blowing in unison in a slow, graceful dance. We followed in our boat for several minutes while Rus continued to scan the swells all around. Neither man seemed in any hurry to go anywhere else. "Is this Hein Bank?" I asked. No, Jon said, grinning, cocking his head toward the inflatable. "They're our friends; we just want to watch them."

As Jon turned the boat east, San Juan Island was a distant hump. It was still the closest chunk of land in sight when we stopped at nearly 2 p.m. at a buoy and ate our sandwiches in the bobbing swells. Then we were traveling again, through two- to three-foot swells, until Rus, scrutinizing the GPS, told Jon to stop. We'd arrived at Hein Bank, the most reliable minke-sighting spot of the summer of 2005.

But not this day. The animal's profile is so low, Rus explained, that it's hard to see in flat water, let alone in conditions like these, with heavy swells and water chopped by the wind into gray and black and white slices. Between that and the whales' always unpredictable behavior, Rus said, "We'd waste a lot of time and gas" looking. Rus made a cursory scan of the sea's surface before Jon started us moving back toward San Juan Island.

Before rounding Cattle Point, however, we made one more stop: Salmon Bank, another good spot in the 1980s. "We used to always find minkes at Salmon Bank, but now it's rare," Rus said. "The only place we reliably find them is Hein Bank now."

Jon cut the motor. Rus stood and circled, around and around, slow rotations, unceasing. Believing. Willing a whale to appear. Or at the very least, making himself present, fully attentive, should a whale grace us with its presence. "Often the first thing is, we just hear them," Rus said, demonstrating the sound of a minke exhaling. Explosive puffs through pursed lips: *POO-hoo*. I snuggled into my fleece jacket in the strait's hazy, cool air. The boat rocked rhythmically. I knew I should be looking, too, but I could hardly keep my eyes open. Jon spotted a small bird ball—a congregation of seabirds feeding, which generally means there's a concentration of fish below the surface. What attracts birds from above may draw whales from below. We motored in that direction.

"I think the whales may have turned around," Jon muttered, meaning the orcas. I asked him what the significance of that was. "The tour boats follow them," he said simply. "It messes my vibe. Can't have that." Some tour boats guarantee whale sightings, Alison had explained the night before, so they'll do anything to show their passengers a whale, any whale, even if it means detouring down to the waters off Lopez Island, where an apparently ailing gray whale had been lingering recently. Its nickname, among the local whale-research community, was "Whales Fargo."

The water formed ridges, small mountains, a landscape that we banged through. It slapped the sides of the boat when we stopped. I nearly nodded off in my seat. Jon stretched out in his seat; hard to tell if he was awake behind the Ray-Bans. Rus turned and turned.

Then suddenly, "Whale up!"

"What?"

"Whale up!" Rus repeated. "Probably about a kilometer." Rus scrambled for the clipboard—4:13 p.m.—while Jon turned the key and threw the boat into gear. We raced to the northwest for thirty seconds, then stopped, engine off, and resumed the vigil, Jon and I suddenly as alert as Rus, scanning, turning, scanning, turning, binoculars up, binoculars down, in silent concentration.

Twenty-five minutes passed this way. Finally Rus flopped into his seat. "It really *was* a minke," he said—as much to himself as to us. Jon started the motor and turned us toward Cattle Pass and Friday Harbor.

The previous day they'd had numerous sightings of two or maybe three individual whales and even followed one for an hour and a half, Rus said. "A nice-looking, very distinctive whale," Jon added. "We could show you pictures on the computer when we get back."

"Just so you believe us," Rus said, mustering a grin.

The forecast for the next day was grim: gale-force winds and rain with heavy seas. On the off-chance the forecast was wrong—I was in no hurry to leave the San Juans—I decided to spend another night on the island, thinking of the old photography maxim, *F8 and be there.* Be open. And show up.

I slept again on the wooden deck at the yurt, awakened several times by mosquitoes. Each time I awoke, the skies were clear, black, and shot with thousands of stars and the Milky Way's shimmering brushstroke. But when I woke for good at dawn, a thick cloud enveloped the yurt. It seemed to be a serious change of weather, and I decided to cut my losses and catch the first ferry out. I'd be back in the San Juans in a couple of weeks for a family vacation and could sneak off then for another day on the minke boat; Rus would be back in England, but Jon would still be here. I stuffed my sleeping bag—heavy with dew—into the back seat of the car, drove down the mountain, and parked in the ferry line at Friday Harbor: an hour to kill before the next eastbound sailing.

Just one vehicle was parked ahead of me: a big, slightly battered, black pickup truck, its driver slouched in his seat, a work-shirted elbow resting in the open window. I wandered over, asked if he'd heard a weather forecast. Swells four to six feet, high winds, he confirmed. Did I live here, he asked? I told him I lived in Oregon. So did he, he said. He made his living hauling things. He'd arrived late the previous night on the last

ferry, towing a carnival ride; the county fair was starting in two days.
He asked what I was I doing here. I came up to watch whales with some
whale researchers, I said.

"Whale watching," he mused out loud. "I done that once. Now, that's
fun. Especially if you got nothing else to do."

I MET JON AGAIN TWO WEEKS LATER on the lower dock of the marina at
Friday Harbor Laboratories early on a late-August morning, the sky a pale
blue, utterly cloudless, the water barely dimpled from swell or breeze.
Jon's nose was significantly more sunburned than it had been two weeks
earlier—fried, in fact. There would be four of us on the boat that day.
Jon dropped into the passenger seat this time, and Alison Gill—since her
return from Seattle she'd become a regular on the minke cruises—sat in
a rear-facing back seat. I settled into the other back seat. At the wheel
was a tall, slender young woman, her long, brown hair gathered in a
haphazard ponytail.

"That's Frankie," Jon said over one shoulder, by way of introduction.
He'd mentioned Frankie on the phone, but her role in the Minke Club
wasn't quite clear. In any case, she'd apparently taken Rus's place as Jon's
sidekick, but swapping roles; now Jon had the clipboard, and Frankie was
at the wheel. After fueling up at the marina in Friday Harbor, we headed
out of the harbor and turned south, toward Salmon Bank. Frankie drove
the boat expertly, with a calm assurance, one bare foot tucked under her
like a booster seat.

The previous day had been exceptional—they'd followed one whale
for six hours, Jon reported and Frankie confirmed, as Jon launched into
an explanation of his pet project, analyzing minke movements by means
of theories borrowed from physical science. Random walks, he explained,
are erratic changes of course when the distance traveled between each
surfacing—the "step length"—is roughly the same. Lévy's flights, too,
are unpredictable course changes but with varying step lengths, such as

when a particular minke whale surfaces in one spot, resurfaces elsewhere thirty seconds later, and surfaces again in yet another location five minutes later. This random foraging pattern that minkes use is actually highly efficient, he said. Typically, a minke will forage an area like Salmon Bank in a series of random walks, and then—in what physicists refer to as *rectilinear ballistic diffusion*—suddenly take off to another area in a long "flight" and begin foraging again. It's a pattern of foraging that is altogether different from that of many other cetaceans—gray whales and orcas, for instance, which change course relatively infrequently.

"So it's an evolutionary adaptive strategy," Jon continued, "because it allows an individual to visit a site that likely hasn't been visited and depleted by another individual." It's a strategy used by many other organisms—bacteria, wandering albatrosses, bumble bees. It also happens to describe the same pattern found in radio signals from pulsars and in the distribution of distant galaxies.

"Jon is known for his rather complicated modeling," said Frankie, smiling wryly, her accent distinctly Cambridge.

"People say, 'Oh, is he still talking about his Lévy's flights?'" Alison chimed in, rolling her eyes dramatically. "But it makes so much sense."

"I find it appealing, because nature isn't reinventing itself over and over," Jon said. Adding, unnecessarily, "So this goes against Intelligent Design."

It turned out that, like Alison, Frankie—Francis Robertson—was English, raised in Cambridge by two historian parents. She, too, had earned bachelor's and master's degrees in marine and fisheries science at the University of Aberdeen. She had come to the San Juans to study orcas but, like Rus, found the pull of the mysterious minke more compelling. Jon had recruited her from among the close-knit society of Friday Harbor whale folk to help complete the summer's research after Rus returned to England.

A few minutes past Cattle Point, Jon—holding the GPS device—let Frankie know that we'd arrived at Salmon Bank. She cut the engine, and we settled in for the vigil. Wind chopped the sea's surface a bit, and the swells were low and gentle—nothing that would call off a minke watch. I checked my watch: 10:15.

And there it was, not four minutes later, maybe a hundred yards off the bow: a sliver of black like the edge of a black vinyl record, a dorsal-finned 45, up for perhaps four seconds, then gone, disappeared without so much as the wave of a tail-fluke. Frankie slammed the boat into gear and sped to the approximate spot where the whale had surfaced. A minute later, another surfacing—the same whale?—barely fifty yards away. We raced to the spot and, arriving, could see where it had been: a small whirl of disturbed water in the middle of a still-glassy patch that, seconds later, filled in with chop, erasing all trace.

We floated silently, all eyes scanning, while the skiff rolled slowly in the low swells. Seabirds chattered distantly; far overhead a float plane rumbled by. Then a splash next to the boat, and all of us startled. It was just a common murre, popping to the surface after a dive.

But minutes later, another whale, or perhaps the same whale, surfaced, then another two minutes after that. They revealed so little in their surfacings—not the subtle white of their pectoral fins, not the white and black accordion folds of their throat. Just that dark arc, and just long enough to know it was real.

It's quite different in the Hebrides, Ali said. The tour-boat operators there got to know many individual whales well. Some minkes would routinely approach stationary tour boats, circling or passing under the hull. Some would turn on their side or upside down as they passed: a flash of white in the clear waters off the Isle of Mull. They'd spy hop, they'd bow ride. The islands of the inner Hebrides were remote, with few signs of civilization save the odd castle; the wildlife was the draw of these trips, Ali explained. Passengers would see plenty of minkes, but also dolphins and seals and birds, from parrot-beaked puffins to low-gliding gannets, skimming the sea's surface with the tips of their black wings.

In contrast, Ali had been unnerved to find that few passengers on orca-watching boats in the San Juans asked questions about the orcas, or the birds, or any aspect of the natural world outside the windows. "They point to the island and ask, 'How much is that house worth?'" she said. "They don't need naturalists on board; realtors would be better."

Another sighting, and Frankie scrambled to it. It's probably two different whales, Jon said. Frankie cut the engine. In the silence of that wait, we heard a blow and followed the sound to the surfacing whale. It was just as Rus had demonstrated: *PUH-huh.* I sniff, wondering if minke breath really smells, as Ellie Dorsey had described it, like overcooked broccoli. Ali nodded, smiling apologetically on the whales' behalf. "Stinky minke," she intoned.

"If they don't straighten up and fly right," Jon said, "we won't be able to get tracks on 'em." Random is one thing, but unless he could snap some decent photographs, he wouldn't have the data points he needed for his computer modeling. "We might have to punish them," he added with a mischievous grin, "by crossbow biopsying them."

He was kidding, of course. But crossbow biopsy isn't a joke; it's a tool whale researchers use to confirm the identity of individual whales, a useful technique Jon and Rus had themselves employed, and one harmless to the whale. Fire a hollow plug the diameter of a pencil eraser at the whale's back, and out pops a tiny piece of blubber and skin, floating on the water; scoop it up, take it to a lab for DNA testing, and you've got another piece of the puzzle to figure out the structure of the minke whale population.

Another surfacing. "Oh, good boy," Jon crooned approvingly. "OK, I think this is that white blushy guy."

South of us, between Salmon Bank and Port Angeles on the Olympic Peninsula, a thick bank of fog had formed. Jon had had his eye on it for a while; he hoped out loud that it wouldn't move our way. Or that the whales wouldn't move into it.

"Do you get an idea of how high they come out of the water?" Jon asked rhetorically. "Which isn't very high. Which is why waves like this are a bummer." The waves hadn't seemed very high to me—a slight chop on low swells, nothing like the low mountains of water we'd bumped through two weeks earlier. But I saw his point—and wondered how much more one might see on an even flatter-water day.

Then the fog was upon us, not yet enveloping us but trying to. It was 10:54, and Jon pulled the plug on minke-watching in the strait. As much as he wanted to, it just wasn't safe to stay, he said, with barges and tour boats and yachts all around us, and no one on board disagreed. There would be no visit to Hein Bank, farther out in the strait, that day.

Frankie turned the skiff north. Forty-five minutes later we were looking at Waldron Island's crescent shoreline: low, dun-colored cliffs to the north, dense green forest above striated cliffs to the south. It was hot and windless on Minke Lake.

Conversation turned to the Whale Museum, which all hands agreed had altogether too much information on orcas compared to what it had on minkes. "I suggested they might like to do a minke scheme," Ali said, "and they just looked at me, blankly."

"You'd think they'd want to have *something* on minkes," Frankie said. "It is the *Whale* Museum, after all."

Jon, with gleeful sarcasm: "Or maybe it's *the* Whale Museum."

Frankie, making the most of the relative torpor on windless Minke Lake, had uncurled from her driver's crouch to stretch out full length, resting a bare foot on the back of the rear passengers' seat and tipping her head back to catch the sun. Over the course of the morning's cruise and in no hurry to impress anyone, she had slowly revealed herself as a serious scientist, one dedicated to making a career out of her curiosity about what makes whales tick. For his part, Jon made no secret of his hope that she'd get interested enough to pick up on his and Rus's and Ellie's research on minkes in the San Juans and take it further, perhaps using it as a doctoral dissertation project. She had both the smarts and the bold irreverence that seemed, by the Jon Stern model anyway, to be a prerequisite for pursuing research on an animal in which most other cetacean researchers saw little potential. She seemed, in fact, to be just the right person to inherit the minke mantle.

"I have missed this, in *so* many ways," Jon said with a big smile to no one in particular. It turned out that he had been more than a little sick the previous two summers—he'd been hospitalized for weeks, nearly dead at one point. He had come back to life, slowly, and to fully living his peripatetic scientist's life for reasons doctors couldn't quite explain. He was now thriving, but with a poignancy and an appreciation for the small things—the slam of a skiff through swells on open water, the sight of a low, black dorsal fin above gray waves, the smell of whale breath—that you can only get from going right to the precipice and not falling off. He was spending August at marine scientists' summer camp, riding around in a fast little boat through a stunning northern archipelago, finding whales that almost no one else ever sees let alone heeds, gathering data for groundbreaking computer models that were linking whale behavior with bees and birds and bacteria and neurons and electrons and the entire cosmos. Even on a bad day, there was just nothing whatsoever bad about that.

But my own quest to see live minkes was apparently at a close. We saw no more that day, and we never did see one spy hop or flash its belly or do anything else besides slyly surface, despite Ali's best hopes. I wasn't likely to get a better view anywhere else in the North Pacific. After we docked at the science center marina in late afternoon, I had a little time to kill before catching an early-evening ferry, so I decided to check out the Whale Museum for myself.

It occupied an old building on First Street, just a few blocks up the hill from the ferry terminal. The walls and ceiling in the stairwell leading up to the exhibits were one big mural, seemingly a taste of things to come: orcas swimming in an azure sea, orcas everywhere, even a three-dimensional orca head jutting out of the wall above the door.

Information about orcas did dominate the exhibit area, accounting for probably half the displays. But I was looking for evidence of minkes, and I found it, scattered. A jar held a plug of minke skin and blubber embedded with an external parasite (*Penella balaenoptera*), its soft tassel end limply suspended in a transparent bath of alcohol. Minkes were mentioned in a panel of interpretive text about the interrelationships of species in the Salish Sea—the traditional name for the inland sea here between the Washington and British Columbia mainland and southern Vancouver Island: "Minke whales, for instance, eat tons of forage fish that school near the surface." The better part of one wall was in fact dedicated to minkes, including a poster about rorqual whales in general and a smaller poster featuring a minke. Suspended from the ceiling was the skeleton of a minke calf found in 1985 two miles north of Friday Harbor by the San Juan County Marine Mammal Stranding Network. The stranded whale was 11 feet, 8 inches long and weighed about a thousand pounds; a photograph on the wall showed a much younger Rus Hoelzel standing next to the carcass. In the center of the exhibit area was a glass case filled with skulls and preserved brains of various marine mammals, among them a minke skull with unmistakable bullet holes on one side. What was missing was anything about the groundbreaking minke whale research that had been going on in the waters all around San Juan Island for more than two decades.

Before leaving, I perused the gift shop a bit. Here were lots more orcas: in dazzling photographs, in books, on key chains and coffee mugs and pencils and T-shirts. They're so easy to caricature, with their distinct coloring and tall dorsal fin. Images of gray whales, too, swam through the racks and stacks of gift items. But there were no minke T-shirts to pick up for the kids, no minke mugs for the folks back home. The truth is, they probably wouldn't sell well. People would think they were a mistake, a manufacturing error or the work of an unskilled artisan. On a key chain, a minke whale would look too slender to be a whale or even a dolphin. And it wouldn't have that trademark dolphin smile.

WHAT TO DO WITH A DEAD MINKE WHALE carcass on the beach? Tamara McGuire had had several options, all of them outlined in *Marine Mammals Ashore: A Field Guide for Stranding*—"the bible for strandings," as Tamara described it. You could move it to a lab for necropsy, as had been attempted with the sperm whale in Taiwan, but that option is best left to smaller, fresher corpses. If it's not too badly decomposed, you might have some luck towing it back out to sea—*far* out to sea, far enough that it's not likely to float back in. Just make sure to slit the belly and load it up with enough ballast to sink it, the guidebook advises. Otherwise it could set sail: a gas-filled whale balloon riding the high seas.

You could try blowing it up: an elegantly simple solution, or so it had apparently seemed to the highway engineer tasked with disposing of a large dead whale that had washed up in the fall of 1970 south of the Siuslaw River's mouth, about thirteen miles north of Mile 157. With a half-ton of dynamite, properly placed, the whale would vaporize, he figured, according to a television news report so funny and, on the face, of it, unlikely that for years it circulated as a purported urban legend. But it's true; Google it yourself. ("When I took this job, everyone had to tell me about the exploding whale," Tamara had told me dryly.) The video clip, narrated by the earnest young reporter, shows the engineer packing the explosives and then, from a distance, a quiet boom, a red cloud rising, and shortly, chunks of whale flesh falling from the sky followed by a fine mist of whale blood. No one was hurt, just spattered; the only real casualty was a late-model Oldsmobile Regal, parked in a parking lot full of cars a quarter-mile from the blast; the passenger compartment was pancaked by a three-by-five-foot chunk of whale flesh six inches thick. Far from vaporized, a good-sized chunk of whale carcass remained on the beach and was later buried by bulldozer. Humor columnist Dave Barry, who picked up the story and shared it with newspaper readers from coast to coast, characterized the video of the incident as "the single funniest thing that I've ever seen."

Having initially mistaken the minke on Mile 157 for a baby gray, I took some satisfaction from learning that the exploded whale had been misidentified by nearly all the reporters who covered the event: the TV newsman whose story about the stranded "Pacific gray whale" still circulates widely on the Internet; the Portland *Oregonian* (it also called it a Pacific gray whale); and the *Oregon Journal,* then Portland's other daily ("California gray whale"). Only the *Siuslaw News,* the local weekly paper, got it right: It was a sperm whale, a forty-five-foot male, according to Bruce Mate, then a twenty-four-year-old grad student doing research for his doctoral dissertation on sea lion migration. He was in Coos Bay when he heard about the stranded whale. Immediately he headed to Florence, arriving about a half-hour before the explosion. He had hoped to collect some samples from the whale before it was destroyed—the stomach contents, the gonads, other parts that might reveal clues to the stranding—but the engineer was in no mood to dillydally. He suggested Mate take some measurements and stand back, a quarter-mile away, with the rest of the fifty-odd onlookers. Mate, who had some experience with explosives as well as with whales, backed off a half-mile.

Perhaps blowing up a whale carcass is not the ideal disposal option. How about burying it on the beach? On popular beaches where a decomposing whale becomes—as lawyers put it—an "attractive nuisance" or a catalyst for complaints to city hall about the stench, burial can be an appealing alternative to simply letting nature take its course. ("The whale is composed of several parts," wrote D. L. Stein in an article for *The Log of Mystic Seaport,* quoted in the stranding field guide: "The blubber, and the whalebone and—the smell. The latter seems to be the most prominent feature of this whale.") A whale corpse will deteriorate faster in the open air than buried underground, however, and blubber has a habit of rising in soft, wet sand, sometimes making a surprise reappearance. But burial also appeals to some people's sense of decorum, Tamara says. "A lot of people will call and complain that it's disrespectful to leave an animal on the beach; you need to give it a 'proper burial.'" Proper burial by whom? Why, the scientists investigating the stranding, of course, the field guide's authors observe dryly, noting an apparent "you cut it, you own it" mentality among public officials.

Grave-robbing can also be a problem with a buried whale. Word of a dead whale on the beach circulates quickly in small coastal towns. Although it's less of a problem with a baleen whale like the minke, bury a toothed sperm whale, and the souvenir hunters come out of the woodwork. A biologist had buried the head of a sperm whale on Oregon's north coast a few years earlier, Tamara said, but when she returned to retrieve the skeleton, all the teeth were gone. Someone had dug up the head and used a Sawzall to cut the teeth from the jaw. Sperm whale teeth can fetch several hundred dollars each if you know someone who's buying. "We're trying to find who did it," Tamara said, "but no one's talking."

Which leads to a more pragmatic reason to bury a whale carcass. If you want to preserve the skeleton, standard practice is to bury it and forget about it for a few years, allowing scavengers in the soil or sand to pick the bones clean. Tamara had asked Mike if he wanted the minke's skeleton, but the idea of handling the increasingly rotten whale any further did not interest him. She also checked with her boss at the science center, Bruce Mate, and the center's public marine-education specialist, Bill Hanshumaker. Neither of them was interested. Bill already had one gray whale in the ground in back of the library and a second buried somewhere else—exactly where, he wasn't certain. In fact, it was sort of lost. He'd recorded the location in relation to some landmarks rather than—as has become current practice—with GPS coordinates and hadn't been able to find it when the time came to disinter it. There's a pit at the science center that's sometimes used for this purpose, but it tends to smell in the summer, sparking complaints from the staff. However, burying a whale is only the beginning; once the flesh is off the bones, you need to dig it back up and rearticulate the skeleton if you're going to put it on display—a time-consuming process unless you happen to have some eager marine-biology majors around with time on their hands. Besides, the science center already had an articulated minke skeleton on display. The science center was, as Tamara put it, maxed out on whale skeletons at the moment.

There's at least one more fairly obvious option for disposing of a whale carcass, or several whale carcasses for that matter: burning. When forty-one sperm whales (*not* California gray whales, as the first newspaper article reported) swam onto the beach south of the Siuslaw River's mouth the evening of on June 16, 1979, and died at nearly the same spot where the sperm whale had been blown up nine years earlier, no one suggested blowing them up. But debate did ensue over whether to burn or bury. Burning would pollute the air, state parks officials argued. Yes, agreed Bruce Mate, Ph.D., by this time a professor of marine biology at Hatfield Marine Science Center. But leaving the internal organs of forty-one sperm whales to liquefy and potentially bubble up through the sand, he said, posed a greater threat to public health than a temporary worsening of the air quality. Ten years earlier, the county's director of environmental health had overseen the successful burning of a stranded whale at Big Creek twenty-five miles north. The decision was made to burn.

But first, Mate and some forty other scientists (including Rus Hoelzel) from Newport, Seattle, and around the country (by fortunate coincidence, the American Society of Mammalogists was meeting in Corvallis, sixty miles inland, that very week) scrambled to measure the whales, determine their sex, collect teeth and testes and blood and whole heads, and dissect as many whales as time allowed, racing against decomposition. (Officials let it be widely known that all the teeth were taken, lest anyone be tempted to go corpse-diving.) Any stranding of two or more marine mammals together, other than a mother and calf, is considered by biologists to be a mass stranding, and mass strandings of any size are relatively rare. Mate knew of only two larger than this one. He was interested in studying the social structure of this intact breeding school of sperm whales. The public, on the other hand, was more interested in learning why the animals had stranded. Mate and his colleagues examined tissue samples, counted blood cells, and searched for signs of parasites. Ultimately, all Mate could say with some certainty was that illness didn't appear to have caused the stranding. The whales seemed to have been a perfectly healthy school that, for yet unknown reasons, swam onto the shore.

Four days after they stranded, three days after most had died, the first of the sperm whales was shoved by bulldozer into one of five trenches, doused with diesel fuel and alumagel, and set on fire. More whales were added over the next twenty-four hours until all were on fire. As they burned, their fat was rendered, and soon they were boiling in their own oil. Fatty as the whales were, they didn't burn quite as well as expected; workers tossed in cord wood and veneer peeler cores, old tires, and more fuel to keep the whales burning, while greasy smoke drifted south over the dunes. Four days after the fires were first set, bulldozers covered over the trenches, burying what was left of the burned whales and closing the book on Oregon's largest mass whale stranding to date.

"Few large-scale disposal operations will turn out as planned," the stranding field guide concludes in Chapter 11, "Carcass Disposal." Ultimately, the guide's authors advise, "The simplest way for a carcass to disappear is to turn your back on it and walk away."

Which is exactly what Tamara and Mike did on March 5, 2004, climbing into the Forest Service pickup and driving north up the beach, away from the minke whale. They were probably not out of sight when the first gull or raven landed on the carcass and began pecking at the tough skin or snatching at the intestines lying in a puddle on the darkening sand.

Mike had seen a bald eagle by the whale when he first went to look at it the day before; perhaps the eagle was back, tearing at pieces of flesh through the square plug Tamara had cut. A small, round black bear, drawn by the smell, may have ventured out of the coastal forest's tangle of salal and rhododendron and shore pine for a bite as well. As the tide crept higher, crabs may have scuttled over the tongue.

"Nature does its work with surprising speed," the field guide further observes. We returned to Mile 157 in late April, just six weeks after we had first come across the whale in early March. There had been some big storms in the interim that had scoured tons of sand off the beach and dumped tens of thousands, maybe millions of *Velella velella,* little purple-blue jellyfish, onto the beach where they had expired and rotted in broad, stinking swaths. The minke carcass had been washed about a quarter-mile to the south and shoved up against the foredune. The flesh was gone; all that was left was the skeleton, or most of it. Four months later, in August, we found the jawbone and a few vertebrae lingering at the same spot. By the time we visited again, in late November, all traces of the minke whale were gone.

As for the baleen Mike Northrup took from the stranded minke whale, it remains on display in a locked case in the lobby of the Mapleton Ranger District office in Florence, flanked by photos of the whale on the beach. Originally white in color, the baleen has yellowed to the color of old ivory, curving—in the drying process—into something like a smile.

Chapter Five: The *Sanak*

WE MUST HAVE WALKED BY or even on top of it a dozen times or more over the years before noticing it. A stump of weathered lumber enclosed in a sleeve of rusted metal angled perhaps a foot or two out of the dry sand near the south end of Mile 157. It was Jack who put two and two together. While I strode down the hard sand that sunny March day, he started poking around in the soft sand where the good stuff was always found, then called to me: "Hey, I think this is a boat!"

What we could see above the sand, that first time, was an upright wooden post, grayed and scoured by sea and sand, embraced by an elongated piece of deeply rusted metal, bent lengthwise into a long V, sticking out of the sand at a slight angle. Two courses of horizontal wooden planking, perpendicular to the post, were broken off just a few inches away; there seemed to be more courses of planking below, under the sand. About fifty feet diagonally to the northeast, near the grassy sand ridge of foredune, was another foot or two of weathered dimensional lumber angling out of the sand at about 45 degrees. Between the two were bits of charred wood poking up an inch or two; if you stared long enough, you could see they formed an elliptical shape, like the outline of a boat. Later visits, when the beach had less sand, revealed two parallel courses of rusted bolts in the middle of the oval, jabbing crookedly at the sky (bent head bolts, Jack recognized) and a couple of odd-shaped steel tanks mired in the sand nearby—from the boat, or unrelated? It was definitely a boat, and it seemed to have burned. An accident at sea? A fire, all hands lost (or rescued), the burned hulk adrift and finally coming to rest on this beach?

On perhaps half of our visits over the next several years, all traces of the boat were gone, out of sight under the beach. Sand volume tends to fluctuate seasonally on the Oregon coast. Most winters, high storm waves pull sand off the beach, funneling it with the help of strong rip currents to huge offshore banks that accumulate out where the breakers start. Summer's gentle swells nudge the sand back onto the beach. The pattern varies from year to year—in a mild winter, the beach can actually build rather than diminish. Sand moves north and south, too, pushed by the waves that are themselves pushed by the prevailing winds: the sou'westers of winter, the nor'westers of summer.

But on the beach, what goes around comes around. Virtually no sand moves outside its *littoral cell*—the pocket of shoreline tucked between two headlands. There are eighteen littoral cells on the Oregon coast; Mile 157 is in the middle of the longest one south of the Columbia River's mouth. Coos littoral cell stretches sixty miles from Heceta Head north of Florence to Cape Arago, south of the mouth of Coos Bay. Some eighteen thousand years ago, at the height of the last Ice Age, much of the world's seawater was locked up in polar ice, leaving the sea level more than three hundred feet lower than it is today and pushing the shoreline far to the west of the present-day coastline—seventy-five miles west of Heceta Head. With no headlands to bump into, the beach sand was free to move, allowing the zircon, pink garnet, green hornblende, and other minerals eroding off of southern Oregon's Klamath Mountains to move north and mingle with flecks of dark green augite and brown hornblende sifting down the rivers draining the central Coast Range. But these days, the Oregon coast is what geologists call a "zero net littoral drift zone": sand can shift north and south, it can move offshore and back onshore, but it all happens within the confines of each littoral cell. The beach sand can play musical chairs all year long, but the number of chairs never changes.

A shipwreck here? Mile 157 is not a likely spot for a shipwreck. Boats tend to wreck at river mouths, where tide and wind and current collide in narrow passages. The mouth of the Siuslaw River is thirteen miles north of Mile 157; Winchester Bay, at the mouth of the Umpqua, is ten and a half miles south. The sea is shallow here, and boats of any kind—

container ships, crabbers, Coast Guard vessels—are rarely more than a speck on the horizon from this beach.

But Mile 157, it turned out, had seen shipwreck before. The *Alpha*, a 132-foot three-masted schooner, had run aground at this very site on February 3, 1907. Captain R. D. Trudgett had been navigating by dead reckoning—educated guessing by an experienced sailor—on the trip north from San Francisco; he thought he was about twenty-five miles west of the shoreline and still south of Coos Bay, his destination. In fact, Tahkenitch Creek is a good thirty-two miles north of Coos Bay. Moments before the *Alpha* struck the shore under full sail, a sailor had remarked to the mate on watch that the moon—two days from full—seemed unusually bright. But that brightness wasn't just the moon on the water; it was breakers on the beach. It was high tide; the crew abandoned ship and reached the shore unharmed. The captain stayed with the ship, hoping to save her, but finally he, too, had to give her up. She was eventually stripped of all valuables and left to be dismantled by the waves.

I wondered if what we were seeing on the beach was some remnant of the *Alpha*, extant nearly a century later. But it just didn't add up. What little we could see was definitely two ends of something, wooden but metal, too, some fifty feet apart. No part of a century-old 132-foot wooden schooner could be reduced to those elements.

Calls to the headquarters of the Oregon Dunes National Recreation Area and to the little Coast Guard station at the mouth of the Siuslaw yielded no information about a wrecked boat north of Tahkenitch Creek. Then I remembered Phyllis Steeves, an archaeologist with the Forest Service on the coast who lived with her husband, Scotty, north of Florence. I called her; she was intrigued but she, too, drew a blank. She worked mostly as a liaison between the Forest Service and coastal Indian tribes; she could read a prehistoric midden heap like a book, but wrecked ships were out of her realm. She wished me luck.

Not a half-hour later, though, she called back, excited. "I got to thinking: Scotty and I may have seen it," she said. "This was maybe twenty years ago. We moved to the coast in 1980, and in those early years we did a lot of hiking in the dunes, getting to know the area. Once we followed an old road out through the dunes—I remember that walk so well because we'd been following bear tracks, so our awareness was heightened.

"We walked over the foredune, and we were surprised to find a fishing boat, right at our feet. I remember it had burned to the waterline." She described the motor block with pistons protruding but the head gone. "It didn't look like it had been there more than a few years," Phyllis said. She also remembered reading an article in the local paper about a fishing boat that had run aground. The location sounded like a match; she offered to fax me a map. Minutes later the map emerged from the fax machine, a question mark scrawled between two hash marks, just north of where Oregon Dunes Overlook Trail meets the beach north of Tahkenitch Creek.

Two hours at the library, scanning microfilmed back issues of the *Siuslaw News,* and there it was. "Grounded Boat Being Stripped," read the headline from the September 22, 1983, edition; a photograph showed a sixty-two-foot fishing boat called the *Sanak* resting on the beach, leaning hard to starboard, its hull and spars and mast reflected in the glassy, wet sand. The captain, "John Vesberkmoes," was from Roseburg; he couldn't be reached for comment, but Duane Leafdahl of Reedsport said he'd bought the salvage rights. I called directory assistance, wondering if Vesberkmoes might still be around, but the operator could find no one by that name in Oregon. She did, however, provide a number for Duane Leafdahl.

"The *Sanak?*" Duane echoed, not a little surprised, when I reached him. He remembered it well; his venture into the salvage business had been short-lived, and he still had parts salvaged from the *Sanak*—the condiment shelf from the galley, a life ring, doors—stashed in the shed outside his home in Reedsport more than twenty years later. "There shouldn't be very much left," he said when I told him I'd apparently found its remains on the beach. "The state made me burn it. But every once in a while those boats come back up!"

I hadn't been able to track down the captain, I told him; any idea what became of him?

"John? He's still around, out at the same place in Roseburg, or Oakland, I believe." I arranged to meet with Duane in a couple of weeks, then called directory assistance again. This time the operator I got was more helpful; she tried some alternate name spellings and hit pay dirt with *Verberkmoes.*

I met John Verberkmoes and his wife, Andy, at their home in the rolling hills southeast of Roseburg. After losing the *Sanak*, he'd spent one season halibut fishing in Alaska—his last season fishing; the following winter he got a job selling sawmill supplies. He and Andy had two girls back in 1983, the year he lost the *Sanak*; they later had a third child, another daughter, and in 1990 moved into an old farmhouse alongside Melton Creek, bringing with them the wheel from the *Sanak.* John had hung it in the horse barn. Even in early April, John—now white-haired—had the ruddy complexion of a man who spends a lot of time outdoors; he owned horses and mules and he worked then on the property around his rural home. For my visit, John had assembled a basket full of old color snapshots: Andy, posed under the stern of the *Sanak* in dry dock right after John had bought it, the red-painted keel as tall as Andy; John as a stocky, auburn-haired thirty-something standing on the deck outside the *Sanak's* wheelhouse, one thumb hooked on a back pocket of his jeans and the other hand resting on the edge of the wheelhouse roof, squinting into the sun with a faint smile.

Bryan Gill, John's twenty-year-old second mate back in 1983, was flabbergasted when I reached him at his home in Drain, a tiny timber town between Eugene and Roseburg. His first summer on the *Sanak* was his last as a commercial fisherman; he promptly went to work in the woods, felling timber. "I definitely knew after that experience that I didn't want to die on the ocean," he told me. "That was *not* the way I wanted to go."

The summer before he joined the *Sanak,* Brian had worked as a hand aboard a charter salmon fishing boat out of Winchester Bay. When he wasn't baiting clients' hooks with herring and hosing vomit off the boat's deck, he used to watch, as he put it, "Coast Guard boys standing there, kicked back in their lawn chairs, waxin' their boats up, or—it looked like to me—doing something stupid.

"I can tell you what," he told me, twenty-four years later, "I have so much respect for those guys now that I couldn't even tell you, you wouldn't even understand, how much respect I have for them, after them risking their lives to save us. My attitude toward them has really changed."

YOU COULD BE DOG-TIRED, short on sleep and beat from gaffing one fifteen-pound black cod after another from four or five miles of fishing line. But standing at the wheel of your own fishing boat, motoring down the Oregon coast at twilight on a mid-September night, a low chatter of conversation on the marine radio, listening to the familiar whine and growl of the engine as it climbed the swells and slid down their backsides: that's what it was all about, John Verberkmoes thought. It made all the nights sleeping alone in a little bunk, the fish slime and the cold and the back-breaking work, worthwhile. That, and the money. But there wouldn't be all that much money after this trip, John knew. Which is one reason why, after several days of so-so fishing up north, he'd decided to go back to Winchester Bay, spend a night or two at home, then head back out to see how the fish were biting below Coos Bay.

Any skipper felt the same, late at night alone at the wheel of his own boat, John knew, but the *Sanak* wasn't just any boat. And John wasn't alone in his opinion. The *Sanak* was pretty widely considered the best-looking fishing boat in Winchester Bay, if not the whole coast. Her profile was low and sleek, the gunwales cut down nearly to the waterline to make it easy to drag big halibut onto the well deck aft of the wheelhouse. The wheelhouse itself was low, too, rounded in front and painted white like the rest of the *Sanak* but appointed with teak doors and window trim. A large triangular steadying sail could be stretched out from the mast, not there to drive the boat but just to temper her moves, to right her in a roll with a nudge, not a snap.

That sail and mast were artifacts of the wind-driven schooners from which fishing boats like the *Sanak* had evolved. The first of the Pacific halibut schooners, built mostly in Puget Sound in the early years of the twentieth century as gasoline power was overtaking sail, were big, stout, eminently seaworthy ships, sixty-five to eighty-five feet long, designed for halibut fishing in the harsh conditions of the Gulf of Alaska. They were shallow in the bow and deep in the stern, with the wheelhouse aft and the working deck space forward. But as fishing techniques evolved, fishermen needed a more versatile boat that could be rigged for more than one fishery and more than one gear combination. Salmon and herring seine fisheries developed a smaller boat about forty feet long, moving the small wheelhouse just forward of amidships. As the nets got bigger, the boats—known as western combination vessels—grew, too, and the wheelhouse was shifted up to the bow to allow plenty of working room aft.

The sixty-two-foot *Sanak*, built in Seattle in 1941, was a classic of the type. As for the name, fishermen of that era had a habit of naming boats for places in Alaska known to them, such as Sanak Island, a speck of land just south of where the Alaska Peninsula runs out and the Aleutian Islands begin.

The *Sanak* rode like a dream, unlike any other fishing boat John had run, and fishing was all he'd done since graduating from the University of Oregon twenty-one years earlier. There were no sharp edges to her moves. She didn't rock; she rolled, nice and easy, even in this night's big swells. It almost felt like she floated on top of the waves, instead of grinding through them like some boats did.

The fishing that year, 1983, had been lackluster even in some of John's best spots, each marked with an X or a circle or "bc" or a pair of parallel lines on the navigational charts he kept on a fold-down table at his right elbow. John and his crew of three had spent the summer longlining for black cod—*sablefish*, they called it in the markets—a rich-tasting fish little known in Oregon but in big demand in Japan. It was not the prettiest of fish: greenish-black with a pale gray belly, rounder and a lot smaller than halibut. Forty pounds was a huge black cod; most of the fish they'd been catching were twelve to fifteen pounds. His crew wouldn't eat it—too rich, they said—but John liked to cut it into steaks, salted to firm up the flesh, and throw them on top of a pot of boiling potatoes that were nearly done. It was a strong-smelling fish—not that that was a problem on a fishing boat, where the smell of fish guts and diesel fuel was ever present, in the walls, in every piece of clothing. John's wife, Andy, wouldn't let him cook black cod at home.

There was very little downtime on a black-cod fishing boat. John's routine was to set three parallel fishing lines, each one-and-a-half miles long. Attached every three feet was a gangion, or leader, three feet long ending at a three-inch barbed steel hook. Between sets, the dark orange fishing line was carefully curled inside fifty or sixty big galvanized-steel tubs stacked all over the well deck, on top of the wheelhouse, in every nook and cranny. Before each set, the crew spent the better part of a day baiting those hooks with pieces of squid and shad, then replacing the hooks on the tub's edge in precise order; when the line was curling out of those tubs at six knots, the hooks would fly, and you didn't want any tangles. They would pay out the lines, one after the other, anchoring each end on the seabed and marking it, on the sea's surface, with a buoy. Usually, John soaked his lines overnight, hauling them in first thing in the morning. John had a way of gaffing the gangion with just enough of a twist to tear the hook out the fish's mouth without having to gaff the fish itself, ripping the flesh. On good sets there might be a fish on every sixth hook, adding up to eighteen thousand pounds of fish in a day's catch.

John had grown up in Roseburg, a smallish town in the mountains of southern Oregon east of Winchester Bay, the son of a doctor. With no particular direction in mind, he finished high school and enrolled at the University of Oregon, an hour to the north. It was there that a fraternity brother had introduced him to fishing. The guy had been married, briefly, and had managed to get through college and support himself and his wife just on what he made fishing summers from his own twenty-five-foot salmon troller. Working just three months a year, outdoors, on your own terms—what was bad about that? After graduation, John bought the troller and fished it one summer on his own out of Newport on the north-central coast. As it turned out, the troller wasn't the greatest boat, so after one winter driving a beer truck, he sold the troller, leased a larger boat, and spent a second summer chasing salmon. In the process, he began working his way into the Newport fishing community. Among the fishermen he met was the son of the owner of the *Seasick II,* probably the top crabbing boat out of Newport. John signed on.

The *Seasick II* was a hard-working boat, and John fished all the time: winters off Eureka in northern California, springtime off the Columbia River and Oregon coast, summers up north in Alaskan waters. One year he spent 310 days on the ocean. It was aboard the *Seasick II* that he became a real fisherman. He learned how to crab, how to longline halibut, how to troll for albacore. He learned how to ride out a storm, how to find your way in the dark, on the open sea, with radar and intuition and loran, the long-range radio navigation position-fixing system that fishermen of that era used to find their way on the ocean. He learned a lot about getting along with people. He learned why fishermen say that being on the ocean is like riding a motorcycle; about the time you think you know what you're doing, you fall down. Fishing became his life. Fishing, and carousing with fishermen at the fishermen's bars from Cordova, Alaska, to San Diego, then staggering on board and heading back out to sea.

In 1971 he heard about a boat for sale in Seattle, the *Sanak*. Ernie Matheson was asking $62,000—a lot of money. But three or four years on the *Seasick II* had left him with a nice nest egg; between that and a loan, John was able to swing it. He was twenty-seven years old, making him one of the youngest captains with one of the biggest and quite possibly the nicest fishing boat in Winchester Bay.

His first summers on the *Sanak* he trolled mostly for albacore from sixty to fifteen hundred miles off the Oregon coast. Albacore was a hot commodity then, and it didn't take long to make a lot of money. One year he stumbled onto the *Sanak* the morning of July 5 with a mean hangover, motored out of Winchester Bay, and had his year's income in the bag by mid-September. Then he and the crew would take the boat down to Mexico, enjoy some sun, party at night, and fish just enough to make expenses.

John became known in Winchester Bay as a good fisherman, the best at times, competitive like most but not driven like some. He also had a reputation as a fair guy, a good friend, and a safe captain who didn't take chances that would put his crew at risk. He had never had an accident, never submitted an insurance claim.

It was good times, good for most of the seventies. But in the late seventies the albacore fishing started to fall off. The fish just weren't there. Commercial fishing is by nature a gamble; you hope that the particular fish you seeking will be plentiful, but not quite plentiful enough to drive down the price. What *was* bringing in a good price, Jon noticed, was black cod—a fish not many other fishermen in Winchester Bay were interested in. Back on the *Seasick II* John had spent one summer longlining for black cod off Oregon, so he knew how it was done. It was a lot like longlining halibut: bait miles of hooks, pay out your lines, anchor them to the seabed, then pull them back in and pull off the fish. Black cod were smaller than halibut and they tended to cluster on the sea floor, so you set the hooks closer—every three feet rather than every nine to twelve feet. Hardly anyone else on the Oregon coast knew much about black cod; they thought it was a joke. He took plenty of ribbing as he changed over his gear in the spring of 1979. That summer he made a killing, catching fish like crazy and raking in more money than he knew what to do with.

By the next summer it seemed like every fisherman on the coast was fishing black cod. That second season the price went sky-high, up to 85 or 90 cents for fish in the round, more for cleaned fish. The Japanese sent their own buyers to the Oregon coast to high-grade the fish at the processing plant, picking through the mounds of headless black cod for the prime specimens.

And then, in the roller coaster that is commercial fishing, the price plummeted to as low as 35 cents a pound. The fish were there—John's best year, tonnage-wise, was 1981—but without a decent market, it wasn't worth doing. He went back to albacore fishing for a season. The next year, spring 1983, he decided to take his chances on black cod again.

Standing at the wheel that evening after supper, his thoughts may have drifted to Andy, at home with the kids at their rental house in Oakland, north of Roseburg. They'd been married for four years and already had two daughters. Fishing was hard on family life, there was no doubt about that. John was home for months at a time in the winter, but come summer he was rarely off the boat. Andy had known what she was getting into when they got married—they'd dated for years before they made the leap—but still, it was no picnic being home alone with a baby and a toddler. John had been a fisherman his entire adult life, and the real world, as fishermen called it, didn't hold much appeal for him. Fishing was exquisitely simple: You fish. You get your money. You spend it. You go back out. As John liked to explain it, it was not confusing; it was real simple. No mortgage, no nine-to-five. No, he wasn't ready to think about quitting fishing. Even when fishing was bad, it was better than any of the alternatives.

It had been a long day. Stormy weather had driven the *Sanak* into Newport Tuesday night, where they unloaded the catch and spent the night in port. Then Wednesday evening John and his first mate, Big Jay, pried themselves off their bar stools on the bayfront and rejoined Bryan and Noland, who were too young to drink (in bars, anyway) and were bored to death waiting on the *Sanak*. John pointed the boat west, toward the bay mouth, and they motored under the Yaquina Bay Bridge and back out to sea. The weather had calmed, thankfully, but one night in port wasn't enough; they were ready for a real break. It would still be a five- or six-hour run south to the *Sank*'s home port of Winchester Bay. Then they'd all be back in their own beds for a couple of nights before heading back out to sea.

By the time supper was over, John was ready to call it a night. Bryan, the twenty-year-old second mate, volunteered to take the first watch. It didn't really matter to John who took first watch. They all knew what to do and everyone knew the rules, or so John thought—even Noland, the kid, still green after only a month or so aboard the *Sanak*. There wasn't much to do; no one was to take it off autopilot without waking John. Thinking back later, it almost seemed to John as if he had posted his rules on the boat, though he knew he hadn't. They were easy to understand. They all began the same: *Wake the captain. Wake the captain if you see any vessels on the radar within a couple of miles. Wake the captain if any of the gauges change, like the engine oil pressure or the transmission oil pressure or the head pressure on the refrigeration. Wake the captain if you feel like you need to change course. Wake the captain if you can't keep your eyes open.* John wasn't about to replay the scenario he'd heard about in the Gulf of Alaska several years earlier, where the guy coming off watch goes below, wakes up another deckhand—"Hey, it's your watch"—then crawls into bed; the other guy falls back asleep and the next thing they know, the boat is on the beach. *Wake the captain if you see a light you can't identify. Never, ever take the boat off autopilot without waking the captain, unless disaster—like a collision with another boat—is imminent.* The last thing John wanted was some neophyte navigator taking the *Sanak* into his own hands. *Wake the captain if for any reason you don't feel comfortable.*

If you change watch, always wake the captain.

John checked the autopilot once more, glanced at the radar. Then, leaving Bryan at the helm, he ducked into his stateroom, tucked between the galley at the aft of the wheelhouse and the wheel room up front. He stripped down to a T-shirt and boxers and climbed into his narrow bunk, a bunk lined—like bunks on ships the world over—with a board a foot or so high keep him from falling out should the going get rough, always a possibility at sea. The swells, leftover from the storm, were plenty big that night. But the forecast was for clear weather into the next day. The rhythmic rolling of the *Sanak* in the swells and his own fatigue put him out in minutes.

Bryan had been on the *Sanak* with John since spring. He'd worked as a deckhand on charter boats in the summer, but this was his first season of commercial fishing. Raised in the Umpqua River town of Elkton, he was a year out of high school, happy to find an alternative to setting chokers in the woods and thrilled with the money you could make on a good boat even in a bad year. He was husky and strong, a fast learner and a hard worker—John's best hand, in fact. Fishing suited him; he liked the work, there was always something to do, and the days went by fast.

But night watch at the helm could be deadly slow, especially after a long day. After two hours he wasted no time crawling down to the crew's quarters in the bower of the boat, by the engine room, to wake Jay. It never occurred to him to wake the captain; it was a routine switch. Bryan was asleep as soon as his head hit the pillow.

Big Jay lumbered up the stairs and squeezed through the door to the wheel room; he was a good three hundred pounds and plenty tall. At thirty-seven, he was just a couple of years younger than John but seemed much older—the dues of a hard life living on the ragged edge. It was Jay's second season on the *Sanak*. John knew Jay needed the work— he had no real home off the boat, bummed from place to place in the off-season. He was slower than the younger deckhands when it came to getting the work done. Still, he was smart and he was loyal, which counted for a lot with John.

It was close to midnight when Jay left the wheel room to shake Noland awake for his watch. Noland, eighteen, had joined the *Sanak* just a few trips earlier. He didn't know much yet—but there wasn't much to know to stand watch. The autopilot steered the boat. All he had to do was watch the gauges, watch the loran, watch the radar. And as Jay reminded him, John was just through that door if anything happened, if there was anything Noland didn't understand.

Maybe the autopilot malfunctioned; it's possible. Maybe Noland took the boat off autopilot for a while because he was bored, or sleepy, and he figured steering the boat himself would help him stay awake. Maybe he just wanted to play captain for a bit, while the captain was asleep, and then forgot to turn the autopilot back on when he stepped out onto the foredeck and settled back to watch the waves for a while. The fog was thick that night, hanging in a bank along the shore. The half-moon seemed to light the fog from within, frosting the waves faintly. You'd think nothing could be darker than being on the sea in the middle of the night, but some nights the luminescence on the pressure wave billowing off the bow was so bright you couldn't even see ahead of you—almost like headlights in your face. It was riveting, even a little hypnotic. Then a different kind of wave crested off the bow, and then another. Noland had never seen any waves quite like that at night; something seemed not quite right. He raised himself off the bow deck and returned to the wheel room. He glanced at the radar; it didn't look right, either. Must be the fog.

When the *Sanak* struck the ocean bottom, the jolt threw John out of his bed and onto the floor of his stateroom, instantly dousing him with cold sea water as a wave washed in from the stern, nearly inundating the galley, John's stateroom, and the wheel room. He scrambled to his feet, took his bearings—what bearings he could take, standing in the dark in his underwear and bare feet, dripping wet, in a listing boat—and froze, listening. In those first moments, he was certain about what was coming next: the *slice, slice, slice* of massive propeller blades on a big cargo ship, a ship that had obviously hit the *Sanak*. He listened hard, wondering if he was going to be able to dodge the blades.

But no propeller came; just more waves, pushing the *Sanak* from one side to the other. The next scenario he conjured was nearly as bad. He felt certain he hadn't been asleep long, which meant they would still be north of Florence. He dashed into the wheel room and glanced out the front windows; in the darkness he saw surf, but no beach. Putting two and two together, it added up to a big zero for the four of them. They had to be off the sheer cliffs of Heceta Head, right around Sea Lion Caves, with no place to run. *This is it,* he thought to himself. And then he went to work.

Everyone was in the wheelhouse by this time, John in the wheel room and the three deckhands huddled in the galley, standing in their underwear as alarms rang and waves of 55-degree seawater washed in and out from thigh-high to waist-deep. That first bump had awakened Jay and Bryan, but no water had washed into their quarters down below. Bryan, lying in his bunk, thought maybe one of the big metal stabilizers that hung in the water alongside the boat had flopped up in the swells and hit the side of the boat. Then it bumped again. With the third bump Big Jay was out of bed, through the foxhole in the ceiling, onto the foredeck, and into the wheelhouse in what seemed like one fluid motion. Bryan was right behind him, but not quite fast enough. Just as he popped through the foxhole and onto the deck, a wave struck. He grabbed a big cleat and hugged it, holding his breath while the wave washed over the top of the boat. Then he, too, dashed inside.

That first big wave had doused most of the boat's electronics, including the radar and the big loran. But John had a second loran receiver, a smaller one, that was still working. He expertly twisted the dials, lining up the little triangles again and again to get his time-distance readings, then checked the read-out against the numbers printed in purple all over his navigation chart. They weren't off Heceta Head at all, it turned out. John had slept a lot longer than he thought, and they were already south of Florence, off the beach west of the dunes. No cliffs here: just sand, more than forty unbroken miles of it. *We're going to live,* he thought. *And now we're going to get this boat back on the ocean.*

In his twenty-plus years at sea, John had never dealt with anything quite like this. Once he'd collided with another fishing boat in mid-ocean, a freak incident that was more embarrassing to both captains than it was harmful to either boat, though each had taken five days to limp back into Astoria to make needed repairs before they could resume fishing. The *Sanak* itself had felt the scrape of the sea floor before, however; the boat's former owner had given John a black-and-white photograph of the *Sanak* high and dry on a rocky Gulf of Alaska beach many years earlier. There was no instruction book on how to un-ground a sixty-two-foot fishing boat, but after twelve years with John at the helm of the *Sanak,* the boat was practically an extension of his own body; he knew her tolerances and her capabilities and her quirks. With a little cunning and some luck, he'd have her off the beach and back on the open sea in no time. While one part of his brain worked to get the boat free, another part was figuring how to cover up the whole affair. The last thing he wanted was to become the butt of a long-running joke in Winchester Bay. If he played his cards right, no one would need to know this had ever happened. His biggest problem would be trying to explain how it was that all his gear got washed overboard.

The *Sanak* had run straight onto the beach, but each wave seemed intent on turning her broadside. John threw the engine into reverse and gunned it, cranking the wheel to try to spin her around. He made some progress, but the next wave shoved her diagonally back toward the beach. He kept working it, though, fighting the waves that were trying to beach her and using their buoyancy to let her turn and get her bow pointed back toward sea. There was no possibility of failure in his mind, and he was using every trick he knew. The big swells he'd ridden down from Newport translated to big surf here on the beach. With every wave, he was losing a little more ground—and a little more gear over the side. Soon several miles of dark orange hook-laden fishing line was bobbing in the waters surrounding the *Sanak*, turning the wave froth pink like the aftermath of a shark attack, and tangling in the propeller in a huge wad.

Then the engine died. John had been working it hard, pushing the engine to push the propeller to push the *Sanak* off the sand, and finally it couldn't push any more. Now the game was up, and John knew it. The *Sanak* was broadside to the beach, stuck on the sand, listing hard toward the shore and shuddering with the percussion of wave after wave. He reached for the VHF radio: mounted high, still dry, and tuned as always to Channel 16.

IT WAS SHAPING UP AS AN UNEVENTFUL NIGHT for the radioman in the operations center, the only soul awake at the Coast Guard's Group North Bend air station. Then again, most shifts started that way. It was Wednesday night—no, Thursday morning now, September 15—and what pleasure boaters had been out that day were for the most part back in port and tucked into bed. The loggers were in bed, too; some would be back in the woods before dawn, but they usually waited until the day shift radioman arrived before losing their footing on muddy slopes and sliding under rolling logs, breaking a few bones and crushing a few organs and needing a quick helicopter ride to the hospital. The commercial fishermen were still out chasing fish, but other than some big swells left by the storm earlier in the week, the conditions weren't bad. Most of the tourists were off the beach by mid-September, certainly by now, a Thursday and close to 1 a.m.; otherwise he would be half-expecting a alarmed call about a flare spotted in the night sky (likely as not just a meteor, or fireworks) or a boat on fire out at sea (almost certainly the working lights on, say, a black cod boat). Chatter on Channel 16 was pretty minimal this time of night; not many fishermen were awake, and most knew better than to use the distress channel for personal business. Any such conversations would show up on the console, outfitted with green lights for each of the high-site antennas the North Bend radioman monitored: Yaquina Head, Heceta Head, and Umpqua Lighthouse to the north, Cape Arago and Cape Blanco to the south. North Bend was the only Coast Guard airbase between Astoria, at the mouth of the Columbia River on the northern Oregon border, and Crescent City in northern California; for any air rescue needed in the 220 miles between Oregon's Pacific City and the California state line, North Bend responded.

"Mayday, mayday, mayday," the call sounded, jerking the radioman alert. He glanced at his console, where two green lights were pulsing. The call was coming in through both Heceta Head and Umpqua Lighthouse, putting the source of the mayday somewhere between the two—the waters west of the dunes. The voice scratching through the speakers was all business. "This is fishing vessel *Sanak*, fishing vessel *Sanak*, fishing vessel *Sanak*. My loran reading is north-south 2-7-7-4-0 and east-west 2-7-8-2-0. I'm in the surf with four persons on board. We've lost power. We're getting beat up pretty bad. We need a helicopter just as soon as we can get it."

"Fishing vessel *Sanak*, this is Group North Bend," the radioman responded by rote. "Roger your mayday." On some maydays, the young radioman—not yet six months out of boot camp—might probe a bit or make a call to the duty aircraft commander before taking action. But it was clear from the caller's precise language and urgency, just a notch or two below panic, that this was a hot case. "We'll get a helicopter on the way. Stand by this frequency." He scanned the loran numbers on the nautical chart next to the console and found the spot, just offshore and north of the mouth of Tahkenitch Creek. He reached for the search-and-rescue alarm button.

Immediately a loud staccato BOOP BOOP BOOP BOOP BOOP started up, a good fifteen seconds of it, heard in every corner of the airbase: the massive indoor hangar deck where the helicopters waited, the crew's quarters, the tarmac outside. Then he flipped on the public-address system to make the pipe: "*Now*, put the ready helo on the line, put the ready helo on the line, put the ready helo on the line. Fishing vessel with four POB in the surf, one and one-half miles north of Tahkenitch Creek. *Now*, put the ready helo on the line." And he hit the SAR alarm button again.

By the end of the pipe, the aircraft commander and co-pilot—awake now and lying unmoving in their bunks, listening to the radioman's words—were already silently ticking off a mental checklist: no injuries, no sinking boat, just a short flight so no need for extra fuel. By the end of the second alarm they and the flight mechanic were out of bed and striding to the locker room, conferring with one another about the mission. By the time they were pulling on their flame-retardant long underwear and zipping into orange survival suits, lacing up heavy boots and grabbing helmets, the watch captain and a couple of line crewmen were jumping into coveralls and heading toward the hangar deck, and the quartermaster on watch was on his way to the operations center to confer with the radioman and take over the case. Now no one at the airbase was asleep, and everyone was working toward the same goal: Get the helo in the air.

All three of the airbase's Sikorsky HH52s were flight-ready and parked on the hangar deck. The ready helicopter was a little readier than the other two. It stood just inside the huge hangar doors, its yellow tow bar already attached. The Coast Guard considered the 52 a small aircraft, compared to others in use in its day. It stood fourteen feet tall with overhead rotor blades spanning fifty-three feet. It measured forty-five feet from nose to tail—longer than a school bus—and was painted a crisp white with a red-orange diagonal slash where the aircraft's cabin narrowed to a tail. It had seating for three in addition to the crew of three; it could fit twelve people or more, in a pinch. It ran on a single turbine-powered engine and was capable of water landings, thanks to its watertight fuselage and a pair of sponsons, or outrigger floats. But it was top-heavy, and with the engine off it tended to flip over in even mild swells. What the 52 really did better than any other aircraft of its day, anywhere in the world, was hover above and rescue people in trouble at sea.

While the aircraft commander conferred with the quartermaster in the operations center, checking on weather and what was known about the mission, his co-pilot was on the hangar deck, scrutinizing the ready helo with a twenty-point preflight checklist: intake covers removed from engine *check,* fuel tank caps on and double-locked *check.* The ready crew was required to get the helicopter airborne in thirty minutes or less; they could do it in five, and they moved through the necessary steps with the precision of ballroom dancers. Hit the button next to the hangar doors, triggering the door panels to fold into the walls at either side. Turn on the outside floodlights, illuminating a patch of tarmac just outside the doors. When the aircraft commander arrived, the flight mechanic handed him and the co-pilot the green survival vests that were stored in the back of the helicopter and loaded with everything they might need if things went haywire: waterproof radio, pen flares, hand-held flares, strobe light, signal mirror, whistle, knife. Both pilots slipped on their helmets and jumped through the big cabin door on the helicopter's starboard side. Sliding between two black metal radio racks, they dropped into their seats in the narrow cockpit and began adjusting seat heights and strapping in. The aircraft commander, in the right-hand seat, did the "wipeout," setting all the switches ready for engine start, while settling both feet on the anti-torque pedals that doubled as brakes. The watch commander, meanwhile, had hopped in the little yellow tractor—they called it a *mule*—and begun backing it toward the free end of the tow bar at the helicopter's nose. As the aircraft inched toward the hangar doors, pulled by the mule, line crewmen took up positions under the tips of both overhead rotor blades—"wingwalkers" watching to make sure the fifty-three-foot-long blades didn't clip the doorframe.

The crewman driving the mule spotted the helo in a circle on the tarmac and tossed a pair of triangular rubber chocks under one wheel before disconnecting the tow bar and driving the mule back onto the hangar deck. There he hitched the mule to the external power cart, towing it out to the tarmac and plugging it into an outlet on the outside of the aircraft, while a second crewman arrived pushing a fire extinguisher on wheels. By now the flight mechanic, still on the ground, had his helmet on, putting him in voice communication with the pilots via a long spring cord.

"Ready for start."

"Ready for start."

In the cockpit, the aircraft commander pushed a button on the cyclic control positioned between his legs. With a distinctive whine, the engine began spooling up, under the scrutiny of the flight mechanic, positioned on the tarmac just in front of the helicopter. No fuel leaks, no funny smoke; it looked good to go. At the pilot's command, the mechanic touched his right thumb to his open left palm and jerked it away, signaling the crewman to unplug the power cart. To the other crewman he gave a thumbs-up: time to return the fire extinguisher to the edge of the tarmac. He took a last look to the right and left and underneath the helicopter—no people, no equipment, no obstructions anywhere.

"Clear for rotor engagement."

Inside the cockpit, the commander released the rotor brake. Immediately the three horizontal blades overhead and two short blades on the tail started turning—lumbering at first, but quickly gaining momentum. With a last glance, the flight mechanic pulled the chocks and jumped in the cabin door. As the aircraft began a slow hundred-yard taxi to a clear spot at the edge of the runway, the mechanic drilled down his own preflight checklist, making sure his hoist was in perfect working order, before folding down his aft-facing seat from its spot against the starboard radio rack and strapping in himself.

"Aft, ready for takeoff?"

"Ready aft."

"North Bend area traffic, this is Coast Guard rescue helicopter 1-4-4-0 departing from Coast Guard pad to the northwest."

With the grace of a symphony conductor, the pilot gently twisted the throttle on the collective control in his left hand, setting the power at 103 percent rotor speed, then slowly pulled up on the collective stick while feeding in the left pedal bit by bit and making minute adjustments to the cyclic in his right hand. As the helicopter began its hover, all three men felt the familiar heavy feeling kick in, like being in an elevator starting up a skyscraper. A little more pedal, slow pull on the collective, and a nudge forward on the cyclic, and the helicopter was now accelerating, heading into the northwest wind. Below and to the right, both pilots and the flight mechanic, peering out the still-open cabin door, could see the dark curve of Coos Bay and, alongside it, white vapors rising from the floodlit paper mill perched on the shoreline. Just ahead and on the left was their second beacon: the faint glow from the lamp over the door of the concrete restrooms at Horsfall Beach parking area. Then there were no more lights: just a line of white breakers and the pale gray sand of the shoreline, which they followed north like the white lines on a freeway.

WHILE JOHN WORKED THE RADIO in the wheel room, talking to the quartermaster at the North Bend airbase and a bosun's mate at the Umpqua River motor lifeboat station, the crew of the *Sanak* waited, huddled on benches at the table in the flooded galley in their underwear on a listing boat in the pale light of an overhead bulb, silently wondering if the next wave would be the one that would start breaking the boat apart.

Then Jay broke the silence. "We're gonna die! We're gonna die! I'm gonna jump!" he shouted, and charged out the galley door.

"Jay's going over the side!" Brian yelled forward to John. Then, turning, "Jay, don't be a dumbass!" But Jay kept heading across the well deck, now clear of gear. Then as Bryan and Noland watched from the galley door, another wave hit, jerking Jay off his feet and sending him sliding across the wet deck and slamming into the bulkhead. Noland, watching, started to whimper; this was Big Jay, and Big Jay was losing it, and the panic Noland had been keeping down low in his throat was starting to rise and sneak out in little sobs. Bryan, watching through the galley door, figured it was all over for Jay.

But just as Jay was gathering himself to have another go, another wave hit, pitching him across the slippery deck again, this time past the galley. Bryan grabbed at him, but all he could reach was Jay's long, wavy head of hair, so he grabbed that. "Noland, help me! I've got Jay by the hair!" he bellowed. But by then John had dashed up, and the two men got hold of Jay under the shoulders and pulled him back into the galley and sat him down on a bench. John turned and sloshed back to the radio in the wheel room.

"Goddamn, Jay, what the fuck were you thinking?" Bryan exploded. But the energy of Jay's moment of panic had played itself out, and the picture of what he had almost done was starting to appear more clearly to the big man: the miles of fishing line floating in the waves, the thousands of barbed hooks.

"I don't know, man, I don't know," Jay just mumbled, hanging his head, staring at his feet. "I don't know. I won't do that again."

"You're goddamned right," Bryan said, and not just to Jay. Noland had been getting jittery and seemed about to do something stupid, too. But Jay's little adventure seemed to have sobered everyone. Now Noland sat, silent and still, staring into the blackness outside the windows.

Then John was back, his arms loaded with orange survival suits. The Coast Guard had a helicopter in the air, he reported. It was less than fifteen minutes away, and they all needed to have the suits on to get rescued. Each of them—the kid, Bryan, Big Jay, and John—began zipping into the big one-size-fits-all neoprene suits. Then, with John back at the radio, each deckhand sat back down on a bench at the galley table: feet and hands and head and torso all enclosed in the thick, clammy rubber, isolated by the sound-muffling neoprene hood. The galley was more than a kitchen to the crew of a fishing boat; it was their living room, the warmest place on the boat, where they started their day with a hot cup of coffee, and where, at the end of a sometimes eighteen-hour day, they'd put away a few beers. Now it was their cocoon, cold and wet as it was. Not that that was much comfort. The boat was no longer moving much from port to starboard; it was wedged in the sand and listing hard toward shore. Every wave that crashed down on the boat felt strong enough to start breaking it up. Bryan, for one, had his own Plan B. If a helicopter didn't arrive before the boat started coming apart, he intended to jump off the bow, where he figured there might not be any fishing gear in the water, or might be less. The shore wasn't all that far; he thought he had pretty good odds if he didn't get caught in a rip tide. As he silently worked the plan over in his mind, he felt a warm liquid running down the inside of one leg of his survival suit. *That's interesting,* he noted with a detached curiosity. *I just peed my pants.*

John reappeared with an update. The Coast Guard helicopter pilot had radioed a request that the *Sanak* fire a flare to help the helicopter crew find her in the dark and fog. Jay jumped up, suddenly eager to be of help. "I'll fire the flare!" he announced.

"You do that, Jay—you fire the flare," Bryan spit back, still rattled and a little disgusted by Jay's panic attack. Jay dug out the flare gun, stepped onto the aft deck and fired. The crew watched the flare zip skyward and explode in a giant red ball, bright even in the fog. The explosion of light, the chance to do something about their situation, and the thought that their rescuers were probably close enough to see the flare, too, gave everyone a spark of hope. By this time Bryan had moved to the aft deck, where he was now squatting in the dark, alone. Inside the galley, he had begun to feel less cocooned and more like a trapped rat. Out here, he felt he had a chance to get off, should the sonovabitch start breaking up.

John appeared again, this time with a news flash from the Coast Guard. The helicopter that had been dispatched to rescue them had been diverted: something about another fishing boat in trouble up north. It was the thirty-two-foot *Antigone,* he later learned. Unlike the *Sanak,* which had run aground just offshore, the *Antigone* appeared to be going down in deep waters with two people aboard. Rescue helicopters from both North Bend and Astoria had been dispatched to search for the vessel, as had a C-130 search and rescue plane out of Sacramento and the fifty-two-foot motor lifeboat *Victory* from Newport. The airbase at North Bend had called in its stand-by crew, the quartermaster assured John, and was working to get another helicopter in the air ASAP.

"Fuck them!" Bryan exploded. "What about us?" There was no answer. Everyone fell silent again. *Well, this is cool,* Bryan thought to himself. *They got our fucking helicopter. We had a chance there; we might have had a chance. And now we are probably gonna die.*

The minutes ticked by. The Coast Guard called again; a second helicopter was airborne and on its way to the *Sanak*. Bryan, alone on the aft deck, figured he'd believe it when he saw it—but in fact, the terror he'd felt ever since that first bump in the night was starting to subside just a bit. It seemed like the *Sanak* had been pushed far enough up the beach that it wasn't moving quite so much with every wave. He was almost getting used to the rhythmic pounding.

Then another call came in, this time from the Umpqua River motor lifeboat station. Two forty-four-foot self-righting lifeboats had been dispatched and were right now in the ocean just west of the *Sanak*—spitting distance. The Coast Guard was considering sending a couple of swimmers to pull the crew off by sea.

"No way," John said. With the tangle of fishing lines and hooks surrounding the *Sanak,* they'd probably never make it to the boat, much less get the crew off. It would be a suicide mission. "I just don't recommend it at all," he said.

And then there were lights, blinding floodlights from overhead, and the high whine of a turbine engine and deep thrum of spinning propellers, and wind, and saltwater from the waves spraying at high velocity, stinging the deckhands' eyes and mixing with the tears now streaming down their cheeks. They were all out on the deck now, squinting in the wet wind and bright lights, while John shouted over the din, relaying the instructions the Coast Guard had given him over the radio. The flight mechanic would be lowering a basket to pull them up one at a time, but they weren't to touch the basket until it touched the boat; something about needing to ground out the static electricity the basket picks up en route. Just let it bang on the side of the boat before you climb in, John said. There was no need for a discussion about what order they'd go in. Noland, petrified, clearly needed to get off the boat first; as captain, John would naturally be last. Jay, still trying to live down his attempted jump, was now playing the hero; he wasn't about to get off the boat ahead of anyone except the captain.

Immediately, a rectangular white metal cage, resembling nothing so much as an oversized eight-items-or-less supermarket basket, came at them from above. Just as fast, Noland lunged at it, clawing the air when it swung away. It was probably not the first time a panicked crew member had ignored the no-touch rule; as the flight mechanic worked the hoist from above, trying to keep the basket out of Noland's reach, Noland kept grabbing for it from below. Finally it banged against the boat, sparking, but before the flight mechanic had a chance to settle it on the deck, Noland threw himself at it, getting halfway in before it swung out and over the dark ocean.

Still swinging, with one of Noland's legs hanging out and his hands gripping the sides, the white basket rose in the air, pausing at the helicopter door just long enough for the flight mechanic to pull Noland out and into the cabin. Then the basket was out the door and moving down, back toward the deck of the *Sanak.* Bryan took Noland's ride as a lesson in how *not* to be rescued and waited like a choirboy for the basket to bump the boat and settle onto the deck. While John and Jay held the basket, Bryan climbed in and took his elevator ride to the helicopter hovering in a roar overhead. With Noland and Bryan aboard, the pilot swung the helicopter west, setting down on the beach to let the two of them out before returning to a hover over the *Sanak.*

A third time the basket was lowered; John held it while Big Jay climbed in and was hoisted without a hitch. Finally it was John's turn. There was nothing to do but to climb into the basket. John knew that. But that didn't make it easy. Never had John imagined abandoning the *Sanak,* nor had he imagined any circumstances that would cause him to do so. But here he was. He waited for the basket to hit the deck, and he climbed in, leaning back to give the flight mechanic the thumbs-up.

Then, just at that moment, a wave hit, and the basket with John curled inside went into a slide. It slipped right under a little table on the deck, lodging there. But with the next wave seconds later, the *Sanak* shifted again, and the basket slid again, freeing itself. As the hoist jerked the basket into the air, it pulled John off balance, tipping the basket precariously. John just tightened his grip on the basket's sides as the hoist began pulling him skyward. Seconds later he was in the helicopter cabin; seconds after that he and Jay were stepping out onto the beach. Then, just as quickly, the helicopter was gone.

But they weren't alone. Waiting for them in the dark were two pickups, one with a sheriff's deputy at the wheel, and another with a camper shell on the back and two Coast Guard crewmen in the cab, waiting to drive them to Winchester Bay. The deputy had a few questions, he said, and he separated the four men to quiz them one by one about just how the *Sanak* had happened to end up on the beach. It was a short quiz; they were all still stunned, and no one really knew what had happened anyway. But everyone knew what the deputy was fishing for. In an era rife with rumors of fishermen dumping their boats not-so-accidentally to collect the insurance money, suspicions ran high. As far as John was concerned, it was none of the deputy's business; his authority ought to end at the beach. The suspicions were insulting, given what they'd just been through. But there'd been enough drama for one night. John clipped out his answers to the deputy's questions. Then he slid into the cab of the Coast Guard pickup, while Noland, Bryan, and Jay climbed into the back, and the truck headed south down the beach toward Sparrow Park Road and out to Highway 101.

It was Bryan who broke the momentary silence in the back of the truck. "Like, what happened, buddy? I mean, shit! We almost died out there!"

Noland just shook his head, his dazed eyes staring at nothing. "I don't know. I was sitting on the bow of the boat and a couple funny-looking waves go by, and I went back inside ..."

But there was no point in quizzing the kid. If he ever knew what had happened, it had apparently been scared out of him, or maybe he was too embarrassed to say more. It took about twenty minutes to get to the Coast Guard station in Winchester Bay, and Bryan's first priority was to peel off his reeking survival suit and get under a hot shower. John headed straight to the pay phone to call his wife.

Andy had never known John without the *Sanak*; she and the *Sanak* had come into John's life within weeks of each other, twelve years earlier. If there was one constant in John's life besides Andy, it was the *Sanak*. So the last thing Andy expected was to get a phone call at three o'clock in the morning from John, telling her he'd run aground, taken a ride in a Coast Guard helicopter, and abandoned the *Sanak* on the beach at Tahkenitch Creek.

"You might as well have told me you had a sex-change operation," she told him later.

DUANE LEAFDAHL HEARD ABOUT the *Sanak* the same way he heard about lots of goings-on in Reedsport: on the marine scanner he kept on continuously at his shop. He'd launched A Dock Repair about a year earlier; it was his first business enterprise. The idea was to repair some boats, buy salvage rights to boats that wrecked, and between the two support himself and his wife and kids. He had set up in a little corrugated-tin shop on the Umpqua River just upstream of the highway bridge, tucked behind the shipyards and next to a boat ramp. Between jobs in the woods, in lumber and paper mills, on a salvage tug, in the Reedsport shipyards, at a Chevy dealership, on a tow truck, and on commercial fishing boats, there wasn't much Duane couldn't fix. He loved collecting stuff, and he loved connecting: a wrench with a bolt, two pieces of metal, two people, or a person and the things he might need. One ear was always tuned to the scanner; never know when you might hear something useful. And from the moment he walked into the shop on the morning of September 15, 1983, the airwaves were full of the *Sanak* running aground north of Reedsport.

He was acquainted with John Verberkmoes and the *Sanak*, though not well. Winchester Bay was a little harbor community three miles downstream from Reedsport at the mouth of the Umpqua. Everyone in Reedsport and Winchester Bay knew everyone else, especially in the fishing community. Duane picked up the phone and called Mark Hitchcock, a close friend of John's and—Duane knew—one of John's most trusted deckhands until this season, when Mark had started running his own fishing boat. "The *Sanak's* run aground in the dunes," Duane told him. Mark already knew—in fact, Mark had already been out to see it at daybreak with John, who had called him hours before from the Winchester Bay Coast Guard station. Duane's Chevy pickup wasn't working at that moment—he had been meaning to fix it, any day now—so he borrowed a friend's Jeep, and he and Mark headed up U.S. Highway 101.

Driving on the beach here wasn't strictly legal, and the dunes between the beach and the highway were part of Oregon Dunes National Recreation Area, a stretch of wild coastline undeveloped but for a few campgrounds and picnic areas. Even the hiking trails in the dunes consisted mostly of tall posts; when the actual trail disappeared, hikers just walked from post to post. There was no direct road access to the spot on the beach where Duane estimated he'd find the *Sanak*, just north of the mouth of Tahkenitch Creek. But he knew the coast. He'd grown up in Reedsport, and other than a stint in the Navy, he'd spent nearly his entire life there. He could approach the *Sanak* from the south, but he'd have to cross Tahkenitch Creek in the Jeep, and he wasn't sure about that, what with the borrowed Jeep and all. Instead, he figured the best way was on an abandoned road that started at the highway about a half-mile north of Oregon Dunes Overlook; it snaked west and north for a mile or so, first through a dense coastal forest of spruce and pine, salal, huckleberry, and rhododendron, and then through dune grass and open sand dunes before hitting the ocean. An ordinary truck would sink in the sand on the open dunes, and the Jeep wasn't exactly built for sand travel. But Duane was hoping its four-wheel drive and big wheels and his own know-how would get them across the dunes.

They did. He crested the foredune, dropped onto the beach, and headed south. It was a perfect September morning, cloudless and still, the sun coming over the Coast Range and slanting onto the beach. As they approached the *Sanak,* she looked to be in great shape, as if all she needed was a little nudge to float her again. Her mast and both poles, port and starboard, were intact; there were no holes in the hull that they could see. Duane wouldn't mind getting the salvage contract for the boat, if it came to that, but right now he just wanted to get the electronics and other valuables off the boat before looters got to her, for John's sake.

They looked her over but didn't stay long. Duane hadn't brought any tools with him, but his eighteen-year-old son, Skipper, was handy with a wrench. Duane's plan was to get back to town and send Skipper and a friend or two out here to start pulling off the lorans and the radios and the depthfinder and the other expensive stuff. He and Mark hopped back in the Jeep and headed back to town. There Duane tracked down Skipper, who rounded up a couple of his friends. Duane gave them the Jeep and his tools and sent them back up the road with directions to cut all the wires and start pulling off everything of value. Then Duane went back to his shop and started making calls.

He tried to reach John at his home, but couldn't track him down. Then the phone rang; it was Ray Nulf, the marine surveyor who functioned as an insurance adjuster for fishing boats. The *Sanak* had run aground on the beach, Ray said, and he wondered if Duane would go down with him and have a look. "I'm two steps ahead of you," Duane told him: he'd already been down to see it and his kid was probably already back on site pulling the electronics even as they spoke. Good, Ray said; let's go take a look at it.

The boys were hard at work, loading the Jeep with salvaged electronics, when Duane and Ray reached the *Sanak*. No reason to think she couldn't be refloated, Duane mused; it was just a matter of logistics. As he looked the boat over, an idea began to form. You couldn't attach a line to any one part of the boat to tug it off the beach; it would just break off that part of the boat. But what if you took thick cables, the kind loggers used, and fabricated a kind of bridle to envelope the boat and tug it off the beach that way, all in one piece? He ran the idea by Ray. Ray liked it. So Duane took some quick measurements and headed back to his shop in town, leaving Ray to scrutinize the *Sanak* more closely.

Back in Reedsport, Duane first called Sause Brothers Ocean Towing out of Coos Bay; did they have a tug available? They did. Next, he headed over to Umpqua Industrial Supply, the logging-supply store on East Railroad Avenue, a few blocks from his own shop, and floated his idea: were the materials available, and could they help him build the bridle ASAP? Again, no problem. The shop was also willing to give him everything on credit, which was what Duane really needed to know. He went back to his shop, got his Chevy running, then headed back to the *Sanak*, this time taking Sparrow Park Road, a gravel road just north of Gardiner through the forest to the beach, then driving up the sand to the creek, four miles north. It was September and Tahkenitch Creek wasn't much more than a trickle, just a few inches deep where it spread out at the mouth; the Chevy crossed it easily. From the creek it was another mile and a half of beach to the *Sanak*. He could hardly wait to tell Ray the good news and start lining up all the players to get her back on the ocean.

But while Duane had been in town, Ray had made a disappointing discovery. The horn timber—a solid piece of Douglas fir, like a bow stem but at the stern—had cracked under the battering the *Sanak* had taken in the surf. Between that and the generally poor market for fishing boats, given the depressed state of the fishing industry, saving the *Sanak* just didn't pencil out. He'd be lucky to get $40,000 for it if it were back in the harbor at Winchester Bay and in perfect running condition, and it would likely take all that and a lot more to make it right, Ray told Duane when they met up again on the beach. Ray had decided to total the boat. Did Duane want to buy the salvage rights? Yeah, I do, Duane said, sizing up the *Sanak* again. It was insured for something like $200,000—boat, fishing gear, electronics, everything.

"I'll give you $2,500 for it," Duane said.

"Sold."

Duane was now the owner of a sixty-two-foot fishing boat, albeit it one stuck on a remote beach and not going anywhere but further up the beach with each high tide. And he had some decisions to make. It was his boat now, and if he still wanted to try towing it off the beach on his own dime, he could. Whether he did or whether he didn't, he needed to strip the boat, not only to salvage anything of value but to lighten it in case it could be refloated.

It was early afternoon by the time John and Bryan arrived in Bryan's pickup to look over the *Sanak* again. John had already talked with Paul Risley, his insurance agent. He'd been steeling himself for a formal investigation, for all the questions the company would want answered before they made a $200,000 pay-out for the loss of a fishing boat they insured, run aground for reasons the skipper couldn't quite explain. But Paul had surprised him. "There isn't going to be any investigation," he'd told John flatly. The Coast Guard automatically investigates when there's a death. But there were no deaths, not even any injuries on the *Sanak*. "It's just a simple grounding, John. That's all there is to it. Turn in your claim."

The tide was out, and John and Bryan were surprised to see how far up the beach the *Sanak* was—you could walk all the way around her and not get your feet wet. There was stuff strewn all over the beach: garbage and clothes and fishing line, scattered everywhere. Duane and the boys were crawling all over the *Sanak,* pulling off gear and loading it into a Chevy pickup parked alongside: vultures picking at carrion, John couldn't help thinking. Then Duane spotted John. He jumped off the boat and walked over to where Bryan and John were standing next to the pickup.

By then John was in tears. He was staring at the inlaid hardwood ship's wheel that Duane had already pulled out of the *Sanak's* wheel room and stuck in his pickup, the wheel that John had used to steer her all over the eastern North Pacific for twelve years, that had guided her for thirty years before that. Duane followed John's gaze. The wheel was the prize item off the *Sanak,* as far as Duane was concerned—not as valuable monetarily as some other things, but Duane could already visualize it hanging on the wall of his living room back in Reedsport.

"You want the wheel?" Duane asked. John nodded.

"Take it."

Duane pulled it out of the back of his pickup and loaded it into Bryan's truck. Then he handed John four coins—a penny, a nickel, a dime, and a quarter, all dated 1941. Duane had hoped to find a gold coin when he unstepped the mast—most boat builders of that era placed one under the mast, or so Duane had heard. He'd found these instead. John nodded his thanks. Then John took a last look at the *Sanak,* her clean lines lit by the low-angled September sun and reflected in the wet sand. He climbed in the cab of the pickup. Bryan turned the key, and Duane watched as the truck made a slow, wide turn on the hard sand and disappeared south down the beach.

Duane helped Skipper set up camp on the beach near the boat that night and came back early Friday with more food for the boys. He wanted to check on their progress and haul out some of the salvaged gear. He also wanted to look over the *Sanak* again. He'd had a brainstorm the night before. What if he were to float the *Sanak* off the beach with a logging balloon? Bohemia Lumber had recently begun using specialized blimps to lift logs out of the Coast Range woods rather than dragging them down the hillsides. What if he were to hook the *Sanak* to a logging balloon at high tide and use the blimp to help the *Sanak* maintain buoyancy for the short trip down the coast to Winchester Bay?

"Let's do it," said Bohemia's Faye Stewart when Duane called. Faye had been to Sweden to learn balloon logging, and he knew the Swedes did a lot of salvage jobs with balloons: boats, trains, planes, you name it. Faye was just finishing up a logging show out of Coquille, down the coast; he could bring the blimp up tomorrow. I don't know if there's any money in this, Duane cautioned. No problem, Faye said. The publicity alone would make the operation worthwhile, he said. Besides, it was something new. He wanted to give it a try.

But the weather took a turn that night, scattering rain on the tent sheltering Skipper and his friend and kicking up the ocean. Duane got a call from Faye Saturday morning; the blimp had blown into some trees, poking holes in it. It would be a week or so before he could get it repaired and up to the *Sanak*. Duane drove out to have another look at the *Sanak*. The storm had hammered the boat, too; it was looking pretty beat. It turned out that the engine was shot as well. John had already told Duane that the block was cracked—had been for years—but when Duane lifted off the head he could see that the block was now cracked all the way around and was beyond repair. No doubt it overheated while John worked it overtime, trying to get the *Sanak* off the beach when it first hit bottom. Duane realized that, despite all his great ideas, there was probably just one way the *Sanak* was ever going to leave that beach: piece by piece.

After a couple of days of wind and rain, the balmy fall weather returned. Duane came out every day, bringing food, helping pull gear and haul it back to the shop, and sometimes spending the night. The electronic navigation and communication equipment had come off first—lorans, radar, depthfinder, radios, antennas—followed by the crew's own personal gear. Duane found six or seven pairs of perfectly good Levi jeans belonging to Big Jay in the crew's quarters. But no one had seen Jay since the Coast Guard had dropped him and the others off in Winchester Bay early Thursday morning. Not being one to waste anything, Duane bought himself his first pair of suspenders and began wearing Big Jay's jeans himself.

Then they set about pulling everything else. While the boys worked the *Sanak*, Duane worked the phone and the fishing community, looking for buyers. The main engine's block was toast; the head was full of water, too, but it was salvageable. The auxiliary engine had some water in it, but Duane cleaned it up and had it running a few days later. He took off the water pumps and fuel pumps and a brand-new diesel stove, a combination cookstove and heater. He took home the electrical panel, a beauty with dozens of switches, factory-built by Hendrix Electronics, and used it in a radio room he'd built upstairs for his youngest son. He cut a hole in the side of the wheelhouse to take out the four-cylinder John Deere generator. He took the rudder and the propeller and propeller shaft. Some parts went to a fellow in Reedsport who was building a boat, and some to another local who was moving to Bellingham to build boats. Duane got acquainted with a couple of guys in Florence who needed to outfit a boat they'd just bought; they loaded up on gear off the *Sanak*. Some of the *Sanak's* fishing gear he sold to other fishermen; some he just stashed in his shop at home, along with a life ring, John's charts, and the solid teak door and the Dutch doors at the galley entrance. The teak condiment shelf, with holes to hold jars of mustard and ketchup and salt and pepper, lived in a series of RVs Duane owned before finding a home above the sink in his shop bathroom.

Meanwhile officials from the state were starting to pressure Duane to pick up the pace. In Oregon, the state's ocean beaches are officially designated highways—thanks to a little legislative sleight-of-hand worked by Governor Oswald West in 1913 to preserve the beaches for public use—so it was the state highway department that had authority over the beaches. That didn't mean you could drive on the beach; in fact, by 1983 cars were allowed on very few of Oregon's beaches, and

Tahkenitch Beach west of the Oregon Dunes wasn't one of them. So Duane applied for, and was granted, a permit allowing him to drive on the beach long enough to get the boat salvaged. Then officials asked him what he intended to do with the fuel and oil in the boat; how was he going to contain it? Good question; according to John, the boat had been full of fuel when it ran aground. So Duane tracked down a company that pumped old oil out of sumps and determined that they'd be able to get a truck and trailer down onto the beach to pump out the fuel. But the highway officials wanted to know how many times a day was Duane driving on the beach? What times of day? He felt like he was getting pecked to death by chickens. Clearly, it was going to be to everyone's benefit—Duane's, mainly—to get the job done and get out.

Finally in early October the last salvageable part was pulled. All that was left was to pump out the remaining fuel, and then it was time to let nature take its course with what was left of the *Sanak:* the hull and the wheelhouse and the machinery that was too big to move or of too little value to bother. But the state saw things differently. You can't leave that boat there, Duane was told; someone might climb on it and it might roll on them and crush them and the state would be liable. Can I burn it? Duane asked. Yes, he was told.

He hated to burn her. Not that he hadn't done well by the parts he'd pulled from her. But Duane wasn't just a salvager; he'd spent time at sea himself, had a fisherman's appreciation for a good-looking boat and the memories she held. It's true she was just a skeleton of her former self, with all her rigging and machinery gone, a gaping hole where her elegant teak door had once been. But she still had her sleek white hull, the lines that had made her the envy of fishermen in every port she visited. Burning would save him some money; rather than pump the fuel out, he could use it to burn the boat. That's when he discovered that there was no fuel. What fuel had been left must have all leaked out the damaged hull.

So he bought some gasoline. He poured it into the fish hold. He took his last look at the *Sanak*. He lit a match, touched it to the boat, and backed off. Then he climbed into his pickup and drove away. He just couldn't stand to see her burn.

The next morning he dropped back by. All that was left of the *Sanak* was the bottom of the hull, scorched around the edges. The engine block and drive shaft were still in place, along with the refrigeration coils and concrete ballast lining the hull's inside walls and other odd bits of machinery. There were a couple of big tanks on the sand nearby; apparently they'd been washed out during high tide. Scattered all around were ashes and the long, square nails that had held the planking in place. A few more tides, Duane figured, and all the ashes and nails would be gone.

They were.

THE YEAR THE SANAK RAN AGROUND—1983—was a particularly low sand year on the Oregon coast. Big storms from an El Niño weather pattern the previous winter had pulled more sand off the beach than usual. Some of it, but not all, had been pushed back on the beach over the summer and fall, before the *Sanak* hit the beach. But the storms during the winter following the *Sanak's* grounding weren't particularly severe, the waves not very high. Over time the vessel swiveled, shifting until the bow was facing southwest, toward Hawaii, the stern toward the dunes. And bit by bit she settled into the sand, the way your feet do when you wade, barefoot, and the sand seems to liquefy beneath your weight. That winter, and every winter for the next twelve years, the storms were weaker than normal and the waves lower, and more sand accumulated on the beach than was pulled off of it. Slowly, what was left of the *Sanak* was buried and local memory of her erased.

Things started to change in 1994, the first of several severely stormy winters, one after another. Worst of all was the winter of 1998-1999, when the Oregon coast was hit with not just one but four of what were characterized as one hundred-year storms: tempests with wave heights greater than ten meters, or thirty-three feet. That winter's biggest storm of all carried some of the highest waves ever recorded on the Oregon coast. That was early on the morning of March 3, 1999. Literally tons of sand were clawed off Oregon's beaches by the storm's waves. Things appeared on the Oregon coast that hadn't been seen in anyone's memory: fossil tree stumps thousands of years old, ancient peat bogs, imprints of ancient Native American settlements.

And, a mile and a half north of the mouth of Tahkenitch Creek, a weathered fishing boat burned to the waterline.

Chapter Six: Mermaid's Purse

THE DAY WAS DAZZLING. A few puffy clouds in a bright blue sky, warm but for a brisk March wind: perfect for a beach walk at Mile 157. Besides, that weekend Oregon's coastal communities—the entire Northwest— was abuzz with the latest developments in the wreck of the *New Carissa*, the empty 660-foot wood-chip freighter that had run aground on Coos Bay's north spit a month earlier, on February 4, 1999. It had begun leaking oil within a few days. Most of the oil was what's called Bunker C oil, extremely thick, thicker than molasses, barely pourable at room temperature, not the sort of thing a seabird or a clam wants to run into. So officials had tried to burn off the fuel oil in a massive conflagration in the surf line, visible for miles inland. The result: the ship cracked, broke in two, leaking more oil in the process. After three weeks, an attempt was made to tow the bow end—the larger of the two pieces—offshore. A towline more than a half-mile long was attached, and the tug *Sea Victory* started pulling. Over the next four days, the 440-foot piece of burned freighter began inching seaward, finally floating off the beach the night of March 2. But timing is everything. That night, when tug and bow were about forty miles offshore, a fierce winter storm struck—the wildest storm of the winter, in fact, the wildest in many winters—and the towline snapped. The ship's bow began drifting north, up the coast, past Mile 157, past Florence, to run aground at sunrise the next morning on the beach just south of Waldport, where it leaked more oil. Some seventy thousand gallons leaked out of the *New Carissa*, all told. Thousands of oiled seabirds and shorebirds were killed or injured in the process. A new tow cable had been ordered, this one four inches in diameter. The plan was to float the freighter bow off the beach with Sunday night's high tide.

We climbed down the foredune and started walking south and immediately noticed (unaccustomed as we were to seeing anyone else on the beach) a group of coverall-clad figures walking slowly, heads down, across the mouth of the creek. One figure was dressed all in black, carrying a box of some kind; it looked like a briefcase or a tool kit, from what we could see of it through binoculars. A second was in a white jumpsuit, and several more were dressed in yellow jumpsuits. The distance and the moisture evaporating off the sun-warmed beach obscured our view of them; they shimmered, seemingly walking in slow motion a few inches above the sand, like wraiths across a desert void. Actually, what they looked most like, to us, was a clutch of scientists at Area 51 heading out across the Nevada desert to investigate an alien spacecraft's crash landing. The hazmat suits they seemed to be wearing were a little disconcerting. Would they dress that way if they weren't worried about encountering something hazardous? We assumed they had some connection to the shipwreck; maybe they were looking for oil on the beach or oiled birds or other evidence of environmental impact from the wreck. But we saw no oil on the beach, no oiled birds, no funny business at all. Perhaps there was something more sinister they were looking for—something you couldn't see or feel or taste until it was too late.

And then we found it.

It was dark brownish-green, and stiff, almost like weathered plastic, but it didn't look manufactured; it had the rough, fibrous texture and color of a palm leaf, but the shape was all wrong: rectangular, almost a foot long and more than half that in width. The corners were flat and curled inward toward each other, the edges frayed. And it bulged in the middle, a bladder full of air or water but not solid when we poked it. It looked to me more like a tropical leaf than anything else, but it rang no botanical bells with either of us. We were stumped.

We decided to cut it open to see what was inside, not completely sure we wanted to know—the hazmat suits had by this time turned around and were slowly moving back down the beach—but we were too curious to resist. Jack pulled out a pocketknife and cut a slit lengthwise down the middle of the green pouch, then cut slashes at either end, like the letter I, and peeled back both sides. We peered inside.

First we saw the yolks—soft and moist, glistening, creamy pink, at least four of them—and then we saw what looked like a blood vessel in a mass of blue-red tissue, throbbing, moving. Whatever it was, it was no plant, and it was alive.

Was alive. But now it was going to die. And we'd killed it. Whatever it was.

Actually, we figured it was probably going to die anyway; we'd just hastened the process. Lying there on the beach, it was clearly out of its element, though we didn't know what its element was. Now, exposed to sun and air and all manner of potential predators, from sand fleas to gulls, it was definitely expiring. And we still had no idea what *it* might be. We left it, a little guiltily, lying on the beach where we'd found it and began the hike back to the car.

Then we received at least a sign, if not an explanation.

We decided to take the long way home, via Waldport and Newport, to get a glimpse—along with everyone else in Oregon, it seemed—of the bow of the *New Carissa*, which overnight had become the state's top tourist attraction. We spotted it through the trees, between the beach and the highway—a dark, looming hulk, attended by more guys in jumpsuits; parked cars jammed the highway shoulder for a mile or more. We didn't stop. Instead we continued driving north to South Beach, where we stopped at a favorite fish and chips shop and ordered at the counter. While I waited at a Formica table for our fish to fry, Jack browsed the reading material strewn on a nearby counter—mostly real-estate flyers and tourist guides. Then he appeared at the table, grinning and holding up the current edition of a local tabloid monthly: the *Depoe Bay Beacon,* "Independent Voice of the Oregon Coast."

"Chicken Lays Message from God!" the lead headline blared.

It seems that on December 4, 1997 (fifteen months earlier—not exactly breaking news), Cheryl Smith, a resident of Neotsu at the north end of Lincoln City, was gathering eggs in her chicken coop when she found that one of her barred rock hens, Spotted G-G, had laid an egg with the letter G almost perfectly formed in relief on the outside of the shell. Smith told the *Beacon* reporter she was "scared to death" at first and thought she was "seeing things" (we knew the feeling). Then, she said, it all became clear to her.

"I know this is God's signature here on earth, and others know it too," she said. More than one person had dropped to his knees upon seeing the eggshell's divine irregularity. She had sucked the yolk and white out of the egg to keep it from spoiling, then had displayed it at both the Lincoln County Fair and Oregon State Fair that summer. The egg was now tucked away in a safe-deposit box. She planned to insure it with Lloyds of London. A date with the David Letterman show, she said, was "still up in the air."

Ms. Smith had put two and two together and come up with an entirely satisfactory explanation for her mystery egg. Jack, still grinning, recounted all our clues swirling around discovery of our eggs: the jumpsuits, the briefcase, the methodical searchers. The explanation is obvious, he said with a self-satisfied smile.

They're alien eggs.

Or they were for the remainder of the day, as we amused ourselves during the drive back over the Coast Range. But at home I started wondering, seriously, what on earth the thing was.

Whom do you call when you find big hen-sized egg yolks inside a pocket of leafy green on the beach? A bird expert, of course. So I called an acquaintance who taught field ornithology classes at the University of Oregon. He recognized my description right away. It was probably an egg case from a shark or a skate, he said; sometimes they get detached from the ocean floor and wash up on the beach.

Which explained everything, of course, except the ensuing questions: Was it from a shark or a skate? What exactly is a skate, anyway? And how did a skate's, or a shark's, egg case end up on this beach?

THE SEABED STRETCHING WEST from the shoreline along the central Oregon coast tapers gradually over forty or fifty miles to a depth of some six hundred fifty feet before dropping off sharply toward the deep Cascadia Basin. This relatively shallow terrace is the continental shelf, but during the last Ice Age, fifteen thousand years ago, when the sea level was much lower, the continental shelf *was* the beach: the dry land defining the continent's edge. Out past the breakers, past the point where the sand shifts onshore and offshore with the seasons, the shelf stretches as a nearly flat plain, little disturbed by weather and waves, a soft, sandy seabed dotted with snails and clams and sponges. Crabs and shrimp scuttle by; speckled flounders settle in the silty sand. And here and there, in congregations a mile or several miles in diameter, lie hundreds or even thousands of identical leathery olive-green rectangular pouches scattered in pairs on the seabed. Waiting.

Once I knew what to look for, a cursory search of marine field guides had quickly confirmed the origin of the egg case we found that day. There are plenty of sharks in the waters off the Oregon coast—some fifteen species, from the small brown and filetail catsharks patrolling the seafloor and the mild-mannered, plankton-eating mammoth basking shark to the great white shark, the bane of surfers. Though many sharks are *viviparous*—meaning, they reproduce by giving birth to live young—some, including the catshark and its second-cousin the ratfish, are *oviparous*; their young hatch from eggs or, rather, from tough egg cases deposited on the sea floor for gestation periods lasting months or, in the case of the catshark, more than two years. Even some viviparous sharks encapsulate their fertilized eggs in some kind of case—a stout one, or a thin, flimsy one—that they retain inside their body for part or all of their pregnancy before giving birth to a little swimming shark. Other sharks use a strategy partway between live birth and egg-laying, great whites among them. These *aplacental viviparous* species begin life in thin-skinned eggs within the mother's body; when their initial yolk supply runs out in the second half of their year-long gestation, the mother produces millions of unfertilized eggs on which her developing litter of shark pups feed until birth.

Not much is known about the life history of most species of Oregon sharks. Some are known to migrate south for breeding. Catsharks and ratfish lay egg cases in waters off Oregon's shore, but they tend to deposit the cases in relatively deep water at the edge of the continental shelf or beyond, so their egg cases don't often wash up on the beach.

Nor is much known about the life history of most species of *skates,* another group of fishes closely related to sharks. Squarish and flat, skates are hard to tell apart from their better-known cousins the *rays.* Several species of skates inhabit the waters off Oregon, from the little fine-spined skate—all of two feet long including its long, skinny tail—to *Raja binoculata,* commonly known as the big skate, measuring five or six feet long or longer from the tip of its pointed snout to the end of its whiplike tail, and nearly that wide from wingtip to wingtip. Skates, like sharks and rays, get their shape not from bones, as most fishes do, but from cartilage: tough, rubbery, fibrous tissue like the tissue that gives shape to your nose and ears.

All rays reproduce by means of live birth. But all two hundred-plus species of skates found in the world's oceans—including the twenty species known to inhabit the eastern North Pacific from Alaska to California—are oviparous. When an egg case such as the one we found washes up on an Oregon beach, chances are it came out of a skate, not a shark. And the big skate's egg case is unmistakable, once you know what you're looking for. At a length of eight to ten or even twelve inches, it's believed to be the largest egg case in the world, certainly larger than any other found on an Oregon beach; the starry skate's egg case, for example, is only about four inches long. The big skate's egg case has to be large; the skates growing inside it reach seven to nine inches long by the time they "hatch." That's *skates,* plural. As a rule, shark and skate egg cases each hold only one egg, with two exceptions: one skate species found in Japanese waters, and *Raja binoculata,* whose egg cases typically hold anywhere from three to eight baby skates.

If you've been to an aquarium, you may have seen skates. If it was a West Coast aquarium, some of those skates may have been *Raja binoculata,* such as those inhabiting the Passages of the Deep exhibit at the Oregon Coast Aquarium, adjacent to Hatfield Marine Science Center on the south shore of Yaquina Bay in Newport. The 1.32-million-gallon tank that once housed Keiko, the celebrity orca, is now bisected by an acrylic pedestrian tunnel, granting views overhead, at either side, and even underfoot of swimming creatures: coho and Chinook salmon, red Irish lords, China and blue and vermilion and canary rockfish, spotted ratfish, leopard and sevengill sharks, resting near the bottom of the tank or undulating from side to side to push themselves through the water.

Not the skates. They move not side to side but up and down, by flapping their "wings"—muscular pectoral fins attached to either side of the skate's head. Up and down, up and down, the wings flap with a languid grace, the tip of each wing curling at the apex of the stroke. A long, narrow tail nearly the length of its body trails behind, like the string on a kite.

They're shaped a little like kites, too—the old-fashioned, four-cornered kind. Their undersides are pale, with a kind of smiley face at one end: full "lips" outlining a crescent mouth near the snout, and just above the mouth, two small round openings that look like eyes but are really nostrils. Seen from above, the big skate's dorsal side is sand-colored with light mottling, like light refracted through waves playing on the sandy seafloor. It is further camouflaged by large circular "eyes" on the middle of each wing—dark spots resembling the eyes of a larger fish, the kind of fish that might deter a potential skate predator. But the skate's actual eyes, the eyes it sees with, are beady little things positioned close together on either side of its cartilaginous skull.

If you didn't know better (and didn't read the signs posted at the display tank), you might assume the aquarium's big un-fish-like fishes flapping silently on the other side of the clear tunnel, moving in and out of shafts of diffused blue light, were stingrays. To the untrained eye, skates and rays are not easy to tell apart. Both generally have square, flat bodies and long, trailing tails. They're close cousins taxonomically, sharing an evolutionary path that goes way, way back. Unlike most rays, skates tend to have small, bump-like dorsal fins along the back half of their tail. Skates' tails are fleshier than the rays' narrow, whip-like tails, and skate tails don't carry stinging spines as most rays' do. But what really sets the two groups apart is their reproductive strategy: one lays eggs, the other doesn't.

Skates even lay eggs cases on the floor of the aquarium's Passages of the Deep tank. Divers retrieve them, and the egg cases are exhibited separately for the duration of the baby skates' gestation. Curators sometimes cut a little square window in the tough shell of the egg case and replace it with a piece of clear acrylic, through which the world can watch the yolks get smaller and smaller and the skates get bigger and bigger until, one day, the pale little skates wriggle out.

Occasionally, after a storm, a beachcomber will bring to the aquarium an egg case that is still viable, like the one we found. Packaged and protected so effectively in that fibrous green case and further nurtured at the aquarium, baby skates from such cases sometimes survive. More often, however, the egg cases found on the beach are dried out, finished, darkened nearly to black by the time they're found, their inhabitants hatched and their purpose fulfilled. Beachcombing guides call them "mermaid's purses"—a nickname as odd as it is apt. I'm not sure what need she'd have of a purse. Isn't escape from such terrestrial concerns as commerce part of the charm of the mermaid's life? But there is a poetic truth to the term. If a mermaid needed a purse, this soft-sided green clutch seems much more practical than a hinged clamshell. And unusual as it is, the egg case is an intricate and elegant answer to the question every single species on earth must address: What's the best way to assure our survival? How can the female skate best wrap and carry that which is undeniably her most valuable possession—the next generation?

THERE'S A LOT MORE IN THE WORLD of animal reproduction than laying eggs, as birds do, or bearing live young, as mammals do. And perhaps the craziest and, ultimately, most successful reproduction happens among the elasmobranchs—the subclass of animals comprising the sharks, skates, and rays.

"It's been called the ultimate solution to sibling rivalry," marine biologist R. Aidan Martin told me with a wide grin. He's talking about the sand tiger shark, which like many sharks is a product of aplacental viviparity—the "middle-of-the-road technique," Martin calls it. But unlike the great white and many other sharks, which feed on their mother's unfertilized eggs after their yolks run out halfway through gestation, the dominant baby sand tiger shark actually devours its embryonic litter mates *in utero*, employing the sharp little teeth already lining its jaws when it's just an inch long. "So what you end up having is a mother that might be three meters long giving birth to two pups"—the shark has not one but two uteruses—"each about twenty centimeters long, with *huge* bellies because they've been feeding on the lesser sibs!"

I met Martin at his North Vancouver home, a quaintly charming townhouse in a small development adjacent to Victoria Park and just a few blocks above Burrard Inlet. I was lucky to catch him at home. He was just finishing up a paper on the behavioral ecology of whale sharks that he planned to present at an international conference in Perth, Australia, the following week before heading to his ecotourism project in the Maldives, off India's southern tip, and shortly thereafter to Jawsfest 05 on Martha's Vineyard, commemorating the thirtieth anniversary of the 1975 movie that put a generation of swimmers on edge. Between such events, he spent time on a project researching great white sharks off South Africa's Seal Island—a project memorialized by a British Broadcasting Corporation photographer who used a 1,000-frames-a-second camera to catch a great white shark with a mouthful of fur seal in mid-air for the landmark documentary *Planet Earth*.

Pitch him a topic, and Martin talked nonstop—articulate comments on elasmobranch phylogeny and behavioral ecology peppered with off-the-wall wisecracks and the occasional *crikey,* all delivered in an Australian accent unmarred by more than a decade of living in the United States and, mostly, Canada. Around his neck hung a silver chain, and from it, his wedding band and a silver shark tooth, cast more than twenty years earlier from "the first reasonable-sized shark I ever caught"—a bull shark near his childhood home in Queensland.

Once I started poking around for skate information, Martin had quickly loomed as someone I wanted to meet. Others were doing more serious long-term work on skates' life history—Wade Smith and his colleagues at the Pacific Shark Research Center at California's Moss Landing Marine Laboratories, Jerry Hoff and Chris Gburski at the National Oceanic and Atmospheric Administration lab in Seattle, Sandy McFarlane at Canada's Pacific Biological Station in Nanaimo, on Vancouver Island. But as far as I could tell, Martin was the only ichthyologist who had worked his way through grad school doing stand-up comedy.

It was his mother's daily warning—"Watch out for snakes! Watch out for sharks!"—that had first piqued Martin's interest in sharks, he told me. Growing up in a little beach town near the southern tip of the Great Barrier Reef, he was a "seaside fanatic," snorkeling out his back door, awestruck by the sea life on the reefs but always looking over his shoulder for the shark that might eat him. Finally, at the ripe old age of eight or nine, he decided it was time to "know the enemy." He went to the public library to read up on sharks—and learned that they weren't nearly as dangerous as he'd been led to believe. "Which in and of itself was kind of a letdown," he recalls, "like finding out that T. Rex isn't around." He began hanging out in the seaside mangrove swamps near his home to observe the behavior of the little black-finned reef sharks that glided through the shallow water there. It was a time, he recalls, of "absolutely rapturous discovery," one that set him on his life's course: a quest to better understand the life history and, particularly, the behavior of sharks and their kind.

Until the day when he and his wife had to ask for help carrying a polystyrene-wrapped, 850-pound dead shark into their garage, he says, "None of the neighbors knew what I did. Not a clue. Not a clue!" It was a salmon shark, a close relative of the great white, and Martin was looking forward to dissecting it after a fish-processing plant in Alaska had caught it accidentally and offered it to him. ("Anne allows me to dissect sharks on the kitchen island," he had told me earlier, by way of introducing me to his wife. ("How many wives would? That's love!") "The amount of blood washing down the driveway," he ruefully recalls: "Now everybody knows I'm the crazy shark guy!"

And not just sharks: elasmobranchs of all kinds. He led me into his study, where I showed him a photo of the egg case I'd found—"Yep, that's *binoculata*," he confirmed at a glance—and he reached into a cabinet, pushing aside piles of dried shark jaws to pull out his own collection of egg cases stored in two flat boxes and a large gallon-size Ziploc bag holding a single specimen from *Raja binoculata*. He pointed at another olive-green capsule just one and a half inches long, with fine tendrils corkscrewing off each of its four corners. "Puffadder shyshark," he said. "Found that at our research site in South Africa."

"Here's one from Coos Bay," he continued, pointing to a small, dark, lumpy rectangle. A woman there had called after she found his Web site and read his request for egg cases. "This lady said, 'Are you interested in the fresh thing?'" he recalled. "I said, 'Yeah!' And she said, 'Well, it's very wet.' So I explained to her how to dry it out, and she did a beautiful job. You do it in stages—do it in the garage, let it sit, put it on a bed of paper towels and periodically change those. Eventually it'll dry out."

He took another look at my snapshot showing the inside of the skate egg case we had cut open on the beach. "There's an embryo there," he pointed out. "This thing is not terribly far along. I can't see the external gill filaments yet. The yolks look very large. There's very little blood network around them. They're at a fairly early stage of development."

That would put the conception of these skates, somewhere out in the ink-dark waters off Oregon's continental shelf, at about the same time that the *New Carissa* first ran aground. *Raja binoculata* is found in waters anywhere from six to twenty-five hundred feet deep, but most are found at depths of a thousand feet or less—waters such as those above Oregon's 650-foot-deep continental shelf. Their reproductive life is relatively short; males reach sexual maturity at age ten or eleven, females at about thirteen, and researchers have found no big skates older than twenty-six. And it's a busy life. Some skates have a fairly narrow spawning season, especially those found in colder waters; in Alaska, big skates seem to spawn from April through September, perhaps longer.

But off Oregon and California, the laying of big skate egg cases seems to go on nearly year-round.

Birds do it, bees do it, most fish don't, but skates and sharks do: internal fertilization is one part of a reproductive strategy that sets sharks, rays, and skates apart from their fellow fishes. They *do it* by means of claspers—the functional equivalent of a male mammal's penis—that transport sperm into the female skate's reproductive tract. The claspers, stiff with internal cartilage and armed with tiny spurs and spines, "open like a flower," as one scientist puts it, digging into the female during mating on the ocean floor or in a mid-water tryst and ensuring that the sperm gets where it's intended. Having shared his seed, the male skate flaps away—and before long, another male will sidle up to the same female for more of the same. Monogamy is a luxury skates can ill afford.

Skate claspers are "mind-bogglingly complex compared to those of other elasmobranchs," Martin said. From an evolutionary perspective, this complexity may help keep skate species separate—species that, frankly, aren't very different one from another, compared with the wild diversity of the shark world. "Kind of a lock and key thing," Martin explains, cocking his head with a *you get me?* grin. "If the penis don't fit," he quips, "you must acquit!"

Construction of the case that will hold a litter of big skates for a year or more starts even before ovulation, before copulation. It's about one-third complete, and white in color, by the time the fertilized eggs drop in. Hours later, the now firmer, darker finished egg case drops down into one of the skate's two uteruses, where it stays for some twelve hours before *oviposition*—the skate equivalent of laying an egg. First the left-side egg case and then the right one is expelled and left on the ocean floor. And with that, the mother skate flaps away. She'll never see the faces of her offspring—unless she happens to encounter one by chance somewhere at sea.

But she hasn't left those egg cases just anywhere. Most, if not all, oviparous skates and sharks position their egg cases in "nurseries"— breeding grounds where hundreds or thousands of egg cases are clustered on the ocean floor. Some nurseries are used by more than one species, but big skates seem to prefer sticking with their own kind, in single-species sites. Scientists with the Canadian Bureau of Commercial Fisheries stumbled upon two such nurseries while conducting an exploratory scallop cruise off the coast of Oregon in 1963. Both nurseries were at a depth of about two hundred feet of water—which, off the Oregon coast, tends to be about two or three miles offshore. Dragging an eight-foot scallop dredge along the ocean floor at varying depths, they sometimes brought up one or two egg cases, or none. But in two sites, both at a depth of two hundred feet, the dredge yielded more than a hundred egg cases, all of them from big skates. One was just off Tillamook Head, between Seaside and Cannon Beach on the northern coast. The other was between the mouths of the Siltcoos and Siuslaw Rivers, less than ten miles north of Mile 157.

Some sharks are thought to pick up egg cases with their mouths and shove them into rock niches or coral crevices. Others may use their mouth or snout to anchor the capsule on the seafloor by painstakingly winding the tendrils of fiber curling out of the capsule's four corners to a rock or a plant. Not so big skates, whose egg cases are lots bigger than their mouths, and whose nurseries, located on the silty, sandy continental shelf, may have nothing much to anchor an egg case to. The egg cases of big skates are still soft and pliable when they're first expelled, the better to wedge into the sand, or a rock outcrop, or even the neighboring egg cases, as if locking arms. Covered with loose, sticky fibers, they tend to pick up rocks and sediment, perhaps to help weigh them down, perhaps to help camouflage them. Meeting seawater, the case quickly starts to harden and darken, blending in with the dark waters surrounding it. There, with luck, it will sit undisturbed for a year or more.

The structural integrity of the skate egg case—a little underwater biosphere, its design fine-tuned over hundreds of millions of years—has been the subject of close study by scientists attempting to unravel all the elements that contribute to its success. Durable, flexible, with amazing tensile strength, it's built in layers of laminate, the fibers pointing in different directions like plywood. It has pores just large enough to let out ammonia and urea—skate pee—but small enough to keep harmful environmental pathogens from getting in. After several months, a jellylike substance plugging the capsule's four corner "horns" dissolves, probably triggered by chemical cues from the baby skates' brains. The openings allow seawater to leak in and embryonic fluid to leak out, assisted by the thrashing of the little embryos' tails, cleaning house and helping the skates slowly acclimate to the ocean environment. Even at this stage, the babies are already developing the fine sensory awareness for which adult skates are known.

"If you take an electrode that simulates the electrical field of a potential predator and bring it near the skate's egg case—bear in mind it's still sealed in this little life capsule—it will actually freeze," Aidan Martin explained. The tails stop swishing; the little four- or five-month-old embryos fall absolutely still, attempting to avoid detection by such predators as snails, sea stars, octopus, seals, or sea lions. "It can detect the presence of a predator with its own electroreceptors and freeze, even though it can't see it. I thought that was a really cool piece of work!" he gushed. "There are so many things about skates that are just amazing."

There is no larval stage for skates; there are no "skate tadpoles." After a year or more inside the egg case's increasingly tight quarters, the baby skates have exhausted their yolk supply. A narrow seam opens in the capsule, one just large enough for the inhabitants to wriggle out. Pale and translucent, the size of an outstretched human hand from tip of nose to tip of tail, with a little cream-colored belly button where the yolk stalk once attached, the miniature adult big skates are now entirely on their own.

MUCH OF WHAT LITTLE IS KNOWN about the life history of skates is focused on their reproductive system, for understandable reasons. It's easier to scrutinize an egg case in a laboratory tank than an adult skate in the open ocean. Besides, the skate reproductive system is compellingly weird—and amazingly successful. Keeping one's babies out of harm's way until they're fully developed—either inside the mother, or in a practically bombproof capsule she's built and left you in, with food for a year and the door set to open just at the right moment—has been an exceedingly successful survival strategy. Unlike other fish that may lay billions of eggs, only a small fraction of which will develop, hatch, and reach adulthood without getting eaten or otherwise killed, skates (like sharks) lavish attention on a relatively small number of offspring, letting them loose in the world only after they've grown quite self-sufficient. Think of the vulnerability of a just-hatched baby bird, beak clapping, hoping for a regurgitated meal, or a fawn, teetering on wobbly legs, suckling its mother. Think of yourself, newborn: blind, hungry, helpless. Then there's the baby skate, a miniature version of its parents, independently grazing the ocean floor as soon as it hatches.

Skates have been around for one hundred fifty million years or so, longer than the first birds, the first flowering plants, and well over a hundred million years before the first hominids, our ancestors. They are descended from sharks, which have been around for some four hundred million years. As a class of animals, skates and sharks survived four of the five worst mass extinctions in Earth's history—extinctions that killed off much bigger, stronger, nastier animals, such as the huge marine reptiles with whom they once shared the oceans. Through it all, skates hung on to the egg capsule concept—simply adding variations.

Sharks and skates are a challenge to paleontologists, who read the past mostly in the fossilized bones preserved in rock. But chondrichthyes—the ancient class of cartilaginous fishes to which skates belong—have no bones, and cartilage doesn't last like fossilized bone does. About all that remains from the earliest chondrichthyes is the teeth, the fin spines, the hard, flattened scales, and the occasional imprint of a jaw, a skull, or fins left in rock-hard ancient mud.

Chondrichthyes are the oldest surviving group of jawed vertebrates on planet Earth. Four hundred million years ago, in what geologists refer to as the Devonian period, our home planet was dominated by ocean, as it is today. The continents were arranged quite differently, clustered together mostly south of the equator, but hardly anything lived on them: some bacteria, a sprinkling of small plants, no animals at all. The sea, by contrast, was by this time teeming with life: fish galore and, by the end of the Devonian, the first fishes with a cartilaginous skeleton. They slipped through the second mass extinction, which wiped out one-fifth of all marine families; the first major mass extinction identified by paleontologists occurred before anything resembling a shark had appeared.

Fossils tell tales of the early shark-like *Cladoselache,* with its fast, slender body and big mouth at the front of its head rather than tucked underneath as with modern sharks. Soon (in geologic time—thus over the next one to two hundred million years), weirder, bigger sharks evolved, more than at any time before or since: sharks with jutting snouts and scissor-like jaws; sharks with extra teeth on their forehead and a scrub brush-like appendage growing from the shoulder; sharks with whorls of teeth spiraling out from their lower jaw that presumably rotated out as the shark grew; sharks with a bony spine like a gun barrel jutting above their head and serving a purpose scientists have yet to puzzle out. Sharks like these must have been worthy foes for the ocean's other fierce inhabitants of the Paleozoic era: *Dunkleosteus,* bristling with teeth and as big as a school bus; *Ichthyostega,* an amphibian resembling a huge crocodile; and *Eusthenopteron,* a big fish with muscular lobed fins, which most paleontologists believe was the first vertebrate creature to leave the sea and try life on land.

And then they were gone—most of them, anyway. The third of Earth's huge mass extinctions was the biggest, the most catastrophic of them all. It came late in the Permian period, the end of the Paleozoic era, 245 million years ago. An estimated 95 percent of all species disappeared. Three-quarters of all amphibian and reptile families, half of all marine families: gone. Many early shark species disappeared. But some—ancestors of today's sharks—survived.

What happened? There are no widely accepted answers to that question. The extinction could have been triggered by the impact of a comet or asteroid hitting Earth, though no direct evidence of such an event has been found. Some scientists note that there is a periodic rhythm to mass extinctions such as this one, which seem to have occurred about every twenty-six million years. Among the speculations based on this are some of suitably geocosmic proportions. One is that a large reservoir of cosmic debris exists in what's called the Oort Cloud on the fringes of our solar system; it may get stirred up on a regular basis, possibly by the orbit of an undetected tenth planet or a solar companion astronomers sometimes refer to as the Death Star. According to this theory, if these celestial bodies exist, the disruption their gravitational pull would exert as they passed through or near the Oort Cloud could be enough to kick loose a comet or two and send them hurtling to Earth just about every twenty-six million years. Don't start hyperventilating or put your house on the market yet; if that theory holds true, we're not due for such an event for another twelve million years or so. Even if an asteroid did start the cosmic chain of events, this and other mass extinctions weren't sudden events; the extinction of entire species, of entire *classes* of species, played out over hundreds or thousands or even millions of years.

The sharks as a class survived this mass extinction and at least two more. The extinction at the end of the Triassic period eliminated about 20 percent of marine families. The Triassic was followed by the Jurassic, better known as the Age of Dinosaurs. As huge reptiles roamed the earth, reptile species were burgeoning in the seas too: toothy, dolphin-like ichthyosaurs, long-necked plesiosaurs. Sharks flourished as well—the first modern sharks, with long snouts and low-slung mouths.

The last of the great prehistoric extinctions, at the border between the Cretaceous and Tertiary periods, was sixty-five million years ago: the "K-T extinction," scientists call it (*Kreide* being the German word for Cretaceous). This extinction, the one that did in the dinosaurs, was triggered when—many scientists now believe—an asteroid the size of Mount Everest traveling at about a hundred thousand miles per hour collided with Earth at the northern edge of the Yucatán Peninsula, creating what's called the Chicxulub Crater. The earth would have been enveloped in a dust cloud, blocking sunlight for weeks. Perhaps the aftermath of the asteroid collision was even more dramatic: a rain of fire from the vaporized asteroid, igniting continent-sized fires that may have burned for years. There would have been plenty to burn, too, on land masses now blanketed with plant life, thanks in part to the emergence of the flowering plants in the Cretaceous period.

Without sunlight, there's no photosynthesis, and without photosynthesis, plants die. The earth's surface temperature would have dropped below freezing for months as well—an impact winter, not unlike the nuclear winter of modern nightmare scenarios. *Strangelove Ocean*: that's the phrase Chinese scientist Kenneth Hsu coined in a 1985 paper, in a nod to Stanley Kubrick's provocative, darkly comic 1964 film *Dr. Strangelove, or: How I Learned to Stop Worrying and Love the Bomb.* It was his way of describing the largely sterile marine environment that resulted from the death of phytoplankton, along with everything that depended upon it, during the K-T extinction, shutting down the carbon cycle for thousands of years.

But one species' disaster is another's opportunity. The oldest known fossil records of skates' ancestors date from early in the Jurassic period, the period leading up to the K-T extinction. Most families of sharks and, by now, skates and rays survived that extinction, or regrouped and reemerged to thrive anew. In fact, skates may have thrived *because* of the Strangelove Ocean conditions that killed off so many other marine animals. With phytoplankton dying and drifting to the bottom of the ocean, with the corpses of sea creatures that used to eat the phytoplankton drifting down as well, the seafloor gained a thick layer of muddy, nutrient-rich silt. It was the perfect environment for the bottom-dwelling precursors of today's skates and rays to graze and hide.

In the beginning, there was oviparity. Skates evolved from sharks that produced young by enclosing them in sturdy egg cases left to hatch on the ocean floor. Most modern sharks and all rays have evolved past that phase to bear live young. But some still encapsulate their embryos in an egg case of some kind, keeping the capsule inside the mother's body rather than laying it on the ocean floor as her ancestors did and as skates (and some sharks) still do. Can we credit the egg case for the chondrichthyan fishes' evolutionary success? It's that, say paleontologists, along with the weird and wonderful array of reproductive techniques that they've devised, allowing them to exploit a wide variety of ecological niches in the world's oceans. Clearly, in one form or another, egg encapsulation has served this venerable group of fishes well. If it ain't broke—elasmobranch DNA seems to have been saying for the last four hundred million years or so—tweak it, maybe, but don't fix it.

THESE DAYS, EXTINCTION IS DELIVERED by much less dramatic means than flaming asteroids. In fact, the sixth great extinction is occurring right now, under our noses. It's known as the Holocene extinction event, and the fact that it has happened concurrently with the rise of humans— humans hunting, farming, logging, fishing, paving, driving—is no mere coincidence. Scientists estimate that tens of thousands, perhaps as many as two million, of plant and animal species have gone extinct in just the last century, more than half of those in the last fifty years. It's the fastest mass extinction in Earth's 4.5-billion-year history, even faster than extinctions triggered by a speeding comet. As paleontologist Michael Novacek puts it, we are our own asteroids.

Though some species' numbers have been declining, so far skates in the North Pacific seem to be holding their own. Some kinds of threats— such as global climate change that raises the temperature of the oceans and, as a result, alters the delicate balance of marine ecosystems—are big-picture threats, affecting all of us. Others are more species-specific, as when we humans take an interest in an animal for its fur or its flesh and, in our zeal, kill every last one of them. Skates needn't worry about that, not right away. True, there's a small skate fishery in Alaska, and big skates' wings are especially prized by consumers, not only for their size but for the quality of their meat, excellent grilled or quickly pan-fried with a few capers and a squeeze of lemon. But more skates are landed as accidental "bycatch" by fishermen longlining or trawling the ocean floor, off Alaska as well as off Oregon's coast.

Trawling is the biggest threat, especially as practiced today in places like the North Atlantic, the Gulf of Alaska, and the Bering Sea. Fishermen drag heavy nets, sometimes one hundred fifty feet wide or wider and lined with big rollers, along the ocean floor. It's a very efficient way to net bottom-dwelling "groundfish" such as cod and flatfish. But in the process it devastates the seafloor's fragile ecosystem, virtually bulldozing it and sweeping away the deep sea corals and sponges upon which the long-term survival of much ocean life depends. And it's hell on skate nurseries and baby skates, some born just a little too big to slip through those nets.

"Every stage of their life is potentially impacted by trawling, from egg cases to adult skates," says Wade Smith, who researched skates at California's Moss Landing Marine Laboratories until landing in a Ph.D. program at Oregon State University. He was drawn to the work after watching the collapse of species, including skate species, as a result of overzealous fishing in the North Atlantic. "I think we're a little ahead of the game here," he says of the Pacific Ocean off the West Coast's lower-48, where trawling hasn't been practiced to the same extent. Not that bottom trawling isn't making an impact here. Another OSU researcher videotaped the seafloor off southern Oregon from a submersible in 1990 and found 30 percent fewer fish species and 20 percent fewer total fish in areas where heavy nets had been dragged along the ocean floor.

How many big skates or longnose skates or Aleutian skates would have to be taken, on purpose or accidentally, before the population starts to collapse? These days, Wade Smith and others in British Columbia, Alaska, Washington, Oregon, and California are puzzling out this and many less-sweeping questions about skates' mysterious life histories with greater urgency. Jerry Hoff of the National Oceanic and Atmospheric Administration motored out to the same spot in the middle of the Bering Sea every two months over a year and a half to drag the bottom and collect data on the development of Alaskan and Aleutian skate egg cases in a nursery more than eleven hundred feet deep. Chris Gburski, hunched over his microscope just down the hall from Hoff at the Seattle NOAA campus, has counted growth bands on skate vertebrae, one pair for every year, like rings in a tree. What's the normal lifespan of various skate species in various oceans? How old are they before they start to reproduce? How often does a female skate lay eggs? How many young skates will she produce in a year—in a lifetime? Finding answers to questions like these, they hope, will fill in many gaps in our knowledge about skates and may fend off overfishing problems before they happen.

THE SCRAPE OF A RUMBLING DRAG TRAWL, the drilling of holes by small, deliberate snails: Of the many potential threats to an embryonic skate snug in its green submarine, getting kicked up and spit onto the beach by an angry ocean isn't chief among them. Jerry Hoff, who dropped in on those Bering Sea skate nurseries with the regularity of a doting uncle, has examined thousands of egg cases, and he thinks the streamlined shape of *Raja binoculata* in particular serves to help keep it on the ocean floor. Lumpy and shapeless when discarded and dried out, it's as streamlined as a spaceship when it's underwater, packed with live embryos. No mere pouch, it's got a V-shaped apron at one end, tapering to a pair of scooped-out corners at the other. The result is a hydrodynamic design that, Hoff believes, invites moving water to stream over it and push it down rather than dislodge it.

As for clustering their egg cases in huge congregations rather than scattering them singly or in pairs, it's back to the checks and balances of group living, tempered with the question good parents of every species ask themselves: what's best for the kids? There's a clear downside to putting all your skate eggs in one basket. Tough but otherwise essentially defenseless, the egg cases filling a skate nursery must seem like an all-you-can-eat buffet to certain predators. So, there must be an upside—a compelling reason that a community of skates would risk wholesale predation of thousands of their offspring.

Jerry Hoff thinks it boils down to real estate: location, location, location. The ideal nursery lies in a dark, quiet place that's close to food sources that baby skates will need but not too close to the shoreline haul-outs of hungry seals and sea lions. A peaceful place with little or no current, leaving the egg cases just where their mothers dropped them. A safe place, not too deep but deep enough to be undisturbed by the storms that invariably lash the shoreline in the winter of the skates' year-long gestation.

Waves don't look so benign when they're crashing on the beach, but they are a phenomenon of the ocean's surface, nothing more. Sun warms the earth, heating it unevenly and causing low- and high-pressure areas. Wind rushes into the low-pressure spots, and where it passes over the ocean, that wind stirs up swells. Those swell waves can travel the surface of the sea for thousands of miles before collapsing on a beach. The West Coast—like the western coast of every continent, thanks to prevailing west winds worldwide—is under constant assault by waves: in summer, gentle five-foot waves, on average, and in winter, waves averaging closer to eleven and a half feet.

Five- to eleven-foot waves are no threat to an egg case lying two hundred feet below. How deeply disturbing a wave is depends on two factors. One is its height, which is driven in part by how strong the wind is. The main factor, however, is the wave's frequency—the distance between successive wave crests, which is primarily a function of how far the wave has traveled across the ocean. As a rule of thumb, waves will affect the ocean bottom only where the water depth is less than half the wavelength, so the farther apart the waves, the more deeply disturbing they are. Waves off Oregon's coast tend to roll in at a distance of about three hundred feet or less between crests, stirring up the waters no more than a hundred fifty feet down. But waves of the long-traveling kind exhibit what oceanographers call "frequency downshifting": the frequency of the waves is reduced, meaning the distance between waves increases.

The storm that broke the towline on the *New Carissa* was by any definition a whopper. When it peaked early on March 3, 1999, four days before we stumbled across that still-viable egg case on the beach, the wind was hitting fifty miles per hour, and the biggest waves were as much as fifty feet tall from trough to crest—the height of a five-story building, almost five times the usual winter wave's height. Waves were rolling in every fifteen seconds or so. By one oceanographer's calculations, such waves would stir up oscillatory currents on the ocean floor more than two hundred feet deep, currents moving at up to five and a half feet per second. That's almost twice as fast as the rip currents that routinely drag unsuspecting swimmers off Oregon beaches. It's much too strong for most of us to swim against.

An untethered skate egg case sitting on the ocean floor couldn't help but be moved.

Epilogue

MARCH 16, 2007: A boisterous late-winter storm had been followed by an unseasonably spring-like day, a little showery but warm and not too breezy, perfect for walking Mile 157. Debris on the beach spelled out the storm's epitaph; it was littered with Asian bottles, dead birds, huge wads of kelp, one tattered shoe, and not one but two large egg cases: *Raja binoculata,* without a doubt.

And agates—the best I'd ever seen. Not just the usual sand-polished orange and white agates as big as the end of my thumb, but two geodes each the size of a child's fist, bristling with crystals. I'd read that agates formed in pockets of host rock, usually that formed by ancient lava flows; there's plenty of that along the Oregon coast. Where exactly did these geodes come from? Did they break from chunks of undersea bedrock? Did they tumble out of a river, wash downstream, and linger offshore for a year or a thousand years until a storm pushed them up onto this particular strand?

The questions brought Aidan Martin to mind. He'd been in my thoughts all day, in fact; I'd just learned of his unexpected death at age forty-one the previous month. The news made this day's gifts—shafts of sunlight between showers, a beach strewn with intriguing debris, the companionship of someone I loved—seem that much more precious. I particularly remembered something he'd blurted out in his rapid-fire Aussie accent toward the end of our conversation two years earlier.

"The thing I like about science, if I can blather on like an idiot, is that, unlike the perception you get when you are in high school, science is actually an *intensely* creative process. I like the process of starting with a question and using what little knowledge I've got, what expertise I can sponge from other people, my creativity, my playfulness, *anything,* and come up with some kind of answer that's satisfying.

"I mean, that's what I call the *intellectual orgasm!"* he'd beamed. "That's why you do it, that moment of, *now-I-get-it* is why we do it!

"Who would have thought?" he had mused, pointing at my snapshot of the skate egg case. "I mean, all of this from a little piece of flotsam on a beach!"

For Further Inquiry

INTRODUCTION: A THOROUGHLY MODERN MIDDEN
The Beachcomber's Guide to Seashore Life in the Pacific Northwest, by J. Duane Sept (Harbour Publishing: 1999).
Beachcombers Guide to the Northwest, by Walt Pich (Walter C. Pich Publishing: 1997).
Beachcombers Guide to Marine Life of the Pacific Northwest, by Thomas E. Niesen (Gulf Publishing Company: 1997).
Beachcombing the Pacific, by Amos L. Wood (Schiffer Publishing: 1987).
Seashore Life of the Northern Pacific Coast, by Eugene N. Kozloff (University of Washington Press, 1983).
www.oregonshores.org

CHAPTER ONE: *GOMI*
Beachcoming for Japanese Glass Floats, by Amos L. Wood (Binford & Mort Publishers: 1985).
Glass Ball: A Comprehensive Guide for Oriental Glass Fishing Floats Found on Pacific Beaches, by Walt Pich (Walter C. Pich Publishing: 2004).
Glass Floats of the World: The Collector's Identification and Price Guide Handbook (second edition), by Stuart Farnsworth and Alan Rammer (West Wind Books: 2005).

CHAPTER TWO: COMU
Beached Birds: A COASST Field Guide, by Todd Hass and Julia K. Parrish (Wavefall Press: 2000).
www.coasst.org

CHAPTER THREE: HAVOC, SIZE 11
Beachcombers' Alert newsletter, edited by Curtis Ebbesmeyer; to subscribe, visit www.beachcombers.org.
The Columbo Bay, by Richard Pollak (Simon & Schuster: 2004).
Extreme Waves, by Craig B. Smith (Joseph Henry Press: 2006).
The Floating World, by Curtis Ebbesmeyer (forthcoming from HarperCollins Publishers in 2008 or 2009).

CHAPTER FOUR: THE FLIGHT OF THE MINKE
Marine Mammals Ashore: A Field Guide for Strandings, by J. R. Geraci and V. J. Lounsbury (The National Aquarium in Baltimore: CD-ROM version 1998).
Minke Whales, by Rus Hoelzel and Jonathan Stern (WorldLife Library: 2000).
www.northeastpacificminke.org
www.projectminke.com

CHAPTER FIVE: THE *SANAK*
The Guardian (DVD from Buena Vista Home Entertainment/Touchstone: 2007).

CHAPTER SIX: MERMAID'S PURSE
The Book of Life: An Illustrated History of the Evolution of Life on Earth, edited by Stephen Jay Gould (W.W. Norton & Co.: 2001).
www.elasmo-research.org
www.elasmodiver.com
www.rajidae.tmfweb.nl

More Good Reading

In the course of my interviews, some people spontaneously recommended their all-time favorite books, which I share here.

From biologist Jon Stern: *The Log from the Sea of Cortez*, by John Steinbeck (Penguin Books: 1951).
From biologist Frankie Robertson: *Heart of the Raincoast: A Life Story*, by Alexandra Morton and Billy Proctor (Horsdal & Shubart Publishers Ltd.: 2005). On Frankie's bedside table: *The Curve of Time: The Classic Memoir of a Woman and Her Children Who Explored the Coastal Waters of the Pacific Northwest*, by M. Wylie Blanchet and Timothy Egan (Seal Press: 2002).
From *Sanak* captain John Verberkmoes: *Voyage: A Novel of 1896*, by Sterling Hayden (Sheridan House: 1999).
From boat salvager Duane Leafdahl: *The Grey Seas Under: The Perilous Rescue Missions of a North Atlantic Salvage Tug*, by Farley Mowat (The Lyons Press: 2001). Duane also recommended *The Hungry Ocean: A Swordboat Captain's Journey*, by Linda Greenlaw (Hyperion: 1999) and *In the Heart of the Sea: The Tragedy of the Whaleship Essex*, by Nathaniel Philbrick (Penguin: 2001).

Acknowledgments

The following individuals welcomed my questions, invited me into their homes and offices and boats, generously shared their knowledge and personal experiences, and in many cases reviewed the text for accuracy. Thank you for entrusting me with your stories:

Bryan Duncan, Stuart Farnsworth, Walt Pich, and Gayle Hansen; Tomoko Wahei, Masaki Harada, and especially Yoshi Asahara of Otaru, Japan; and Emily Casey of Canberra, Australia.

Julia Parrish and Jane Dolliver in Seattle, Val Knox and the rest of the Baker Beach COASST survey group, and Bob and Shirley Loeffel.

Curtis Ebbesmeyer, whom I stalked over six years in two states, and his colleague Jim Ingraham, for sharing their expertise and their stories and for engendering a groundswell of interest in beachcombing, the dynamics of ocean currents, and the growing issue of ocean debris.

Leo Leung, Steve Yeh, Yolly Cuarisma, J. J. Juang, Mike Napolitan, Mike Collier, and Peter Nickerson.

Clark Casebolt, Alison Gill, Rus Hoetzel, Tamara McGuire, Mike Northrup, Frankie Robertson, and most of all, Jon Stern.

Chiefs James Armstrong, John Bush, and Michael Frame of U.S.C.G. Group/Air Station North Bend; Capt. Lewis C. Dunn, U.S.C.G. (ret.); Kurt "Smoke" Mason, U.S.M.C. (ret.); Bryan Gill, Duane Leafdahl; Mark and Lisa Hitchcock; Phyllis Steeves; and in particular, John Verberkmoes.

Ted Brekken, Merrick Haller, and particularly Wade Smith of Oregon State University; Josie Thompson; Jerry Hoff and Chris Gburski of NOAA; and R. Aidan Martin, remembered fondly.

I am also indebted to many others for their support of this project:

Phillip Johnson, founder of Oregon Shores Conservation Coalition's CoastWatch program.

Jack Long, for his hiking companionship, long friendship, and turkey sandwiches.

Jim Weber, who reappeared just in time to offer his expert editing and unabashed enthusiasm.

My father, George Henderson, for correcting our grammar and encouraging adventure, my mother, Jan Henderson, who could find a story in anybody and who never hesitated to fall in love with her subjects, and my siblings, for their enthusiasm and support from start to finish.

Donna and Mike for the use of their lake house—a writer's dream—and the
   support of many other friends, including Leslie, Kathleen, and the Cysters.
The staff of OSU Press, whose personal interest and enthusiasm for the book I
   deeply appreciate, and Annamieka Hopps for her inspired illustrations.
And Charlie, who helped in so many ways to make this book happen.